# Poetry and Ethics

*Inventing Possibilities in Which We Are Moved*

*to Action and How We Live Together*

# Poetry and Ethics

*Inventing Possibilities in Which We Are Moved*
*to Action and How We Live Together*

Obiora Ike, Andrea Grieder and Ignace Haaz (Eds.)

Globethics.net Global No. 16

Globethics.net Global
Series editor: Prof. Dr. Obiora Ike, Executive Director of Globethics.net in
Geneva and Professor of Ethics at the Godfrey Okoye University Enugu/Nigeria.

Globethics.net Global 16
Obiora Ike, Andrea Grieder and Ignace Haaz (Eds.), Poetry and Ethics:
Inventing Possibilities in Which We Are Moved to Action and How We Live
Together
Geneva: Globethics.net, 2018
978-2-88931-242-9(online version)
978-2-88931-243-6 (print version)
© 2018 Globethics.net

Assistant Editor: Samuel Davies

Globethics.net International Secretariat
150 route de Ferney
1211 Geneva 2, Switzerland
Website: www.globethics.net/publications
Email: publications@globethics.net

All web links in this text have been verified as of June 2018.

# TABLE OF CONTENTS

Introduction ..................................................................... 11

Part I: Poems, Maxims and Aphorisms ......................... 13

1 Our Game More Resembles a Dance:
The Tennis Commune ....................................................... 15
*James Luchte*

2 Nakedness and Ecophenomena:
Ethical Emotions from African Poetries ....................... 17
*Christian Anieke*

    2.1 Ideas are Naked ..................................................... 17
    2.2 Ecophenomena ..................................................... 18

3 Saisir un rêve légitime pourtant inaccessible ............. 21
*Ange Sankieme*

4 Maximes sur l'amour et la parole ............................... 23
*Alexander Savvas*

5 A Scene of Kidnapping in an Apocalyptic
Approach: Conflict, Ethics, Post-Conflict
in the Colombian Context ............................................... 25
*Deivit Montealegre*

6 Transpoesis: Kigali Vibrates with Poetry ................... 31
*Andrea Grieder, Janvier Nsabimana, Ange Theonastine Ashimwe,
Lion King and Anisie Byukusenge*

6.1 Transpoesis and the Young Poets from Rwanda:
Janvier Nsabimana Writing Home .................................................. 31
6.2 A Cry for Normality ................................................................. 33
6.3 Ange T. Ashimwe: Poems on Disability .............................. 34
6.4 Lion King: I am Cyacyana! ..................................................... 37
6.5 Anisie Byukusenge: With the Eyes of my Heart .................. 40

# 7 Aphorisms: The Best Thing to Give to Our World .... 43

*Obiora Ike*

7.1 I Am a Child .......................................................................... 43
7.2 The Cost of Peace and the Cost of War (in Comparison) ........ 44
7.3 A Smile Costs Nothing ............................................................ 44
7.4 On Forgiveness ....................................................................... 45
7.5 A Friend ................................................................................ 46
7.6 The Best Thing to Give to Our World ..................................... 46

# 8 All in the Name of God ................................................. 47

*Dicky Sofjan*

# Part II: Essaies ............................................................... 53

# 1 Nursery Rhymes, Fairy Tales and Cartoons: A Miasma of Values, Violence and Social Reconstruction ............................................................... 55

*Divya Singh* ................................................................................ 55

1.1 Introduction .......................................................................... 55
1.2 Discussion ............................................................................. 57
1.3 Conclusion ............................................................................ 69
1.4 References ............................................................................. 73

# 2 Sense through Senses: Ethics and Aesthetics ............. 79

*Christoph Stückelberger*

2.1 Introduction: The Five Senses ............................................... 79
2.2 Christian Culture: Incarnation as Enculturation .................... 80
2.3 Christian Literature and Art ................................................... 82
2.4 Being Centred: Christ-Centred Means Love Centred ............. 82
2.5 Love as the Centre of Literature, Art and Ethics ................... 85

## 3 Représentations symboliques de Jésus dans le Nouveau Testament, entre appellation et acte symbolique : le cas d'étude du quatrième évangile ......... 89

*Mulolwa Kashindi*

3.1. Introduction ...................................................... 89
3.2. La méthode symbolique dans le quatrième évangile ............ 91
3.3 Premier exemple : l'eau changé en vin (Jn 2, 1-12) ............. 95
3.4 La guérison du fils de l'officier royal (Jn 4, 46-54 //
Mt 8, 5-13 // Lc 7, 1-10) ............................................. 102
3.5 La guérison du paralytique le jour du Sabbat (Jn 5, 1-9) ...... 106
3.6 La multiplication des pains (Jn 6, 1-15 // Mt 14, 13-21 //
Mc 6, 30-44 // Lc 9, 10-17) ......................................... 109
3.7 Bibliographie ...................................................... 115

## 4 Biomimesis and Self-Poiesis: A Renaissance in the Beauty of the Caring Nature ......... 117

*Didier Blasco*

3.1 Introduction ....................................................... 117
3.2 Nature Draws a Path to Sustainable Values ..................... 118
3.3 A Promenade through the Philosophical Roots ................. 119
3.4 A Soft Walk around Sciences .................................... 123
3.5 Systems Are Everywhere! ....................................... 125
3.6 General Principle of Biomimetic Action ........................ 126
3.7 Self-Poiesis and Other Ways to Articulate Bio-Mimesis ..... 129
3.8 The Reconquest on the Desert of Yacouba Sawadogo ......... 132
3.9 Conclusion ........................................................ 135

## 5 Litotes, Irony and other Innocent Lies: Trusting Truth Stronger Than Not Trusting Lies ....... 137

*Ignace Haaz*

5.0 Introduction: Why Could Litotes and Irony Be Considered
as Innocent Lies? .................................................... 137
5.1 Trusting Truth Stronger than Not Trusting Lies:
Is There Such Thing That of a Total Loss of Credibility? ......... 139
5.2 Brief Philosophical History of the Argument of the Misuse
of the Language and the Lie in the Classical Religious
Context ............................................................... 141

5.3 The Romantic Logic, Epistemology of the Lie
and the Value of Games and Spans for Knowledge Formation
and Values ........................................................................... 154
5.4 Bibliography ................................................................... 157

## 6 Literature, Poetry and Reconciliation: Why Wait Until War is Over? ................................... 161

*Alexander Savvas*

6.1 Literature and Poetry Assist in the Healing Process .............. 161
6.2 Why not Use Writing to Endeavour Preventing Misery ........ 163

## 7 Underdevelopment as Ideology: Racism, Ideological Lies and Africa's True Potential of Development ....... 167

*Ernest Beyaraza*

7.1 Nature of Underdevelopment ............................................. 167
7.2 Africa Underdevelopment ................................................. 172
7.3 Racial Theorists .............................................................. 178
7.4 Racism as Ideology ......................................................... 197
7.5 Racism as Class .............................................................. 204
7.6 Human Development ........................................................ 206

## 8 Responsabilidad social, solidaridad, comunicación y cultura empresarial: un mecanismo de reconciliación social ....................................... 211

*Edison Tabra*

8.1 Introducción ................................................................... 211
8.2 Fundamentos teóricos de la práctica solidaria en la vida
empresarial ........................................................................... 214
8.3 La solidaridad y la empresa: la empresa "solidaria" ............. 221
8.4 La responsabilidad social "solidaria" como instrumento
de reconciliación de los stakeholders en el sector minero .......... 228
8.5 La poesía y la escritura poética como instrumento
de reconciliación social en el sector minero ............................ 231
8.6 Síntesis ........................................................................... 232
8.7 Bibliografía .................................................................... 233

**9 Value Construction through Poetry in Rwanda: Poetic Voices Imagining the Space Beyond Normality**.......................................**211**

*Andrea Grieder*

9.1 Introduction ............................................................... 239
9.2 To Sustain Poetically in that History .................................. 240
9.3 The Poetic Moral Self.................................................... 241
9.4 Poetic De-Construction ................................................. 242
9.5 Exploring the Space of the Possible ................................... 243
9.6 Poetic Voices in Rwanda................................................ 244
9.7 Conclusion................................................................ 244
9.8 References ............................................................... 245

**Conclusion** ...........................................................**247**

**List of Contributors**............................................**257**

# INTRODUCTION

'Tis thus, by crystal fount, my muse hath sung,
Translating into heavenly tongue
Whatever came within my reach,
From hosts of beings borr'wing nature's speech.
Interpreter of tribes diverse,
I've made them actors on my motley stage;
For in this boundless universe
There's none that talketh, simpleton or sage [...]'

*Fables XI, Epilogue,*
*Jean de La Fontaine*

When Andrea Grieder came to Geneva in 2016 to present the results of her PhD research, *Collines des mille souvenirs* (Hills of a Thousand Memories, 2016 Globethics.net, ISBN: 978-2-889311-019, 410pp. www.globethics.net/theses-series) She planted the seeds for this book project.

In her doctoral dissertation, which was published as a book with Globethics, she presents a deep point of view that successfully bridges the gap between anthropology and literature relating to the post-genocidal society in Rwanda. She describes the context through portraits, mainly of survivors, and shows that the performance of poetry helps in strengthening mutual recognition, healing and reconciliation. Her book is a deep testimony on 'living after and with the genocide perpetrated against the Tutsi of Rwanda'. She has established herself as an international expert with experience in the field of art, poetry and reconciliation in the context of post genocide Rwanda. Her work is an important contribution to art and anthropology with innovativeness in exploring social reality, art and cultural management and the process of individual and collective transformation.

The present book has been initiated as a new contribution, in a first part, by twelve authors, of original poems, expressing ethical emotions and aphorism related to a philosophical questioning of the grounding of our values for life. Coming from four continents, poetic emotions are sources of inspiration for future work in the field of anthropology, art and conflict resolution. In a second part, nine authors tackle, in the form of short essays, how poems, symbolic representations, metaphorical narratives, lies and corporate culture impact the space of possibilities, in which we are moved to action, knowledge formation, and how we imagine the world together.

The plan of this book project in the Globethics.net Global Series on the topic of *Ethics and Poetry* should gather, through the international contributions from different continents, and the scope on applied ethics related to poetry, a favorable reception from philosophers, ethicists, theologians and anthropological researchers from Africa, Asia, Europe and Latin America, allowing for a comparison of their findings on the healing power of words, in various religious, spiritual and philosophical traditions.

**Keywords:** poetry, rhetoric, fairy tales, nursery rhymes, cartoons, incantations, symbolic language in the Bible, declamation, living metaphors, performing poetics arts, rap, reconciliation and mutual recognition through the production of art and literature. China and Christian art. Truthfulness, lies and trust. Self-poiesis, nature and bio mimesis, CSR: corporate culture and communication.

Obiora Ike, Andrea Grieder, Ignace Haaz

Geneva, June 2018

# PART I

# POEMS, MAXIMS AND APHORISMS

*Expressing Ethical Emotions*

# 1

# OUR GAME MORE RESEMBLES A DANCE: THE TENNIS COMMUNE

*James Luchte*

We play tennis differently[1].
We give little heed to traditional rules.
Of course, there are limits, otherwise
It would cease to be a game called tennis.
But, our game is not just another mask
Of regimented & belligerent anarchy.

The rackets & balls are for instance 'ours.'
We choose the racket that suits us best.
At the outset of play, the ball must stay within
The green space & go over the net –
Unless, of course, we decide to
Play with the net down.
Another rule is that the ball is in play
As long as it can be hit – no matter
How many times it has bounced.

We do not keep score.
Our tennis is not about the

---

[1] Dr James Luchte is a philosopher, author, writer and poet. Visiting Professor of Philosophy at Shanghai University of Finance and Economics from July 2014-August 2017, he is also on the Board of Advisers of the Nietzsche Circle, a global philosophical community, based in New York.

Wrath of gladiatorial combat,
With one warrior subduing another.
In our game, there are only winners.
Our tennis is about our enjoyment of motion,
Kinetics – not who can defeat the other,
But how long the ball can be
Kept in play by the players.

Instead of aggressive combat,
Our game more resembles a dance.
As the motion of the dance unfolds,
Even the green space & its rigid
Dividing lines cease to be limits.
All that is left is the dance in its
Choreography of cooperative action.
Our game eschews the boundaries &
Protocols of the gladiators for the
Dionysian joy of the dance.
We play tennis differently.

# 2

# NAKEDNESS AND ECOPHENOMENA: ETHICAL EMOTIONS FROM AFRICAN POETRIES

*Christian Anieke*

## 2.1 Ideas are Naked

Ideas are naked[2]
Naked floating bodies enjoyed in privacy
Naked bodies surveyed in the bedroom of uncensored freedom-
Curves, lines, spots, colours, all before you alone
With a bonus of smells, tastes and sounds

All seen, heard, tasted and enjoyed privately.
But ideas sometimes desire to step into the public sphere
So they put on their clothes
Wear the clothes of language
Language incandescent and cloudy
Language mythic and banal
Language false and true.

---

[2] Rev. Prof. Dr Christian Anieke is professor of English. He is the founder and current Vice Chancellor, Godfrey Okoye University, the University of the Catholic Diocese of Enugu, Nigeria.

Once in the public domain private enjoyment vanishes
The savoring of naked ideas in the bedroom evaporates;
Once out of the private room ideas can be trampled upon
Ideas can be slapped
Ideas can be raped
Ideas can be transformed into monsters.

As a baby in the womb swims in the liquid warmth of the mother's
        tummy
A chick enveloped by the eggshell curls undisturbed
A tortoise like soldiers withdraws into its armoured shell
Delicate human organs are hidden by skin and bones
So are ideas untouched in the innermost chambers of the creator's mind
But once out of the private room they must be ready for human punches!

## 2.2 Ecophenomena

You cried and I cried
You yawned and I yawned
You laughed and I laughed
You clapped and I clapped
This is ecophenomena!

But why do I echo your actions
Why does the oak tree of my identity bend
Why does my tummy rumble when yours drums
Did we eat the same primordial soup at the night of creation
Are we the fruit of the same semen and ova from a forgotten primordial
        intercourse?

Now I see why dictators triumph
Now I guess why fanatics are applauded
Now I understand mass suicide
Now I see the roots of human bonding
This is ecophenomena!

Social media experts and users understand it
Politicians build their empire on it
Pastors and fiery preachers know its power
Orators aim their love arrows at its heart
This is ecophenomena!

As scientists tumble over heaps of research
Let me say this: we are held inescapably by the hands of ecophenomena!

# 3

# SAISIR UN RÊVE LÉGITIME POURTANT INACCESSIBLE

*Ange Sankieme*

Marcher vers des horizons lointains[3]
Loin des regards désespérés des siens
Saisir un rêve légitime pourtant inaccessible
Inaccessible destin enfoui dans l'insolence d'un monde bafoué
Personnage atypique, indésirable ou aliéné du savoir acquis et éprouvé
Épouvante recherche d'une affirmation personnelle

Passionné d'une éthique morale empreinte d'humanité
Humanité et dignité méprisées et méconnues
Fils, frère, père et époux d'une famille aux attentes légitimes
Attentes nourries par une espérance soutenue
Soutenue par les efforts d'un père et époux en quête
Quête et attentes déçues par un mépris séculaire d'un stéréotype humain

Décor planté pour faire couler de semblables humains dans les
        décombres de la vie
Y répondre par une affirmation de soi ou s'afficher en hypocrite
        acceptant des renoncements aux droits même les plus
        fondamentaux
Exercer un métier et ne rien gagner en retour

---

[3] Ange Sankieme holds a double doctorate: in Law from the University of Berne, in African, Congolese, European and Swiss law, and in Theology from the University of Basel on migration in the European Union and Switzerland.

Réclamer un soutien légal et se faire rabrouer
Se rabattre au plus bas de l'échelle et être qualifié d'irresponsable
La vie devient un algorithme sans solution.

# 4

# MAXIMES
# SUR L'AMOUR ET LA PAROLE

*Alexander Savvas*

L'amour-propre est une question d'équilibre. En manquer nous rend misérable, en avoir trop nous empêche de nous affranchir de notre condition[4].

Une histoire d'amour qui se termine, c'est un monde qui disparaît.

Il n'y a pas d'amour impossible. L'amour est toujours possible, c'est un signe et un don de Dieu. C'est un océan de jouvence, de bonheur, d'abnégation et de dépassement de soi dans lequel il faut plonger tête baissée. Seule la solitude est impossible.

Quelle disgrâce d'être battu par les armes !
Quel délice d'être vaincu par l'amour !

Dans la vie comme devant un tribunal, quel triomphe que d'avoir raison, quelle tragédie que d'avoir tort ! En amour, quelle douce ivresse que d'avoir tort, quel désespoir que d'avoir raison !

---

[4] Alexander Savvas was born in Geneva in 1967. He studied International Relations and French in the United States and Switzerland. His main influences rest with the XVIth century French moralists. A Schoppenhauer enthousiast, he particularly relishes the works of Voltaire and La Rochefoucauld. He was moved by American poetess Sylvia Plath and novelist Flannery O'Connor. He has been working in the financial sector since 1997.

On ne mérite souvent pas plus d'être aimé que de gagner au jeu. Certes, on gagne, mais l'amour est offert innocemment, parfois inconsciemment. C'est un cadeau fait de fierté, d'honnêteté, de sincérité et d'espoir. Il se nourrit de lui-même et ne demande rien d'autre que d'être perpétué au sein de l'espèce.

Le monde est ainsi fait qu'à peine un homme apprend-t-il à parler, qu'il doit apprendre à se taire

Les hommes regrettent souvent leurs paroles, rarement leurs silences

Un homme qui s'accommode de l'ignorance s'habituera naturellement à l'injustice

Nietzsche écrivait : « Nur Narr nur Dichter ». Le poète n'est-il qu'un prédateur sentimental qui frotte plein d'amertume son âme d'écorché à la vie ? Les larmes de ses victimes lui offrent-elles assez d'encre pour coucher sur le papier toute l'essence de son mal et de sa propre consolation. N'est-il pas au contraire, le magnanime artiste et musicien, qui œuvre comme pionnier sur la voie de la connaissance de soi, lui qui démêle avant tout autres chaque émotion mieux que le psychologue, loué par les rois, les ambassadeurs et les hommes d'église, sur les terrains accidentés de la vie.

Pour l'homme, Dieu existe obligatoirement ! Blaise Pascal en voulait pour preuve la magnifique complexité de la création et la multitude de signes qui rendent l'absence de Dieu inconcevable. En effet, la vie terrestre est en soi un non-sens. Nous dérivons constamment d'une vanité à l'autre, nous voguons d'une futilité de l'esprit à une action misérable, imaginant ainsi échapper à la vacuité, à l'absurdité de notre condition. Ce faisant, nous nous trompons continuellement, bercés par l'illusion de rêves qui ne se réaliseront pas. Seules importent alors la sublimation de la volonté divine et la qualité de nos échanges avec nos semblables.

# 5

# A SCENE OF KIDNAPPING
# IN AN APOCALYPTIC APPROACH:
# CONFLICT, ETHICS, POST-CONFLICT
# IN THE COLOMBIAN CONTEXT

*Deivit Montealegre*

## 5.1

1. This is the revelation that the omnipotent God, God of life and everlasting sovereignty has decided to reveal himself to his servant Nahuel, who gives testimony that this word is true and has been confirmed in deeds and words of omnipotence[5].

2. Nahuel greets the Colombian church and all those who inhabit the earth of the three arms of the Andes, grace and peace to you; companions of the route of life that is, was and will be, that has in its hand the manifestation of the light and that has in its dominion the wisdom of history[6].

3. Hope arises as standard.

4. Light shines with burning rage.

---

[5] Deivit Montealegre is currently Programme Executive Globethics.net South America and PhD. Candidate at the Instituto Superior Evangélico de Estudios Teológicos (ISEDET) in Buenos Aires (Argentina). His training and previous formation include the Tao Fong Shan Centre, Hong Kong, in governance and management for the economy of the life, and Deivit is a specialist in ecumenical studies from the University of Geneva.

[6] Translation from the original Spanish by Amélé Ekué.

5. The Divine and loved one by the people is on his way.

6. I, Nahuel, your sister, the one that chose life before death; the one that resists to serve him as excuse to Works of the abyss for the mission of the evil.

7. It happened in front of the river which holds the name of Amazon, in the twelfth month of my captivity when I was touched by the power of the presence of the sovereign,

8. I saw suddenly that the skies were opened and I heard a voice like of trumpet that shut up the noise of the light sparkles which caused that humans' life ended.

9. Hearing it, I came to see who speaks to me, and when doing so I saw the night retire before his/her face, and the death to flee before his/her words.

10. Holding the form of the son of mankind and his face was like the one of a child capable to communicate peace and tenderness without pronouncing a single word. When seeing it I fell like dead.

11. The dust of the earth touched my lips, but he, while he touched me with his hand on the shoulder, said to me: Rise and write to the nation of the three arms of the Andes which I will show to you, because the earth which is today barren and without any fruit will become fertile again for its people living in it.

**5.2**

1. Listen to the words of terror; as moving out of my quiet fear I will no longer repress the terrible horrors death.

2. In the open sky appeared a great sign; as I never saw before: an army of thousands ready for the frontal assault,

3. While I saw the multitude descending, I saw it appeared to be only one man, but who was divided into three. Each one took up a defined shape and was headed by a terrible beast.

4. The soldiers had in front of them a seal that distinguished them, while their arms as if they were of iron, caused death, flight, hunger, suffering, questions, answers, poverty, distress, pain, passion.

5. The one who spoke to me said: the three beasts that you have seen, have been a single one before; now its ambition has separated them and transformed them into monsters.

6. The first monster took the form of a human being, but its outer appearance was like a wolf and its arms like the roots of trees enable to transmit life to the rest of the body.

7. Nonetheless, around its roots no water circulated, but gold, upon opening its mouth, and promised many benefits to those who listened to him.

8. In a period I order the tropical garden, but now lies and contradictions invaded its nature.

9. The second beast had the form of a dragon, its head was a single one, but it was not always so, before it had much more.

10. However, the time passing and due to its constant fight with the first beast, caused that it has lost them.

11. When it advanced with much noise, everything around it shook and was destroyed.

12. From its mouth came words of protest.

13. Under their steps the innocents wished not to have been born and the witnesses filled the lake of pains with their tears.

14. This is the beast which catches human beings, marks them and makes them captives.

15. When I was about to observe the third beast, a light beam left the earth and a lamb rose of its bed.

16. At its side a woman dressed with justice and a veteran of peace raised the right hand to the sky, crying out in adoration.

17. The lamb directs itself towards the man and walks ahead, while everything under its steps turned green again. The stars shone brighter.

18. The one who spoke to me said: This is the one who once died, and now is alive, this is the hope amidst of pain and to whom the captives cry for the day of their liberation.

19. Suddenly, a noise resonated as of an abundant waterfall; when returning to see from where it came, I saw the third beast.

20. It had the form of a horse, its colour was red like blood, its height was three times the one of a normal horse and when it walked it changed its colour.

21. This horse could be confused in the middle of the army with the other two because it resembled them.

22. His mouth spoke about revenge for the injustice against the right ones and his galloping produced a roar that shook mountains.

23. The one with the eyes of hope spoke to me and said: the red colour of this beast is not his colour, before it has not even existed; it is not like the other beasts that always have been there, this beast was born of the monstrous fight of the two previous ones, the blood of its birth is the reason, and the revenge for which it cries out is an endless task.

**5.3**

1. Thereafter I saw as each one of the armies and their leading beasts touched the earth, the valleys, the mountains, the rivers, the cities, the towns, the small villages, the neighbourhoods, my house.

2. All this was object of his power and apparent kindness.

3. The woman of justice who raised her hand at the side of the lamb, cried out in a heart-tearing complaint: you are the captive, who has been dressed off the liberty, the one that takes in her chest the marks of the absent mother, the assassinated father and the sons and daughters who yearn for the return of the disappeared.

4. However, you are not the unfortunate one without hope.

5. As those words were pronounced, I saw as from the four ends of the earth, of the three arms of the Andes, wove a great linen cloth of many colours.

6. Each thread with which the linen cloth was woven was necessary so that the rest of the weave behold its form.

7. There was not any loose plot; everything was part of the same frame, all the threads were connected, the weave had its own life.

8. The peace veteran kept silence and his silence opened the linen cloth before my eyes.

9. The shout of a faithful and excluded multitude appeared in the middle of the weave, the beasts and their armies did this also.

10. My legs shook, as much as I could no longer hold myself and I fell demolished.

11. In that moment, below and above, sky and earth, everything was part of the same system.

12. The voice that has spoken to me, the one that has the feet for a long way, asked me: who tiles the linen cloth? I articulated my answer to him in a whisper: 'I did not know'.

13. And the voice asked me again: 'who tiles the linen cloth?' Amidst my astonishment I responded: 'the coloured threads', and the voice asked again:

14. 'Who maintains the coloured threads?', 'I do not know': I responded.

15. I took over the linen cloth, and I could see those who maintained the threads; they were all, the multitude, the beasts, the armies, myself.

16. The lamb which became a human, without ceasing to walk, rose over everything.

17. Shining like the rising sun, a new army assembled at its feet, and with a silver dress it pulled out of a scabbard its sword directed towards the linen cloth,

18. It stopped at the centre of the weave and being on the verge of tearing it, directed its eyes of fire to the witness, who in silence was always present.

19. He gave his sword and said to him: 'you do justice'.

20. The witness took the sword from two edges and went towards the beasts, fighting with them and on the verge of killing them and tearing the veil of peace, the veteran of peace opened his lips and in a song proclaimed:

21. 'If justice takes control of the sword,

22. If the sword touches the linen cloth,

23. Enslave those who compose it,

24. Kill those that have fought to weave it,

25. Punish those who sometimes cried out at their accomplishment.

26. There is no justice for the faithful and excluded multitude if the linen cloth leaves its weave'.

**5.4**

1. Thereafter, I saw as the faithful and excluded multitude ceased to lament and with firm voice started to organise themselves.

2. A troop of love, respect, value, with hands and words bathed of crystalline pardon regrouped threads of the weave,

3. Not the way it has been at the beginning, but according to a new form in which the pestilence of the beasts was no more.

4. With the sword of the witnesses the beasts were judged, condemned to the abyss, from where they will not be able to leave again.

5. The voice that spoke to me said: the fight is finished; the dead will return to life, the captives will have the hug of love and friendship. The solitude will step back, when seeing life governing the footpaths of the anguish.

6. The omnipotent, the ethnic groups, towns and nations brought the justice to rain over the shores of the river called Amazon, the dry earth gave its fruit.

7. A new sky and a new earth rose, a new weave manifested.

8. The witness who has taken the sword to the feet of the veteran of peace, proclaimed a praise song:

9. 'Happy are those that did not insist to tear the linen with the sword.

10. Happy, those that the beasts judged.

11. Happy those that see the words of this prophecy and implement them.

12. Happy, those that find life and peace outside revenge.

13. Rejoice, you captives, because your liberation is already enclosed in this list.'

14. I received these words when I was in captivity; a place where the hope rises over against death.

Amen

# 6

# TRANSPOESIS: KIGALI VIBRATES WITH POETRY

*Andrea Grieder, Janvier Nsabimana, Ange Theonastine Ashimwe, Lion King and Anisie Byukusenge*

## 6.1 Transpoesis and the Young Poets from Rwanda: Janvier Nsabimana, Writing Home

Janvier Nsabimana is young poet that lives in the Nyibiheke Refugee Camp in Easter Province of Rwanda. His poems are based on an autobiographical self-narrative. Since he was a child, and now as a young man, Janvier has been moving from one place to another, leaving home behind again and again. In the poem *My home, why don't you care for me*, we discover a cry to be heard and understood, which expresses both a melancholic voice and nostalgia of a home—a far distance and distorted testimony of war and violence.

Born in 1994, in the Democratic Republic of Congo (DRC), Janvier Nsabimana's life is a journey, where the non-security of different places is the driving force to live one provisory 'home' for another one. 'We were born seven' says Janvier, who adds within the same sentence 'three of us remain'. Sitting in the living room of a 'ghetto' (a term used for basic houses) in Kabeza/Kigali, he draws the main line of his journey. In 1997, his mother and siblings came to Rwanda, but they 'continued to Uganda' because they 'didn't feel safe'. In 2000, they heard that peace had been established in RDC, so the family went back to Masisi. The peace time lasted only for a short period. In 2003, the Mai-Mai Rebel Group and Ex-Interahamwe were the key actors responsible of the insecurity in the region and the three children with the mother moved back to Rwanda. After one year in the transit camp, Nkamira in Rubavu District, the family then moved to Nyibiheke camp where they still live today. The story of Janvier is one of being moved by force through history and social context; insecurity.

Making the best of a journey on boat, Janvier writes poetry. 'It helps me to control my anger', he says. He considers the hypocrisy of many traditional communities, which feeling ashamed, attempt to stop a poem from speaking out, because fear leads their lives. If someone starts sharing shameful stories, they become public. As Janvier puts it in a poem 'I know my Identity brings shame but who is able to be blamed? I wonder why my home does not care for me.'

Andrea Grieder director of Transpoesis, who created the programme Kigali Vibrates With Poetry, a yearly poetry competition in Kigali Rwanda, explains the very essence of poetry as a philosophical ethical therapy. 'My home, why don't you care for me?' is the question Janvier perseveres in asking, as if the pain is given voice and remembered each time a place is no longer safe enough for a child to go to school and to play. By stating: 'I believe in poetry' the young poet pronounces 'I believe' with the same intensity as someone expressing faith in God, thus Poetry could be symbolically considered as a bible that is rewritten with every new experience[7].

---

[7] Janvier refers to *Kigali vibrates with Poetry*: 'I heard your voice at the radio,' he told to the director of Transpoesis, when they met, travelling in the bus, from Kigali to the camp. Janvier laughed and expressed the highly symbolic power he recognizes in poetry. 'I wrote your email address on my school report'. A laugh that says, that he didn't hesitate to use the 'sacred' school report to write down what became a key to open a door public recognition of his talent, and to an imaginary audience of what he wants to say, that will become soon reality.

# 6.2 A Cry for Normality

'I never give up' says Janvier in April 2018, after he had an accident while riding a bicycle. He was in hospital with a broken bone in his chest after having been hit by a car. He asked the doctors to let him sit his exam at University. 'I know how to motivate myself'. It may be a strength that is rooted in that inner conversation with the poetic soul, he learned already at an early age. How can the situation of refugees change today? 'Don't give them food that will end one day, give them education' they advise. School began for Janvier in the refugee camp. Later on, he continued in Rwandan Schools, facing poverty, hunger and collective stigmatization as a refugee. But he remembers having always had a need to write history, his own history, in order to find a place within History—his dream was to deal with History until the end of his education[8].

### I Just Want to Be Normal

When I say I want to be normal
I don't mean to graduate, in four years
Get a job
Get married, have two to five kids
When I say I want to be normal, I mean
Not suffering
Not in agony
Not drowning in despair

---

[8] After P6, Janvier sat national exams. He his results were very good and he received a recommendation which took him to the Rwandan schools. Lacking the finance to pay for the school fees, he spent one year at home and only attended secondary school after the introduction of education for all programme. Thanks to a Scholarship from DAFI, today he is following his studies in Business of Hotel and Tourism Management. At secondary school, he studied History, Geography and Economics. Knowing that government institutions, sometimes even the private sector, are not willing to hire refugees, he decided to go for Tourism.

Not refugee camps
Not stuck in mind.

When I say I want to be normal, I mean: I just want to be okay, I just
    want to be healthy
I just want to feel at home,
I want to live not just survive,
When I say I want to be normal,
I just want to be
Like you.

To be normal is a call for the respect of a shared humanity. It is a call
to transcend social status and prejudices. Construction of a new social
order where to be normal—to be seen normal is not determined by status
or facts, but may only be done by the normative value of being a human
being. Transcending the lack of being with someone with whom to share
his stories, Javier's poetry is written out of a space of loneliness, but
finds the social other in the public audience, the anonymous public,
collective and distant at the same place. Maybe the lack of the capacity
to share in early years is reflecting that distance (of poetic sharing), in
terms of emotional relationships and, at the same time, it creates the
potential for a collective audience and soon opens the door for a
collective impact.

## 6.3 Ange T. Ashimwe: Poems on Disability

'Tomorrow, will I be recalled?' questions Ange Theonastine
Ashimwe in the poem that made her famous. The young poet, studying
at Secondary School is permanently confined to a wheelchair[9].

---

[9] Born in 1999, 'normal like any other child', she started walking, but later she
became weak until she could no longer walk. At the age of five, she started
using a wheel chair. Over the last 12 years, Ange tried different hospitals but
they couldn't find the problem. She recalls her journey of pain and hope, and
Ange chooses the path of acceptance: she gave up looking for a cure. Instead,

Her poem writes against the judgments based on her physical appearance, the prejudices of being seen as unable[10].

In her *Narrative Hermeneutics, History, and the Possible* (2018), Meretoja who teaches the theory of poetry, presents the idea of the ethical potential of storytelling in the development of our perspective-awareness and capacity of perspective-taking: how poetic stories can enlarge or diminish the space of possibilities[11]. We see in our concrete case of Ange's 'Tomorrow, will I be recalled?' that the first spatial circle of the possibilities could be seen as a voice against judgments, it is an ante-predicative level of experience, an unconscious reactive posture, claiming to be seen as a normal human being. Still, to be able to express all its potential, an artist needs to be able to go beyond the longing of normality, to reach a space of unique and authentic being. Genius artistic expressions arise only when the unique voice of the singular self reaches the sphere of a universal truth. Ange knows the taste of that metaphysical zone although without knowing the exact shape of it.

### Tomorrow, Will I Be Recalled?
Oh, God! You have created me[12].
You put me on this earth.
Can you allow me to live as nobody?
I want to make a thing out of nothing
I want to be somebody out of nobody
I want to construct out of destruction
Is it too late now, will I be recalled?

---

she started looking at how she can live with it, as she says in an interview for *The New Times*, the leading English newspaper in Rwanda.

[10] 'The computers I used are judging me, the social networks I used are judging me, friends, families, preachers and teachers are judging me.'

[11] Meretoja, Hanna. 2018. *Narrative Hermeneutics, History, and the Possible*, Oxford: UP. Cf. further reflections in Ch. 8 of this book.

[12] Watch the video: Tomorrow, will I be recalled?
https://www.youtube.com/watch?v=oceNNBWF_t8

Or will I just die and the world would forget me as if I never lived?
Tomorrow, will I be a hero out of zero?

Darkness and sadness are natural twins - since I was born,
I was aspired to do the best but the worst took over me!
I was irritated and demolished from inside,
All I can think is pain and hate,
The darkness is pulling me down in a cage full of sadness!
The pain flows inside me as blood flows in vain,
The normality is expressed through 'normal' relationships,
Boys, will you ignore how I broke your heart and recall me?
Women, will you ignore how I stole your men and left him penniless?
Only, tomorrow can save me.
Only tomorrow can make me be recalled.
Yesterday is pulling me down: the past is haunting me.

Today is judging me on the past, it doesn't understand,
Yesterday is saying I was never good enough;
Today is saying I am not good enough,
Tomorrow, make me a giant, and prove today and yesterday wrong,
People are judging me based on the only chapter they know about my
    life
Tomorrow save me from being nothing
I have life, it's what everyone is looking for,
I'm gonna make the most of it, so that I won't leave nothing on earth.

Tomorrow is that imagined space of the impossible possible, where
fame and recognition will soften the pain and hurts. 'Expressing, not
impressing' became her leitmotiv. Other than poetry, she is modeling[13].
As Ange formulates it:

---

[13] She goes on stage, to show the world that people with physical disability are
also capable of performing, and can do small things in a great ways. She also
does it to establish hope and confidence in all the people living a life with
disability. Going to school seems often a nightmare in itself. Studying History,
Economics and Geography at Senior Five (Secondary School), Ange had to
choose a school not for its quality in education but for its access to wheelchairs.

'It hurts to have dreams and die without even accomplishing a quarter of it. I know it is hard to step in my dreams but I also know it is possible because even the world possible means I'm possible.'

'The pain is too deep. Every time I write, my ink drips pain, not poetries...' Ange is expressing that her words are embodied experience and not just words[14].

## 6.4 Lion King: I am Cyacyana!

'If someone calls you Cyacyana, it's like they are saying you're someone useless' says Lion King. Cyacyana is an aggressive way of calling a child referring to a dehumanized world, as if a child would be an object instead of being a human creature. Ironically, the poem 'Cyacyana' is written by Lion, a rising star[15].

---

[14] She made the word of social media her own; we read these words on Instagram. In April 2018, Ange writes on her Facebook account: 'Back then [referring to her poem *Tomorrow, will I be recalled?*] I wanted to be remembered badly but today I just want to be happy, to live the reality of now not some fictionalized version of me. I want to chew every inch of the universe, I am not trying to build a legacy, to be loved or to fit in. I'm trying to live, to love and to share. See, 'it doesn't matter how the world will remember me. What matters is how I'll remember the world' because I lived every moment I was given not trying to be the idol of the town, not trying to be perfect just really; Perfect is just an illusion.' The young woman shows an important shift of her creative perception with these words, passing from the desire to be admired to be fully engaged with the world.

[15] King was awarded with the Nyirarumaga Trophy, in July 2017 with an overall and overwhelming convincing poetic performance. 'The crowd was screaming in unison every time he paused in between performances. When he left the stage, the cheers and screams went on to praise the new start'. The journalist Moses Opobo asks: 'Just who is this guy, and where has he been all long?' Before his

A poem about judgments of appearance instead of actions or human values, the poem speaks about King's own life. 'People usually judge based on appearance' he says. Because he didn't cut his hair, people had always walked to him and told him that he doesn't have a future.

In Rwanda, hair seems to be a metaphor for conformity. As much as long hair, Rasta or dreadlocks is often an artistic statement, as much the social judgment can be harsh. Students cannot miss disciplining comments by fellow students or official school authorities to get in line with standards. Falling between the norms of simplistic social status, Cyacyana has the value of openness and sees life within different perspectives. Written out of a space of marginalization, King's poem points at social stigmatizations by the majority. Cyacyana refers to a group of people who recognize each other mutually by sharing their difference.

*Cyacyana*

My appearance makes you judge[16]
But your actions make me laugh
Coz the biggest criminals don't wear tattoos
And dread locks
They are smart people they wear suits and ties[17]
It's Cyacyana yes it's him he threw all morals
I am Cyacyana who doesn't have where to get morals
We all follow one line
But when it comes to back biting, we are the first in line

---

performance, the 19 year old rapper and poet was only performing for a few fellow students at school.

[16] Watch the video: Cyacyana: www.youtube.com/watch?v=7s3_YxORzTI

[17] The poem is written in English and Kinyarwanda, reflecting the mixture of language in the everyday language of today's youth: Ngo ni cyacyana ego nicyo, Cyacyana cyataye indero, Cyacyana cyataye umuco, Oya ndi cyacyana cyabuze umuco […].

I live with an open mind
The world ever changes angles
Am ever ready let it come
Stay true like I've always done
The good the bad
The truth and the lies see
I have seen a lot and
That's why sometimes I write
And sometimes, I am Cyacyana

I am Cyacyana in the group of Byabyana
that never worry about what they say
Byabyana who admitted to called ibyana
Because of what they like
Byabyana that never sleeps
Byabyane that write day and night
Love is their weapon
They put God first.

King as a rapper by heart: 'It is not a culture from America,' he says. It is a mentality. It is music that is poetry, with a lot of rhythm and rhyming. 'People call it flowing because it is done with a beat.' His talent of flowing makes him an authentic artist and performer. What he says and performs is one, expresses his poetic self, a being beyond any standard. His poetic affinity seems to have grown out of this outsider life at school[18]: 'Every school I went to I'd always be the new guy that nobody wanted to mess with. So I'd be the lonely guy.' He remembers: 'I would just sing and after getting tired of singing, I'd get a pen and write as a way of making me happy but also whiling away the time.'

---

[18] King's school curriculum and grades reflect also his nomadic life. He studied Kindergarten and primary school in Rwanda before his family moved to Burundi where he repeated the first year. Back in Rwanda, he attended different schools for his second, third and fourth year. His family moved then to Uganda where he was integrated to third year instead of P5.

King's testimony of the inside looks to gain knowledge; it's the intimate conversation between pen and paper, one's poetic soul. Poetry is the capacity to bring the margins to stage. It is the voice from the silent space where the relationship between the self and the world is explored and digested.

## 6.5 Anisie Byukusenge: With the Eyes of my Heart

Anisie Byukusenge who has graduated in translation and interpreting at the University of Rwanda in 2017, is visually impaired since the age of 5. The 24-year old woman is a talented poet and the manager of *Seeing Hands Rwanda*, a spa for blind people. In her poem: 'What have I done wrong, Mother Nature?'[19] She cannot stop asking herself 'What have I done wrong, Mother Nature? I was just a kid, smiling at the enemy?'[20]

***What Have I Done Wrong, Mother Nature?***
The path of acceptance goes with the experience of rejection[21].
Everyone I tried to touch, just pushed me away
Everything I try to hold on, goes away and I fall
I thought I was born with bad blood
But I didn't stop
I went to start with Primary,
And continued with Secondary
Now see, I've finished University
But trouble: Never come! Never stay
In that trouble that came to me,
I've seen the good and the bad sides of humans

---

[19] 'Nacumuye iki Nyiribiremwa?'

[20] At five years old, Anisie stopped eating because her hand moved empty spoons to her mouth. The young girl was missing eyes to add food on it. In her struggle over her destiny, she has survived a suicide attempt.

[21] Watch the video: What have I done wrong, Mother Nature? www.youtube.com/watch?v=IjjOq2ASPXo

I opened the eyes of my heart as they are the ones I remained with

And now, even if I stumble over not knowing to differentiate night and
    day
I've decided to become a light to the world
Even if my heart is full of agony and irritation
I am ready to love and be loved
To give birth and raise kids surrounding me.

Don't run away from me,
Don't be against me
I've opened my arms for you
I've come towards you
To share my kindness

You, the creator,
I can't be unbearable,
Even if you didn't tell me the reasons
Even though you failed me
I testify that there is none,
Cause I was innocent

In conversation with God, the creator:
Now, I come toward you.
To give you all my sorrows.
I've come so you teach
How to accept and be grateful of how you created me
See, there is no kindness beyond that
*Teach your creatures not to be against me*
How you created me
However help me where I need hands.

Anisie is struggling with God for having her created blind. At the
same time, she asks him to become the mediator between her destiny
and the people around her. Beyond the agony, she defines her place in
the world as a light. What we also find in her deeply moving poem is the

wish to be seen as a woman, in her female and mothering capacities. We hear the echo of Sojourner's voice: 'Ain't I a Woman', the call to be a woman beyond stigmatization. In Rwanda, if the situation of disabled people has tremendously changed within the last years, in terms of rights and public acceptance, still the intimate and relational space is mined by prejudice. Anisie herself was encouraged by her own mother to give up the love with a young man, a light of joy in her life.

As with Ange, we understand the act of expressing poetically the pain as an important moment of accepting the unchangeable reality of being blind, of being condemned to the wheelchair, of becoming grateful for our own life. Elaine Scarry wraps up this fundamental self-awareness as related to the notion of beauty: as a beauty towards one's own being[22].

---

[22] Cf. Scarry, Elaine. 2014. Poetry Changed the World. Injury and the Ethics of Reading. In: *The Humanities and Public Life*, ed. Peter Brooks. New York: Fordham University Press.

# 7

# APHORISMS:
# THE BEST THING TO GIVE TO OUR
# WORLD

*Obiora Ike*

## 7.1 I Am a Child

I am a child, I want to sing a song to your heart, in the name of many other children[23].

I am a child; the fruit of your life; the testing of your love; my world is so small and yet so big like yours; even though I cannot conceive the idea. Come, help me! Take my hand and lead me over the street that leads to the school of life.

Convert your world and my world into our world. You were also a child with joy, sorrows, wishes --- we are both children of this earth — children of one GOD.

---

[23] Prof. Dr Obiora Ike is Executive Director of Globethics.net in Geneva and Professor of Ethics at the Godfrey Okoye University Enugu/Nigeria.

You are big and I am small. What does that matter? Your hard slap on my face is painful, not only to me. It concerns life, what have I done to you.

Say yes to my life and to your life. I need your love, your warmth.

As you are to me, so shall I be to those children who come after me. They shall laugh, they shall weep, as I do.

Dry my tears, share my joys, forget your death. Have some time for me, your child.

## 7.2 The Cost of Peace and the Cost of War (in Comparison)

When we speak of the cost of PEACE, we cannot forget the cost of WAR. The world is getting very different now. For man holds in his hands the power to abolish all forms of human poverty and all forms of human life. Let mankind of every nation, every tribe, every race, every tongue, creed, religion, colour, ideology and philosophy, culture or whatever world view explore the problems that UNITE us, instead of be labouring those problems which DIVIDE us. This is the price of peace which must be paid if ever we shall attain peace. Peace is the last state of happiness and the noblest price we can gain in this valley of tears. But the cost of peace is so dear that only the patient can ever attain it. Yet peace in spite of its cost is better than war even if it seems the easiest way out. PEACE!!!

## 7.3 A Smile Costs Nothing

A smile costs nothing but gives much. It enriches those who receive, without making poorer those who give, it takes but a moment, but the memory of it sometimes lasts forever. None is so rich that he can get along without it, and none is so poor that he can be made rich by it. A smile creates happiness in the home, fosters goodwill in the business world, and is the countersign of friendship. It brings rest to the weary, cheer to the discouraged, sunshine to the sad, and it is nature's best antidote for trouble.

Yet it cannot be begged, borrowed, or stolen, for it is something that is of no value to anyone until it is given away. Some people are too tired to give you a smile. Give them one of yours, as none needs smile so much as he who has no more to give.

## 7.4 On Forgiveness

To return evil for evil is a disgrace vengefully disgraceful;
To return evil for good is devilish;
To return good for good is just human!
To return good for evil is Godlike;
To be thankful for little is to possess great riches;
To keep silent about evil is to implant it;
It is man-like to revenge but God-like to forgive.
Virtue is not secure till its practice becomes a habitude and is free from the opposition of the contrary inclination. All noble things are as difficult as they are rare.

## 7.5 A Friend

A friend is someone with whom you can share your thoughts without fear of his walking away in condemnation seeking his understanding.

A friend is someone with whom you can be naked in body without fear ridicule or rejection of your imperfection seeking his harmony.

A friend is someone with whom you can probe his soul without fear of your acceptance seeking his knowledge.

A friend is someone with whom you can lie next to and hold without fear of his attitude toward your intentions seeking his warmth

A friend is in truth a human being where there is no fear that your life, which is precious, is shared seeking your peace.

## 7.6 The Best Thing to Give to Our World

The best thing to give your enemy is forgiveness.
To an opponent tolerance;
To a friend sincerity;
To your wife heart;
To your father humility;
To your mother conduct that will make her proud of you;
To your child a good example;
To yourself respect.
And to all men charity;
To God your creator adoration.

# 8

# ALL IN THE NAME OF GOD

## *Dicky Sofjan*

I have travelled afar to nearly 30 countries of the world[24]
Venturing to the East and West as well as the North and South
Only to realize that the world comprises many faiths and beliefs
With each one earnestly struggling to attain relevance in today's
    conflictive world

The Islam I know is a religion of peace
A religion brought about by an orphaned, illiterate Prophet
Muhammad was his name
Peace be upon Him, His Progeny and Faithful Companions

The Angels and all inhabitants of the Heaven
Praise Him and send their blessings
For He is the 'Seal of the Prophets'
Testifying and affirming all the Prophets and Apostles before him

The *Sunnah* is the Way of the Prophet
Far from being the 'Way of the Sword'
For the Sufi mystics, His name preceded existence
His eminence sits beside his Lover's beautiful name

---

[24] Dr Dicky Sofjan is core doctoral faculty, Indonesian Consortium for Religious Studies (ICRS), Graduate School of Universitas Gadjah Mada (UGM) in Yogyakarta, Indonesia.

Allah is the God of Islam
The One and Alone
The Most Beneficent, the Merciful
The Sovereign on the Day of Recompense

'Say: He is Allah, the One
He is the Eternal Refuge
He neither begets, nor was born
Nor is there to Him any equivalent'

He partners with no one
Yet provide sustenance for everyone
He neither forgets
Nor discriminates

Every hill, mountain and planet
Every lake, river and sea
Every cell, plant and tree
Every living being in the multiverse

All chant His name in glory
*Allahu akbar!* God is Great!
*Allahu akbar!* God is Great!
*Allahu akbar!* God is Great!

The Quran is Islam's Holy Scripture
It is a Book about which there is no doubt
'*Laa ikrahaa fiiddiin,*' laments the Quran
There is no compulsion in the matters of faith.

*** 

I was born into a faithful Muslim family
It was not so much my personal choice
As we can't possibly choose our parents
But I feel Heavenly blessed with it

In all honesty, I could truly recognize and feel its spiritual prowess
And understand why the Quran
Refers to Islam as 'a blessing for the multiverse'
For I indeed have witnessed such blessing throughout my own lifetime

I pronounce my faith every now and then
And conduct the obligatory prayers and supplications on a daily basis
I try my best to always fast during the month of Ramadhan each year
And regularly pay my religious alms and give charity to the poor

Yet, I have come to know that for others
My Islam is impure, unauthentic and inadequate
For they desire a uniformed kind of Islam
An Islam that could only be fitting for beardy, male chauvinistic Arab
    men

They consider people like me as almost Muslim
An aspiring Muslim, at best
Or a Muslim wannabe
A person whose religion or faith seems strange, if not ludicrous

Call it al-Qa'idah or Daesh or an-Nusra
Call it IS, ISIS or ISIL
Call it whatever you want to
But how dare you associate it with Islam?!

How is it even possible that Islam could terrorize people?
When its God is the Most Beneficent, the Merciful?
Or, when its Prophet is an illiterate and orphan, who constantly yearned
    for love?
And whose essential desire was teach us all to love and be loved?

How is it that you insist on it being Islam
When there is neither love nor compassion in their endeavour?
How is it that you persistently perceive it as Islam
When the only thing they teach is violence and mayhem?

Indeed, Islam is the most misunderstood religion
But it is also true that Islam is the most abused religion
For the great many Islam bashers out there
Islam, from its very outset, is a religion of war, conflict and
     hatemongering

A religion that is vicious and nasty, they say
A religion that is full of ambiguity and obscurity
A religion that feeds on irrationality and infidelity
A religion that seeks to destroy the very foundation of humanity.

                    ***

But Islam is none one of them
Because Islam is 'the Straight Path' toward God
A path of love, compassion, redemption and salvation
Of mercy, devotion and benevolence

Therefore, let Him be a witness
A witness to our faith, love, devotion and compassion
For Allah is the Creator of all hearts
And surely He knows what we all conceal in them

The time is ripe for us to come together
To learn from each other
To forgive but never forget
To live and let live

There is really no reason whatsoever to fight among the children of God
Among those who truly believe in His bounty
For His sustenance is boundless and ceaseless
And surely there is enough to for everyone, if we could only tame our
     relentless desires

For greed or avarice is the main source of evil
Creating jealousy and animosity
That result in forgetfulness and insensibleness
Yet, we realize that no man is an island and that no bridge is too far

If religion were to teach us to hate one another
Then, let it be known that I am against religion
But my religion teaches me to love and care for others
And so, I would rather die then to be rid of my religion

It is all too easy, familiar and intuitive
To find religious people speak of harmony, peace and reconciliation
Or, to get religious teachers and scholars to preach about such topics
But seeing the world today, I fear for the future of religion

Religion, they quickly learned, is an effective mobilization tool
To serve the varied interests of political masters and business partners
        alike
Whether to gain votes or attain public office
Or to profit from the military industrial complex

Today, the politicization of religion is the new normal
The Way of the Post-Modern World
Politics and business are hidden beneath the cover of religion and piety
While the faithful naively believe they are working to manifest God's
        Divine Plan

Religious parochialism and particularism are definitely on the rise
And fast becoming humanity's cutting-edge ideology
With many calling upon God's name
To justify their annexation and colonization.

                    ***

They say that killing one person is murder
And killing tens of thousands of people is foreign policy
The question is:
How many deaths does it take to constitute a crime against humanity?

Religion provides the perfect pretext to ruin the lives of many
Because the Almighty seemingly permits it
The Holy Scriptures appear to always find their way in
To rationalize the death, destruction and mayhem

What excuse have we got?
When we are later brought before God's supreme court?
To explain the unnecessary and wanton killing of many innocent lives
Or, to defend our constant want and desire for all the material things in
     life

In every conflict, every battle and every war
Innocent blood is spilled
Women, children, the aged and non-combatants
They simply dismiss them as 'collateral damage'

Chaos and strife seem to rule the world now
With unwise kings, presidents, prime ministers and generals all blinded
By the lure of material benefits and political domination
And all is done in the name of God.

# PART II

# ESSAIES

*Inventing Possibilities in Which We Are Moved
to Action and How We Live Together*

*Nursery Rhymes, Fairy Tales, Religious Art, Symbolic Representations,
Mimesis, Metaphorical Narrative, Lies, Literature,
Ideology and the Poetic Voice*

# 1

# NURSERY RHYMES, FAIRY TALES AND CARTOONS: A MIASMA OF VALUES, VIOLENCE AND SOCIAL RECONSTRUCTION

*Divya Singh*

## 1.1 Introduction

*Have you ever wondered why your young son or daughter is afraid of the dark; or displays inexplicable signs of aggression and what role you may be playing in introducing these fears and behaviours?*[25]

The wicked stepmother in Snow White exuding malice, the giant in Jack and the Beanstalk threatening the village, the violent deaths of two of the three little pigs, the loneliness, isolation and ill-treatment of poor Cinderella, the vicious attack on the three blind mice who have their tails cut off with a carving knife,

*sing a song of sixpence a pocket full of rye, four and twenty blackbirds baked in a pie, when the pie was open the birds began to sing, now wasn't that a dainty to dish to set before a king?*

---

[25] Prof. Dr Divya Singh is Chief Academic Officer at STADIO Holdings, Divya Singh holds an LL D, a Master in Tertiary Education Management. Among her keynote experiences, she is advocate of the High Court of South Africa and former vice Principal at the University of South Africa.

Really? Cooking the birds alive? What these often-repeated rhymes and stories have in common - explicitly or by implication - are words like wicked, evil, kill, and/or poison that a fertile little imagination without the appropriate cognitive filters, can build into its own experience and expression of terror. What is also significant is that in many of the stories where there is emotional loss with concomitant feelings hurt, injury and pain, the cause of the harm is neither reactive or retributive: rather, it is perpetrated on innocent victims *whose families and carers seem unable to protect them.*

Children today are exposed to violence almost every day and in early childhood much of it is inadvertent by the very people tasked with caring and protecting the child. Do you ever wonder if your child, whilst lying in bed, is afraid of the evil witch offering her a poisoned apple, or the ugly giant climbing down from the beanstalk, or the troll who lives under the bridge, or being left motherless and alone like poor Cinderella, or locked in a tower like Rapunzel, or being caught by Father Bear or the big bad wolf? So many images and of course we all know that in contemporary society, there are no 'handsome princes' so unlike Sleeping Beauty or Rapunzel or Snow White who will be their hero? Is it possible that Superman's nemesis will scale the walls of the house to enter in the night?

The literature abounds with expert opinion on the impact of reading violent literature or watching media violence of the cognitive and affective development of young children: however, what was not available was a holistic impact study of all three influences on the child - starting with nursery rhymes, progressing to fairy tales and allowing unsupervised cartoon viewing as the child grows older. One would be forgiven for exclaiming, 'Innocuous!' but analysing the literal, visual and emotional results as a progressive and collective experience, parents, teachers and caregivers may think twice about the life's lessons to which we are exposing our children. How often does one hear the question: '*Why are children so violent today?*' This article focuses on the ordinary wording of these oft-repeated media experiences and their potential effect in many young children's lives. It highlights the unprecedented levels of violence to which children are exposed - unintentionally - before the age of ten years. As one focusses on social and moral regeneration of the individual, home, and society, this discussion introduces a critical field for further study.

## 1.2 Discussion

### 1.2.1 Nursery Rhymes

Nursery rhymes and fairy tales, as spoken by most adults to their young children or by teachers to young charges, are primarily intended for fun or to amuse. Seldom do we take the time to consider the words or the message that is being shared and what a young mind may understand and interpret from the little songs and stories. So, let's take a quick look at some of what we read to the children:

> *Baa Baa black sheep have you any wool? Yes, Sir ... Yes, Sir ... Three bags full. One for the Master, and one for the Dame, but none for the little boy that lives down the lane.*

In *Baa Baa black sheep,* the both adults get something, but the little boy gets nothing. Immediately two vices present themselves: spite and selfishness – both of which are decidedly antithetical to the values that caregivers deliberately foster in impressionable young children. Another version of the rhyme has a changed last line which reads '*But none for the naughty boy crying down the lane.*' In this latter version there is a lesson in the story namely that if you're naughty, you will not be rewarded. Yet a third version reads, '*And one for the little boy who lives down the lane.*' In this version, everyone gets to share – both the lesson and the messaging are far more positive in impact. One immediately notes how the rhyme has been amended from the original to promote better social acceptance.

> *Ding dong bell, pussy's in the well.   Who put her in? Little Johnny Flynn. Who pulled her out? Little Tommy Stout. Oh, what a naughty both was that who tried to drown poor pussy cat who never did him any harm but killed the mice in his father's barn.*

Again, there is a lesson that it's wrong to drown the animal but still the main imagery is that of the cruelty to the animal.

> *Tom Tom the Piper's son, stole a pig and away did run.   The pig was eat and Tom was beat, and Tom went crying down the street.*

Of course, there's a good lesson that stealing is wrong and will generate punishment but equally the story is quite the expression of (a) inappropriate conduct in that the stolen pig was eaten and not returned; and (b) unfairness because everyone made common purpose with the criminal act and benefitted from eating the pig but only Tom was still 'beat' for his action.

Other more violent and morbid examples include:

> *Davey Davey dumpling, boil him in the pot.   Sugar him and butter him and eat him while he's hot!*

> *Goosey Goosey Gander, where shall I wander?   Upstairs and downstairs and in my lady's chamber.   There I met an old man who couldn't say his prayers, I caught him by the left leg and threw him down the stairs. The stairs went crack, the man fell back, and all the ducks in the house went quack, quack, quack.*

Whilst the original story is materially different from the rhyme shared with children,[26] what the young mind hears is a theme of physical violence.

> *Rock-a-bye baby on the treetop. When the wind blows the cradle will rock. When the bough breaks the cradle will fall and down will come baby, cradle and all.*

> *There was an old woman who lived in a shoe. She had so many children, she didn't know what to do. She gave them some bread without any broth and whipped them all soundly and sent them to bed.*

> *Ladybird, ladybird, fly away home. Your house is on fire, your children all gone. Except for the little one and her name is Ann, and she crept under the frying pan.*

One of the most inconceivable rhymes to read/teach to a child because of its depressing and melancholic message:

> *Poor little Johnny, his mother was dead. His father was a drunkard who couldn't buy him bread. He sat by the window playing his banjo, thinking of his mother far, far away.*

In a nutshell one has read about drowning and other forms of cruelty to animals, ridiculing the blind, babies falling from trees, hunger, beating, children displaced (and perhaps lost) by fire, deliberately injuring others by pushing them down stairs, power relations, boiling people and eating people (cannibalism). One the one hand, some

---

[26] According to Burton-Hill *Goosey Goosey Gander* is really the story of religious persecution reflecting a time when Catholic priests would have to chant their forbidden latin-based prayers in secret and often in the privacy of the own homes (Burton-Hill, 2015).

nursery rhymes are blatantly cruel,[27] whilst others give a hint of prohibited conduct: however, rarely is there any punishment for the wrongdoer. The lesson in these instances is perhaps an indication of naughty, but then there are seldom repercussions for the wayward conduct.

The synopsis shared certainly begs the question: why would nursery rhymes aimed at children be framed with such negative imagery? The answer lies in the fact that nursery rhymes were never intended for children and the stories/themes/ideas are therefore not child orientated. Research agrees that nursery rhymes as we read them today were actually part of an oral-based tradition that sought to record political events and social and moral contestations dating back to about the fourteenth century. According to Roberts, 'Childhood is a relatively recent phenomena' emerging over the last 'couple of hundred years [where] children are seen as very separate from adults.' (2005: 2) It was only in the nineteenth century 'when Victorian society sentimentalised childhood and romanticised 'quaint' times from the past, that most nursery rhymes were written down and presented as for children only' (Sizer undated: 2).

With this explanation, one more readily understands the content and tone of many nursery rhymes but equally the anachronism that is evidenced in several of the rhymes. However, Prosic-Sanovac stresses that

---

[27] An Afrikaans lullaby, Siembamba, was originally a poem about the death of children on the concentration camps: however, in the contemporary age the song sung goes:

*Siembamba, mama se kindjie*
*Siembamba, mama se kindjie*
*Draai sy nek om, gooi hom in die sloot*
*Trap op sy kop, dan is hy dood.*

Translated: Siembamba, mother's baby… Siembamba, mother's baby. Twist his neck, throw him in the ditch. Stamp on his head, then he is dead.

'[r]hymes need to be considered from the point of view of the relevance of their content to the children's world and their age appropriateness, and whether they provide material for encouragement of discussion and exploration of values, as well as the means for overcoming a variety of problems children may encounter in their daily lives' (2015: 1).

Many of the nursery rhymes that are shared are unacceptable in today's values and equality culture and it behoves parents to be much more selective in what they read to their children. In today's learning milieu, rhymes enforcing stereotypes, especially the timidity, servility and fragility of girls should be re-considered in the same way as rhymes describing racial labels. For example, *Georgie Porgie Pudding and Pie kissed the girls and made them cry. When the boys came out to play, Georgie Porgie ran away.* Similarly, *Little Miss Muffet, Peter Peter Pumpkin Eater*; and the classic illustration of obsolete thinking:

*What are little girls made of? Sugar and spice and all things nice – that's what little girls are made of. What are little boys made of? Frogs and snails and puppy dog tails – that's what little boys are made of.*

Similarly, the rhyme which premises the adage 'children should be seen and not heard: *A wise old owl lived in an oak. The more he saw, the less he spoke. The less he spoke, the more he heard. Why can't we all be like that wise old bird?* Today, the value of this proposition has been widely questioned, with significant literature emphasising the importance of communication and engagement in the child's development. Perhaps, however, the explanation is again to be found in history. Peter Gray notes that

'For hundreds of thousands of years, children educated themselves by play and exploration. [...] With the rise of agriculture, and later of industry, children became forced labourers. Play and exploration were suppressed. Wilfulness, which had been a virtue, became a vice that had to be beaten out of children' (2008: 1).

Notwithstanding the above, it is important to avoid over-reaction and throwing the baby out with the bathwater - nursery rhymes have a very well-documented benefit for children's language, comprehension and cognitive development and, emphasises Cook, insofar as children's learning process are concerned, 'a good deal of language remains primarily driven by sound rather than meaning' (1997: 228). The repetitive rhythm, visual colour, short length and simplicity of the rhymes make them appealing and easy to remember. They are indicated as promoting language skills, expression, and vocabulary in a far more positive and fun learning environment than the traditional classroom setting (Crystal 2001:28). Palmer and Bayley emphasise the importance of nursery rhymes, particularly those with music, pointing out their developmental function in significantly aiding a child's 'mental development and spatial reasoning' (The Express Tribune: 1).

Therefore, whilst acknowledging the negative impact of the literal expressions of violence and abusive imagery of many nursery rhymes, if dealt with in a responsible and developmentally suitable manner by the teacher/parent, the learning potential of rhymes may be extended beyond the literal to introducing children to the important skills of dealing with emotion. Prosic-Santovac maintains that psychologically, selected rhymes can be used to provide children with the tools for acquiring necessary knowledge both about themselves and in their social spaces. (2009: 47) This, of course, pre-supposes proper engagement between the reader and the child explaining what is being read and seen pictorially. Unfortunately, this is not always the practice and in fact, with nursery rhymes, the reader will often laugh at or enact the violence creating a sense of positive reinforcement for what is unacceptable or even frightening conduct.

### 1.2.2 Fairy Tales

When the child grows a little older, we start reading fairy tales – Snow White and the Seven Dwarfs, Cinderella, Little Red Riding Hood, Rapunzel, Hansel and Gretel, the Three Little Bears, and Jack and the Beanstalk. As with nursery rhymes, the same themes of good and evil, loss, naughtiness and despair are repeated, and the same values-based enquiries - as with nursery rhymes - are apposite. Fairy tales are often used by parents and teachers to introduce and reinforce behaviours. For example, in the Three Little Pigs the wolf's demise in the pot of boiling water and the witch's violent end in Hansel and Gretel are intended to show the triumph of good over evil and illustrate the repercussions of malevolent conduct. However, notwithstanding the messaging, the use of fear and violence as an instrument to educate children remains questionable. Sanpruskin claims that statistics show that today 'parents are no longer read[ing] fairy tales to their children due to the prominent themes of violence' (2015: 1).

Creasey, however, takes quite a different view to the effects of the repetitive themes of evil and violence, advancing the hypothesis that violence, if used appropriately, has its place in children's literature in that it exposes children to the realities of violence and helps them develop and understand coping mechanisms (Creasey 2010: 1). And Creasey's is not a unique opinion - Moustakis agrees emphasising that even in the absence of the 'literary culprit' and in cases where children were completely protected from 'tales of ogres and monsters' in the attempt to 'make bedtime easier', they still took form in the children's imaginations (Moustakis 1982: 13). This is the 'power of a child's imagination to create violent situations even when parents and teachers try hard to steer children from any material that would inspire such behaviour,' confirms Williams (2004: 4). Further defending violence in fairy tales Moustakis points out that 'Fairy tales handle justice and retribution in a manner that young children can understand (1982: 6). In fairy tales 'often the violent tales contain violence to emphasise of moral value' as opposed to haphazard gratuitous aggression (Creasey 2010: 4). Citing Bettelheim, Sanpruskin notes that those of the Moustakis school of thought believe that violence and fear found in the majority of fairy tales is always answered and overcome by the forces of good (2015: 2).

Taking no definitive side in the debate, it is suggested however, that for optimal advantage to the moral values in the fairy tales, there must be some intervention that allows children to *understand* the real emotions of others and the effects and impact of what is being read. Furthermore, it is important to acknowledge that, as with the traditional nursery rhymes, the stories of Hans Christian Anderson and the Brothers Grimm are more than 200 years old. In all the traditional fairy tales one sees the racial and gender biases with a total absence of diversity, an emphasis on physical attributes, the stereotyping of woman, and the 'strong and protective' role of men as the 'saviours' of the 'defenceless fairer sex', all of which should be unequivocally rebuffed in the contemporary values-driven society. In the absence of further explanation Sanpruskin's caution must be noted:

> 'There are no redeemable qualities in any of these fairy tales' villains and no indications of their humanity or their suffering, which in turn makes it very difficult for the child to put him or herself in the villains' shoes. Instead of seeking alternative endings, children understand violence as the solution to seek their "happily ever after" and overcome their fear' (2015: 2).

### 1.2.3 Cartoons

Like nursery rhymes and fairy tales, cartoons also have a positive effect on children's development teaching them humour, the brilliance of imagery and again develops the imagination. However, Schneiter points out that children in the age category 6 to 7-years-old are still developing psychologically (2013: 1) and are consequently both impressionable and open to suggestion. Zauche *et al* also stress that early childhood is a critical period for language and cognitive development where children start learning from observation (2016: 318). Research also confirms that knowledge and attitudes learned/acquired at an early age can have far-reaching consequences on the life of a child (Prosic-Santovac 2009: 64). Therefore, story lines in Tom and Jerry, Wile E. Coyote and the Road Runner, and Tweetie and Sylvester - which are built on violence and revenge but where, irrespective of the seriousness of the harmful act, no-one is ever seriously or permanently injured - have the potential to create a cognitive belief that violent responses when angered or in order to 'get your way' are normal and, in fact, funny because 'everyone laughed when it happened on the TV'.

Today with the enhancements in media technology and graphic design, cartoon characters have become increasingly life-like and not much different from real people (Schneiter 2013: 1). This adds to the child's confusion in discerning differences between play-acting and reality. However, Schneiter is quick to emphasise that whilst the real-life character may *aggravate* the problem, it does not *create* the concern as children identify equally with cartoon and real characters (2013: 1).

According to Grose another factor that exacerbates the effects of watching violent cartoons is the 'indiscriminate' nature of the violence and the fact that it is often glamorised and 'perpetrated by the heroes themselves, for immediate reward' (Schoolatoz 2015: 1).

There is consensus in the literature that exposure to violence makes it more acceptable to children and that children exposed to media violence will often try and imitate what they see, presenting with behaviours that are both aggressive and dangerous. Available research also agrees that to the extent of being perpetrated by heroes and role models, it gives children the implicit go-ahead to also do the same. Confirming this opinion, Mandrapa emphasises that children often identify themselves with the characters as role models notwithstanding the inappropriateness of the choices - most often the characters are too aggressive or have supernatural powers that enable them to fly, shoot spider web from the wrist, leap across buildings, fall from the top of a skyscraper and not get hurt, beat up multiple 'bad guys' singlehandedly and walk away unharmed *etc.* (2014: 3). Similarly, the American Psychological Association states:

> 'Children who identify with aggressive TV characters and perceive the violence to be realistic are most at risk for later aggression' (2003: 1).

Explaining why violent visual content evokes an aggression response in the viewer, Daly and Perez submit that the continuing exposure to violence 'desensitises the child to the repugnant nature of the behaviour and violent activity and imitation is conceived as being standard social practice.' (2009: 1) This then manifests in the child becoming increasingly uncaring of and indifferent to the suffering of others, depending on the duration and degree of the violence. They point out that:

> 'Separation of internal thought from external perception marks the emergence of symbolic capacity and directly facilitates cognitive growth and abstract thinking. Until these capacities are developed, children cannot reflect upon or understand the consequences of violent behaviour. As such, children who are developing internal symbolic systems are vulnerable to the images of media, especially when the images are violent' (2009: 1-2).

Another similar study conducted by researchers from the University of Washington points to the fact that children engaged in prosocial and non-violent cartoons were considerably more sociable children than those who were left to watch violent cartoons. The latter cohort of children all exhibited clear and early signs of aggression (Drinka 2013:

2). Interestingly, in a follow-up engagement with the original respondents six months after the study ended, the researchers found that many of the parents had reverted to the old behaviours of unsupervised television viewing and the children had equally started to display violent predisposition (Drinka 2013: 2). Kashaba notes that Huesmann's research raises a further enquiry in the realm of 'imaginative' versus 'imitative' play (2008: 2). For many parents and caregivers one of the reasons that cartoons and fairy tales are introduced to children is to stimulate imaginative play: however, watching violent cartoons has been found to have just the opposite effect and whilst decreasing the element of imaginative play, it increases the imitative play factor. Kashaba notes that children exposed to media violence are far more prone to mimic the various aggressive responses in their play without the necessary cognitive understanding or any creative thought (ibid.). In such cases, the absence of appropriate supervision to explain the differences between reality and fiction, cartoons can be used as 'substitutes for real life' (Mandrapa 2014: 1).

Contextualising the views expressed by Huesmann, Perry points out that by the age of 18-years, the average child will have witnessed approximately 200 000 acts of violence on television. And so, '[e]ven with solid emotional, behavioural, cognitive and social anchors provided by a healthy home and community, this pervasive media violence increases aggression and anti-social behaviour.' (Perry 2001: 3) 'Simplifying this behavioural reality, Drinka uses the work of Donald Hebb on associative thinking explaining that 'neurons that fire together wire together' (2013:2):

'What this means is that when a group of neurons are activated concurrently in a child's central nervous system they begin to form a kind of firing unit. So when a child sees violence used as a means to solve a problem, this lesson becomes hard-wired in the central nervous system. [...] Certain behaviours are not simply learned but neurologically fixed, and therefore hard to change' (Drinka 2013: 2).

Notably, research studies find that interest in *violence* itself does not determine viewership at a young age. In the study conducted by Daly and Perez they found that boys chose to watch the typical Batman, Superman and Power Rangers; whilst girls preferred Little Mermaid, Cinderella and Beauty and the Beast. Both genders watched Shrek, Aladdin and Lion King. When assessed for violent content, Superman scored 69 points whilst Little Mermaid 1 had 134; and Power Rangers had 90 points compared to Little Mermaid 2 with 101 points (2009: 9). However, Huesmann *et al* found that – consistent with the justification theory of behaviour – more aggressive children, teenagers and adults positively seek out media violence because it makes their behaviour 'seem normal. This increases their aggressive schemas and beliefs through observational learning and makes subsequent aggression more likely' (Huesmann *et al* 2003: 217).

The existing body of research is *ad idem* that children exposed to violence may become:

(i)     more desensitised to the harmful effects of violence

(ii)    less understanding of the harm and its effect/impact, in other words they do not fear violence nor are they bothered by violence

(iii)   more fearful

(iv)    more aggressive in their behaviour – Eron et al are categoric that watching violent television in early childhood 'is statistically related to later aggression.' (1972: 257)

This summary of effect is quite fascinating as it sets a continuum of impact. On the one hand is the evidence that exposure to aggression may have the potential to desensitise a young viewer to violence; whilst on the other hand, we learn that exposure to violence generates a heightened sense of fear in the young child. Warburton for instance, is categoric in his assessment of

> 'hundreds of studies that show that if you have a lot of exposure to violent media, including cartoon violence, you tend to develop a belief system that thinks the world is more harmful than it actually is' (Schoolatoz 2015: 2).

It would be irresponsible to create a belief that watching violence always engenders aggression in children. The relationship between media violence and children's development is complex and, as Kostyrka-Allchorne indicates, depends on a variety of factors including the child's individual characteristics, family and social context (2016:2). Cartoons can be 'an important factor in helping or harming healthy psychological development in young children and into the future' (Schneiter 2013: 3). Referencing decades of research, one finds that 'children emulate behaviours – both good and bad - that they see on screen' (Christakis *et al* 2013:3). Therefore, rather than throwing the baby out with the bath water, avoiding the negative repercussions of nursery rhymes, fairy tales and cartoons can be quite easy to remediate by introducing a more managed approach to what children are allowed to view.

## 1.3 Conclusion

Returning to the question about whether exposure to violence in the form of visual and aural media including nursery rhymes, story-telling and cartoons causes fear in young children who lack the appropriate cognitive maturity to interpret and understand what they are hearing and seeing, one finds significant agreement in the affirmative.

Aggression and hostility in many nursery rhymes, fairy tales and cartoons are commonplace, and these values and conduct may indiscernibly and subliminally, or quite directly, imprint themselves on the child's mind. In the infant, violence is probably a spontaneous reaction but as the child matures and the exposure continues, the aggression is presented in a much more co-ordinated pattern of aggression. Eron *et al* note that '[t]he best single predictor of violent behaviour in older adolescents, and even middle-aged adults is aggressive behaviour when they were younger' (1972: 259). Thus, they suggest, 'anything that promotes aggressive behaviour in young children statistically is a risk factor for violent for violent behaviour in adults as well' (1972: 7).

Children who read about violence and watch violence are also inclined to try out these behaviours often not fully cognisant of the repercussions because the wolf is always there on the pages every time you open the book and Tom keeps coming back no matter what Jerry does.

Kunkel takes the discussion a step further framing the concerns as a critical 'public health' issue. In his presentation to the U.S. Senate Committee on Commerce, Science, and Transportation he drew the following comparison:

'The statistical relationship between children's exposure to violent portrayals and their subsequent aggressive behaviour has been shown to be stronger than the relationship between asbestos exposure and the risk of laryngeal cancer; the relationship between condom use and the risk of contracting HIV; and exposure to second-hand smoke in the workplace and the risk of lung cancer. [...] There is a strong consensus that exposure to media violence is a significant public health concern' (2007:2; see also Bushman *et al* 2001).

According to Aliyeva (2013) children who watch cartoons full of violence tend to be nervous, aggressive and disobedient; whilst Christakis *et al* also confirm that 'as aggressive behaviour in early childhood years has been repeatedly linked to violence in later youth and adolescence, interventions that might reduce early aggressive behaviour could have significant societal implications' (2013: 3; see also Huesmann and Miller 1994: 180).

However, whilst recognising the effects of violence, one must be equally alive to the fact that many of the rhymes that we continue to repeat today were first authored centuries ago and repeating these outdated teachings to children continues to reference value sets that are often rather anachronistic.

Therefore, if the question is: what values are we really inculcating in our children with the literary and media diet that we serve them, caregivers, parents and teachers must be concerned about the number of times repetitive themes of violence are shared with children and presented as acceptable. The follow-up question with which one is then confronted is: when children are exposed to violence – from nursery rhymes to fairy tales to cartoon viewing – is it because we have not fully comprehended the impact that it might have on the emotional and psychological health of the child and, by extension, on society?

It will be counter-intuitive to suggest that all nursery rhymes, fairy tales and cartoons should never be engaged because of the negative themes identified. The material benefits on children's development are well-documented: media – nursery rhymes, fairy tales and cartoons – have a positive benefit in developing the young person's imagination and emotion. Just as the characters experience various and disparate emotions, this can assist the child identify his/her own emotions. However, as we focus on the value systems that we seek to inculcate in future generations, parents should become more conscious of the risks and take greater care moderating media programming and *what* is shared with their young children as well as *how* the information is shared. Huesmann *et al* suggest that parents who co-view programmes with their children and discuss the behaviours observed reduce the effects of TV violence on children. They reason that explanations will assist the child to understand that the violence observed is not real and is not something to be emulated because even the observed outcomes are fantasy (2003: 219). Head and Darcy reiterate the view that talking may 'mediate the association between cognitive outcomes and social risks' (Undated presentation: slide 14). Similarly, Daly and Perez state, 'Parents should not undervalue the importance of shared media viewing, nor should they overlook the significance of interacting with their children and explaining violent content to them.' (2009:10)

The truth is that, 'children are affected by violence whether it is animated fantasy or with real people,' says Schneiter, and often when programmes are rated 'fantasy violence' (as opposed to 'normal' violence) it may be misleading as it gives parents a false sense of security that what their children are watching isn't harmful to their psychological health (2013: 3). The research consensus is that young children's ability to regulate their behaviour towards a more prosocial framework would be significantly enhanced by interactive regulatory support with the caregiver and a limit on the amount of violence that is part of the child's visual and aural diet (Daly and Perez 2009: 10). Specifically regarding observed violence, Daly and Perez suggest that the lack of regulation when children watch alone, hinders their self-regulation ability. To back their view, they cite their finding that 'children who watched violent content alone were more than twice as verbally aggressive as those who watched it with their parents' (2009: 9). However, this factor does not stand on its own and as Shonkoff and Phillips point out environmental factors such as the home, and parental behaviours also had a significant effect on the child's development (2000: 226). Likewise, the study by Huesmann *et al* suggests that severe instances of aggression are more likely to occur if there is a convergence of precipitating factors including neuropsychological predisposition, poor child rearing, socio-economic deprivation, poor peer relations, attitudes and beliefs supporting aggression, drug and alcohol abuse, frustration and provocation; and there is significant evidence that 'exposure to media violence is one such long-term pre-disposing and short-term precipitating factor' (2003: 201).

Consequently, if the question is: what values are we really inculcating in our children, caregivers, teachers and parents need to be concerned about the number of times repetitive themes of violence are shared with children and presented as acceptable; similarly, long unsupervised exposure and engagement with violent media themes. There is simply no gainsaying the costly impact of antisocial behaviour at both the individual and societal levels, but important familial differences can mitigate the long-term impact. Parents must talk to their children more [...] interacting with them and explaining the meaning behind what is read and seen. 'Parents must not be tricked into thinking that because a story is presented in cartoon format it has a lesser impact on children' (Shoolatoz 2015: 2).

## 1.4 References

Aliyeva, A. 2013. Hidden effects of cartoons on little spectators. *AZERNEWS*. https://www.azernews.az/analysis/58562.html

American Psychological Association. 2003. *Childhood Exposure to Media Violence Predicts Young Adult Aggressive Behavior, According to a New 15-Year Study*. http://www.apa.org /news/press/release/2003/03/media-violence.aspx

Burton-Hill C. 2015. BBC Britain Special Series. www.bbc.com/ culture/story/20150610-the-dark-side-of-nursery-rhymes.

Bushman, B.J., and Huesmann, L.R. Effects of televised violence on aggression. In Singer, J. (ed). 2001. *Handbook on Children and the Media.* Sage Publications: California.

Christakis, D.A., Garrison, M.M., Herrenkohl, T.,Haggerty, K., Rivara, F.P., Zhou, C., Liekweg, K. 2013. Modifying Media Content for Pre-School Children: A Randomized Controlled Trial. 131(3). *Pediatrics.* 431. www.pediatrics.aappublications.org/content/131/3/431

Cook, G. 1997. Language Play, Language Learning. *ELT Journal.* 51(3). 224-31.                http://203.72.145.166/ELT/files/51-3-4.pdf http://www.luther.edu/oneota-reading-journal/archive/2010/does-violence-have-a-place-in-children's-literature/

Creasey, M. 2010. Does Violence Have a Place in Children's Literature? www.luther.edu/oneota-reading-journal/archive/2010/does-violence-have-a-place-in-childrens-literature/

Crystal, D. 2001. *Language Play.* Chicago: The University of Chicago Press.

Daly, L.A. and Perez L.M. 2009 *Exposure to media violence and other correlates of aggressive behaviour in preschool children.* http://ecrp.uiuc.edu/v11n2/daly.html.

Drinka, G. 2013. *Violent cartoons and Aggressive Preschoolers.* https://www.psychologytoday.com/blog/when-the-media-is-the-parent/2013/07/violent-cartoons-and-aggressive-preschoolers

Eron, L.D., Huesmann, L.R., Lefkowitz, M.M., and Walder, L.O. 1972. Does television violence cause aggression? 27(Apr) *American Psychologist* 253.

Gray, P. 2008, Aug 8. *A Brief History of Education.* https://www.psychology.com/blog/freedom-learn/200808/brief-history-education.

Head, L.M. and Ashley, D.M. Undated. Influence of early language exposure on children's cognitive and language development. Virginia Henderson Global Nursing e-Repository, Emory University. http://hdl.handle.net/10755/602027

Huesmann, L.R. and Miller, L.S. in Huesmann, L.R. (ed). 1994. Long-Term Effects of Repeated Exposure to Media Violence in Childhood. *Aggressive Behaviour: Current Perspectives.* Plenum Press: New York.

Huesmann, L.R., Moise-Titus, J., Podolski, C., and Eron, L.D. 2003. Longitudinal Relations between Children's Exposure to TV Violence and their Aggressive and Violent Behaviour in Young Adulthood: 1977-1992. 39(2) *Developmental Psychology.* 201.

Kashaba, N. 2008. The Negative Effects of Cartoon Violence on Children's Behaviour. *Kashaba Thoughts.* http://nizarkashaba. blogspot.co.za/2008/06/negative-effects-of-cartoon-violence-on.html

Kostyrka-Allchorne, K., Cooper, N.R., and Simpson, A. 2016. *The relationship between television exposure and children's cognitive behaviour: A systematic review.* https://doi.org/10.1016/ j.dr.2016.12.002

Mandrapa, N. 2014. Negative Impacts of Cartoons. https://novakdjokovicfoundation.org/author/nebojsa-mandrapa/

Moustakis, C. 1982. A plea for heads:Illustrating violence in fairy tales. 7(2) *Children's Literature Association Quarterly* 26.

Perry, B.D. in Schetky, D. & Benedek, E.P. (eds). 2001. The neurodevelopmental impact of violence in childhood. Chapter 18.

*Textbook of Child and Adolescent Forensic Psychiatry.* American Psychiatric Press: Washington. www.childTrauma.org

Pinter, A. 2006. *Teaching Young Language Learners.* Oxford: Oxford University Press.

Prosic-Santovac, D. 2015. Traditional Nursery Rhymes and Teaching English to Modern Children. 3(1) *Clele Journal.* 25. www.clelejournal.org/makingthematch-traditional-nursery-rhymes-and-teaching-english-to-modern-children/

Prosic-Santovac, D. 2009. *Home and School Use of Mother Goose.* Belgrade: Andrejevic Endowment. https://books.google.rs/books?id=qrf2CDD7fwsC&dq=home+and+school+use+of+mother+goose&source=gbs_navlinks_s.

Roberts, C. 2005, October 2. The Real Meaning of Nursery Rhymes. In conversation with Debbie Elliot on *All Things Considered.* October 2, 2005. www.npr.org/series/5038037/reason-behind-the-rhyme.

Sanpruskin, M. 2015. *Can violence be completely removed from fairy tales?* https://humn308frankiestein.wordpress.com/2015/03/23/can-violence-be-completely-removed-from-fairy-tales/

Schneiter, D. 2013. The Psychological Impact of Cartoons on Children. *Developmental Psychology.* https://prezi.com/tggwf2Qhquik/the-psychological-impact-of-cartoons-on-children/

Shonkoff, J.P. and Phillips, D.A. (eds). 2000. *From neurons to neighbourhoods: The Science of Early Child Development. Washington: National Academy Press.*

Sizer, M. *The surprising meaning and benefits of nursery rhymes.* www.pbs.org/parents/education/reading-language/reading-tips/the-surprising-meaning-and-benefits-of-nursery-rhymes/

Schoolatoz. 2015. *Does cartoon violence make kids more aggressive?* State of New South Wales Department of Education. www.schoolatoz.nsw.edu.au/technology/using-technology/does-cartoon-violence-make-kids-more-aggressive.

The Express Tribune. 2015, June 13. *10 nursery rhymes that reveal the shocking dark side of children's poems.*

Williams, B.T. 2004. Boys may be boys, but do they have to write that way? 47(6) *Journal of Adolescent and Adult Literacy.* http://www.readingonline.org/newliteracies/lit_index.asp?HREF=/ne wliteracies/jaal/3-04_column/index.html

Zauche, L.H., Thul, T.A., Mahoney, A.E.D., and Stapel-Wax, J.L.S. 2016. *Influence of language nutrition on children's language and cognitive development: An integrated review.* 36(3). *Early Childhood Research Quarterly.* 318. https://doi.org/ 10.1016/j. ecresq.2016.01.015

# 2

# SENSE THROUGH SENSES: ETHICS AND AESTHETICS

*Christoph Stückelberger*

## 2.1 Introduction: The Five Senses

I start with some basics of being a human being[28]. We all agree that we have five senses[29]. We *see* with the *eyes*, we *hear* with the *ears*, we *taste* with the *tongue*, we *smell* with the *nose*, and we *touch* with the hands/body. From a theological prospective it is a great gift to have these five senses. For those who are disabled, it can be very difficult; to be blind or deaf, to have four senses or three senses left. We may not be able to see but we can rely more on our developed sense of hearing or touch. We learn to compensate and that is the great capacity of the human being.

Why do I talk about the senses? Because art, literature, music and dance all have to do with the five senses. For example, the eyes look at

---

[28] Prof. Dr. Dr. h.c. Christoph Stueckelberger is President and Founder of Globethics.net, Executive Director of Geneva Agape Foundation GAF, and Professor of Ethics in Moscow/Russia, Enugu/Nigeria, Beijing/China, Member of Ethics Committees, Advisor to Institutions and Ethics Institutes.

[29] This chapter was originally published in: Christoph Stückelberger (2016): *Global Ethics Applied*, Vol. 4, Geneva: Globethics.net, pp 343-351, reprint with permission of the publisher. The text is a speech from the Opening Ceremony of the Centre for Christian Art and Literature, Normal University Beijing, March 2016.

things in a broader sense when painting and drawing. So art is helping to use this sense in a profound way. The music is using the ears so it is concentrating as an instrument for using the sense of hearing. Food is especially using the sense of taste of the tongue. With our sense of smell we can experience different perfumes, smell opportunities and threats, relations and feelings which is also an art. Then we have the sculptures which are three-dimensional, for example, the works of Michelangelo. They are not only for seeing but for touching or in dancing which we use our touch sense and in fact almost all senses.

You may now ask 'Where is literature? Which sense is provoked or used by literature?' Literature has to do with the so-called *sixth sense* - the sense of understanding, of meaning and of sense. You may be more of a specialists in literature than I am. I am a scientist, an ethicist and I am analytical, but I have a high appreciation for literature. So literature helps us to transform what we see and hear into something meaningful as all activities using the five senses look for meaning, help to understand and interpret the world. Sense through senses.

In this new centre we concentrate on Christian art and Christian literature which is a huge task and scientific opportunity. We can also ask what about the other senses: Is there something like Christian food? How to express faith by food? By dance? By smell or any other special ways? This is a question of Christian culture.

## 2.2 Christian Culture: Incarnation as Enculturation

This leads to my second point about the term Christian Culture. What is 'Christian Culture'? It's a very complex and also timely question for China. Here in China, as like all cultures, we see the importance of embedding and enculturating values and world views in an existing culture which at the same time enriches and transforms this culture to a next level. The current call and efforts of the Sinicization of Christianity means to find a way to have Christian faith as an expression of a special Chinese culture. Enculturation was always happening and has to happen with all religions in order to become meaningful for people rooted in the respective culture. Buddhism in China is different from Buddhism in Thailand or India. Islam in Indonesia is different from that in Saudi Arabia.

Even secular philosophies and world views have the same way of enculturation and the same need. The socialism of Karl Marx was a European socialism but the socialism of Mao Zedong is a Chinese one. That is why Professor Cui Wantian emphasised how we can help to reflect and to analyse Christian literature and Christian art to find the Chinese expression of it and deep roots inside this beautiful, profound and very old Chinese culture. Some people think that Christianity is a Western religion. This is wrong. Christianity is an ancient religion born in the Middle East, in Jerusalem and Palestine which are parts of Asia. Then it was transformed as it spread to Greece, to Rome and it became very much westernised. But there is another wing of Christianity in Africa—Christianity in Egypt and Ethiopia is older than Western Europe, Asian Christianity in Syria is older and in India from the third century almost as old as Western Europe. African, Asian and Latin American Christianity is very different from European or North American Christianity. Hence, Christianity is not a Western religion.

There is a theological term for this way of enculturation which means that every religion has to be embedded in a specific culture. In Christian faith and theology we call it *incarnation* - God became a human being. *Incarnation means enculturation:* Jesus was born as a man, in a village in Palestine, around 2000 year ago in a very specific situation. He was not a global neutral being somewhere in the air. He was in one culture at one time, in one continent in one country.

## 2.3 Christian Literature and Art

The third remark on Christian culture is about *literature*. The psalms
in the Bible are songs that we sing in the churches or in the Jewish
temples. The creation story in Genesis 1 and 2 are myths. The
storytelling gives meaning as to the meaning of creation for human
beings. The creation story: it is not a scientific report about seven days.
It is hymn and a myth, it is a top piece of literature. Even the Easter
story, it is not a historical report or a chronology of events that
happened. The Creation Story and the Resurrection Story gives meaning
to the Christian faith and to life. For the Christians, these are hymns and
it is literature to express the meaning of Christ for the disciples and why
we can have hope in a desperate situation and how we can care for
creation by thanking for the beauty of God's creation.

The same is true if we take Hinduism; the epic stories like the
Bhagavad Gita are mythological stories and not historical reports or a
chronology. Also if we take the Dao de Ching, we cannot understand it
if it is not understood as a poem and a philosophy in the form of poems.
We can better understand if we know the form.

That is why this centre has such an important role to play in order to
have a deeper understanding through access to literature and art.

*Art* helps us to see the world with new eyes and to understand deeper
than if we just listen to scientific analysis. For example, Professor Cui
Wantian is a rare person since he is an entrepreneur, an artist, and a
professor. He understands the meaning of academic work. He
understands not only the meaning of using all the senses but also using
entrepreneurship.

## 2.4 Being Centred: Christ-Centred Means Love Centred

The Christian faith means to be Christ-centred. Christ-centred means
to be love-centred or Agape-centred. I come back to the six senses. We

can use the senses in two different ways. We can use them in a random way or from the periphery or we can use them from the centre. To cite some examples: If I take the sense of seeing: Sometimes when I look at an art work, I have the impression that somehow I am lost with it and it does not affect me. Sometimes I ask myself why I feel an emptiness when I look at this kind of art. My feeling is there is something in the artist who is self-centred, a kind of narcissism. If I express my ideas by drawing, what is the meaning in that, when it is just being self-centred. But when we are centred in Christ and the other human being, then art becomes meaningful and we are touched. I may not figure out what it is, but I know that it is meaningful because it is centred.

There is a famous French author, poet, during the Second World War, named Antoine de Saint-Exupéry. He wrote in his famous story 'The Little Prince': 'We can only see well with our heart.' So it is not our eyes, but it is with the heart, which makes us see. Does an artist speak with his heart? Or just with his hand? The same is true with the sense of hearing. Is music the expression just of my own fantasy? Or is it an expression of love, which in the Christian tradition, we would say, God's love? I would like to quote a verse from the Bible, which may be familiar to you. When people did not understand what Jesus was saying. He said, 'You will indeed listen, but never understand. You will indeed look with your eyes, but will never perceive, for this peoples' hearts have grown dull ...' (Matthew 13:14-15)

So Christian art and literature can help us to really hear and really see not just superficially, to get the deeper meaning. The same is true for the other senses. For example, I like dance, but I am not a dancer. We know that the dancer has to dance from the centre and he has to be very stable. The dancer can do everything as long as he or she is stable then the dance becomes beautiful and meaningful. But if you are lost then you lose your body and concentration and your centre. So this is the centre to do real dancing. You can fall down if you turn with no proper balance; the balance comes when you are stable in your moves.

Let us take the sense of taste. If we have a delicious meal, but my wife is angry whilst cooking it or does not taste it, then what is the meaning of this delicious meal? If it is made out of anger and not out of love? But even a simple meal made out of love and is very meaningful and, of course, heart-warming. The sweetest chocolate tastes bitter if it is served with anger and frustration.

*All this shows us that our senses need meaning by the centre of love or Christ-centred which means love-centred.* That is also the freedom of the Christian faith. Paul in the New Testament says that very clearly when someone asked him why he was not fasting and following the rules. He answered that Christ has set us free, so we are free to eat or not to eat. So the only rule we should respect is the rule of love. If you eat with a vegetarian, you eat vegetarian to respect the other, it's not about vegetarianism but it is for the relation and community. So a Christian food culture is not primarily about what one should eat and refrain from eating, but is about eating in a way which respects the community and the others. This includes respecting nature as part of God's creation. Then, in order to care for creation, vegetarianism may be meaningful.

It is the same with the other senses. With regard to the sense of smell, God does not say that you should use perfumes or not. If it is an expression of good relations then it is fine. The perfume of the person does not judge a person; it's the relationship, it is behaviour which does. But if it is to show that 'Oh, I am a rich woman who can afford to wear an expensive perfume,' then it is not out of love but out of selfishness. So I think we could develop a whole theology of the six senses. Your centre may help!

## 2.5 Love as the Centre of Literature, Art and Ethics

For this fourth and last point, I would like to quote a very well-known Bible verse about love from the Corinthians 13:1-13[30]:

*'If I speak in the tongues of men or of angels, but do not have love, I am only a resounding gong or a clanging cymbal. If I have the gift of prophecy and can fathom all mysteries and all knowledge, and if I have a faith that can move mountains, but do not have love, I am nothing. If I give all I possess to the poor and give over my body to hardship that I may boast, but do not have love, I gain nothing.*

*Love is patient, love is kind. It does not envy, it does not boast, it is not proud. It does not dishonour others, it is not self-seeking, it is not easily angered, it keeps no record of wrongs. Love does not delight in evil but rejoices with the truth. It always protects, always trusts, always hopes, always perseveres.*

*Love never fails. But where there are prophecies, they will cease; where there are tongues, they will be stilled; where there is knowledge, it will pass away. For we know in part and we prophesy in part, but when completeness comes, what is in part disappears. When I was a child, I talked like a child, I thought like a child, I reasoned like a child. When I became a man, I put the ways of childhood behind me. For now we see only a reflection as in a mirror; then we shall see face to face. Now I know in part; then I shall know fully, even as I am fully known.*

*And now these three remain: faith, hope and love. But the greatest of these is love.'*

---

[30] New International Version (NIV)

Today and for our topic we can interpret these verses as follows:

You may be a famous artist, or you may be a famous poet, or you may be a famous cook, but if it is not done out of love, then it is empty, then it is not 'true' art and 'true' literature and 'true' cooking and 'true' ethics.

*Agape* is the Greek word in the New Testament for love as God's love. Different from it are two other words in the New Testament: friendship (*philia*), and the sexual love (*eros*). Agape is the divine and humane love of caring for the other human beings and for the whole of creation.

Twelve years ago, I founded a foundation called Globethics.net in Geneva. We want to find out what our common values are and what are the differences in our values and ethics. I think this corresponds to your experience. We have a lot of common values because we are human beings.

Recently, I made a comparison of the twelve Socialist core values and Christian values. If we compare those with Confucian values and Buddhist values, some of the values are common. For example, the value of caring for each other or having compassion for each other, that is a human value which is common to all of us and in all religions. But there are, of course, clear differences. For example, the value of forgiveness is specific to Christian faith. Therefore, a centre like this new Centre for Christian Art and Literature at the Normal University can really help to dig deep and find out what are our common values of Christian values. Then we may compare them to values in other religions and to the values of other philosophies.

I would like to close with a quote from Saint Augustine, who was a famous church-father of early Christianity in the fourth century. He said in Latin, *'Dilige et fac quod vis'* which means—'Love, and then do what you want'. To decide and live a Christ-centred life is the same as love-centred life. We then act out of the centre, the body-centre and the mind-centre and then we will act in the right way. And we then do not need 10,000 rules and regulations as long as we act from this centre of love. This is the core of Christian ethics.

Let us take this *agape-love* as our benchmark or criteria when we analyse a poem, a piece of literature, an art work, a painting, a meal, a perfume, a song or another piece of music. We then always ask: Is it an expression of love or not? A part of art and literature is 'hate speech' or hate music or destructive art. Or perhaps it is an expression of what we call the narcissism culture of today? Many of us are narcissists, we love first ourselves, we want to be exposed, we have our pictures taken here, it is all about 'me' and 'my' performance. Or if it is a piece of literature or a piece of art which is fatalistic, always repeating that we cannot do anything, the world is bad, everything goes only down: that is not an expression of love. Therefore, as conclusion, let me close with the words of Saint Augustin: 'Love—then do what is appropriate as expression of love.'

# 3

# REPRESENTATIONS SYMBOLIQUES DE JESUS DANS LE NOUVEAU TESTAMENT, ENTRE APPELLATION ET ACTE SYMBOLIQUE : LE CAS D'ETUDE DU QUATRIEME EVANGILE

*Mulolwa Kashindi*

## 3.1. Introduction

Dans nos travaux et lectures du Nouveau Testament et en particulier du quatrième évangile, aussi bien que dans nos enseignements de chaque jour, la christologie johannique nous paraissait déconcertante, à cause du caractère symbolique que revêtent les appellations de Jésus[31].

Ayant trouvé la possibilité d'écrire ce livre, nous avons trouvé qu'une des clés, pourquoi pas la principale même, pour entrer dans la christologie du quatrième évangile, serait d'arriver à repérer les multiples appellations de Jésus, en vue d'une connaissance profonde de la personne sur laquelle, la foi de l'Eglise tout entière se fonde[32].

---

[31] Prof. Dr Mulolwa Kashindi teaches New Testament exegesis at the Faculty of Theology of the Evangelical University in Africa (UEA). He is currently Executive Director of the Higher Pedagogical Institute of Uvira (ISP-Uvira) in RD. Congo.

[32] Le texte publié dans ce volume est une partie d'une recherche plus importante également en voie de parution aux Éditions Globethics : *Le langage symbolique*

Les appellations symboliques dans le quatrième évangile rebutent et tirent en quelque sorte le voile, pour ne pas s'apercevoir de la personne même de Jésus. Par ces appellations, Jésus nous paraît insaisissable. Il nous échappe et s'évade de notre entendement. Il est « *Autre* » qu'on le croyait. Un effort spirituel et théologique, minime soit-il est exigé pour entrer dans la sphère de l'auteur du quatrième évangile afin d'appréhender cette réalité. A beaucoup de chrétiens, les symboles d'appellations christologiques ne disent pas grand-chose. A beaucoup d'autres encore, ces symboles sont significatifs et doivent être bien compris.

Les appellations symboliques impliquent la manière non familière et concrète de désignation. Dans les évangiles, ce procédé est surtout propre au quatrième évangile, et de par ce caractère symbolique du livre, l'auteur laisse entrevoir son intérêt pour la divinité de Jésus. Il importe de dire que l'expression symbolique, d'une façon générale, s'oppose à l'expression rationnelle qui expose directement une idée, sans passer par le détour d'une figure sensible. Il semble qu'il appartienne à la nature de la pensée humaine d'être une pensée symbolique, dans la mesure où sa tendance naturelle, disait DESCARTES, est d'exprimer imaginativement les choses abstraites, et d'exprimer abstraitement les choses concrètes. Plus précisément un sentiment ne peut s'exprimer rationnellement (par le discours conceptuel) : il ne peut s'exprimer directement (tel le sentiment religieux) que par des symboles et des mythes.[33]

---

*: une méthode en théologie*, Focus Series, Genève : Globethics.net, à paraître 2018. Cf. aussi : Kashindi, M. *Appellations johanniques de Jésus dans l'Apocalypse*, Theses Series No. 12, Genève : Globethics.net 2015, 570pp.
[33] K. RAHNER et H. VORGRIMLER, *Petit dictionnaire de théologie catholique*, traduit de l'allemand par Deman et M. Vidal, Paris, Seuil, 1970, p. 459.

Les appellations symboliques de Jésus cachent à notre sens, une certaine vérité que l'auteur du quatrième évangile n'arrive pas à exprimer clairement. Etant pénétré profondément de cette réalité, il préfère s'exprimer par des représentations symboliques.

## 3.2. La méthode symbolique dans le quatrième évangile

Nous avons déjà dit que le quatrième évangile constitue avec 1Jn, 2J, 3J, et l'Apocalypse, l'ensemble appelé « *tradition johannique* ». Une simple lecture faite du quatrième évangile montre d'un seul coup que cet écrit est aussi un texte symbolique. E. COTHENET, L. DUSSAUT, P. le FORT et al. le confirment aussi en ce qu'ils disent : « *En dehors des textes marqués par l'emploi du terme sèméion, tous les auteurs s'accordent à reconnaître à l'évangile spirituel une dimension symbolique du texte.* »[34] Complétant cette affirmation, X. LEON - DUFOUR semble voir derrière l'auteur du quatrième évangile un héritage biblique, ainsi qu'il dit :

> *Il est évident que Jean a un langage symbolique : n'est-il pas d'abord l'héritier d'une tradition biblique pénétré du symbolisme ? Depuis la création, Dieu « vit que tout cela était bon » : la créature, investie par Dieu, peut véhiculer un sens qui la déborde. Ainsi les actions des prophètes par lesquelles se rendent intelligible la parole de Dieu et sa relation à Israël ; par exemple, les expériences conjugales d'Osée, tel ou tel geste de Jérémie ou d'Ezéchiel.*[35]

---

[34] E. COTHENET, L. DUSSAUT, L. Le FORT et al. *Op. cit.*, p. 126.
[35] X. LEON – DUFOUR, « Spécificité symbolique du langage de Jean », in J. - D. KAESTLI, J. - M. POFFET et J. ZUMSTEIN (éds.), *La communauté johannique et son histoire*, Genève, Labor et Fides, 1990, pp. 126-127.

Parlant du langage symbolique, Jean ZUMSTEIN est plus précis. Il s'exprime ainsi :

> *En second lieu, il faut mentionner le langage symbolique (par ex. les paroles en 'Je suis', l'usage de notions telles que 'eau vive', 'pain', 'lumière', 'cep/sarment', 'porte' etc.). Exploitant le double sens inhérent à ce type de langage (le sens premier pointe vers un second), le symbole fournit le réservoir sémantique nécessaire à l'expression de la révélation.* [36]

L'évangile de Jean se distingue bien d'autres évangiles dits synoptiques sur plusieurs points tels que le dit Pierre LETOURNEAU :

> *Cette différence se manifeste sur tous les plans : un cadre littéraire différent, des épisodes inédits, de longs discours de révélation, un Christ plus céleste que terrestre, l'usage massif du symbolisme et de l'ironie, pour ne mentionner que ces quelques points. L'évangile de Jean est un monde qu'on ne peut circonscrire exactement, car sa nature symbolique et ses nombreux jeux se font en sorte que le lecteur y apporte autant, sinon plus, que ce qui s'offre à lire.* [37]

Comme pour tous les autres livres de la Bible, il faut dire que, le symbolisme nécessite une intelligence mais aussi et surtout une illumination pour son intelligence. Qui dit symbolisme, dit intentions

---

[36] J. ZUMSTEIN, « L'Evangile selon Jean », in D. MARGUERAT (sous dir.), *Introduction au Nouveau Testament*, troisième éd. mise en jour, Genève, Labor et Fidès, 2004, p. 356.

[37] P. LETOURNEAU, « Les Ecrits johanniques », in O. MAINVILLE (sous dir.), *Ecrits et milieu du Nouveau Testament*, Paris, Médiaspaul, 1999, p. 175.

secrètes difficiles à percevoir. C'est en quelque sorte une métaphysique.
P. DIEL et J. SOLOTAREFF l'ont bien dit :

> *Le symbolisme est une expression de la pensée intuitive et*
> *analogique : elle se réfère intuitivement à l'insondable*
> *profondeur de la vie. Si l'on prend le symbole sans*
> *transposition, sa diction, pour une expression logique,*
> *l'erreur est inévitable. Le symbole ne veut pas aboutir à*
> *une preuve logique, mais à une conviction intuitive qui est*
> *la foi : la confiance inébranlable dans l'organisation*
> *légale du monde physique et de la vie ; constat possible à*
> *faire pour tout esprit qui sait « voir » ; tout autre chose*
> *est la croyance en l'improuvable, croyance toujours sous-*
> *tendue par le doute.*[38]

Dans le quatrième évangile, la vérité n'est pas exposée d'une manière explicite et conceptuelle. Cela ne va pas pour rien, c'est en connaissance de cause. C'est parce que l'évangéliste est imprégné de la vérité profonde qu'il préfère la cacher et l'exprimer par des images. C'est une habileté ingénieuse qui devrait habiter tous les communs des mortels de tous les âges et de toutes les époques. P. DIEL et J. SOLOTAREFF, l'ont remarqué et s'expriment en donnant cette précision :

> *Si l'évangéliste avait été moins profondément pénétré de*
> *sa vérité, il n'aurait pu trouver l'exactitude symbolique et*
> *il aurait été obligé de s'exprimer à l'aide de la*
> *spéculation philosophique qui fleurissait à son époque. Il*
> *a su dompter à l'aide de la formulation symbolique le*
> *danger de toute imagination spéculative, de toute intuition*
> *incontrôlée.*[39]

---

[38] P. DIEL et J. SOLOTAREFF,*Op. cit.*, p. 8.
[39] *Ibid.*

Il faut donc comprendre que l'intention dans le quatrième évangile est de conduire « *le lecteur à la recherche du sens profond qui se tient derrière le récit, apparemment miraculeux. En employant un langage symbolique, l'Evangéliste veut réveiller la conviction essentielle, la foi. Il veut rendre frappante la vérité proposée, non l'expliquer.*[40]

Il y a un élément qui vaut la peine d'être soulevé dans le quatrième évangile, le dogmatisme des pharisiens auquel Jésus fait face et devant lequel, ses paroles paraissent un blasphème. Devant ce dogmatisme, Jésus s'exprime par l'illogisme du symbole qui vaut la haine des pharisiens : « *Dès lors, les juifs se mirent à murmurer à son sujet [...]* » (Jn 6, 41) ; « *les pharisiens lui dirent alors : 'Tu te rends témoignage à toi-même ! Ton témoignage n'est pas recevable'* » (Jn 8, 13) ; « *Ces paroles provoquèrent à nouveau la division parmi les juifs. Beaucoup d'entre eux disaient : 'Il est possédé, il déraisonne, pourquoi l'écoutez-vous ?'* » (Jn 10, 19) ; « *[...] Mais d'autres s'en allèrent trouver les pharisiens et leur racontèrent ce que Jésus avait fait. Les grands prêtres et les pharisiens réunirent un conseil [...]* » (Jn 11, 46).

En donnant ces versets, notre intention est de montrer le choc du dogmatisme pharisien, face au symbolisme exacerbé de Jésus devant le pharisien dans le quatrième évangile. En effet, pour eux « *tout ce que Jésus dit et fait, toute son attitude, semble insensé [...]* »[41]

Il y a donc à remarquer que dans le quatrième évangile, il y a d'une part l'exacerbation du symbolisme choquant de Jésus, mais d'autre part la mécompréhension pharisaïque, voilà ce qui est caractéristique dans le quatrième évangile. S'exprimant justement à ce sujet P. DIEL et J. SOLOTAREFF précisent ce qui suit :

> *Puisque la cause de toute leur attitude est la mécompréhension du message de Jésus, la vraie foi*

---

[40] P. DIEL et J. SOLOTAREFF, *Op. cit., p. 8.*
[41] *Ibid.,* p. 11.

*implique de dépasser l'apparence et de saisir l'essentiel qui se tient derrière. L'expression symbolique poussée jusqu'au plus haut degré et la perplexité des pharisiens criant blasphème sont donc un moyen pour l'évangéliste de forcer le lecteur à chercher et à comprendre le vrai sens de ce qu'il veut dire et de ce qu'il ne peut exprimer que symboliquement.*[42]

Etant donné que le symbolisme est diversifié dans le quatrième évangile, il est nécessaire de s'arrêter à l'étude de symbolisme qui relève des actes symboliques de Jésus.

En parlant d'actes symboliques dans le quatrième évangile, il peut s'agir des miracles ou d'autres actes réels que Jésus lui-même a opérés de son vivant et qui ont leur réalité historique. Comme dans les synoptiques, ces actes sont nombreux. Quelques uns seulement peuvent être relevés.

## 3.3 Premier exemple : l'eau changé en vin (Jn 2, 1-12)

Ce miracle est le premier de cette série d'actes symboliques dans le quatrième évangile.

### 3.3.1 Contexte

Comme le texte le montre clairement, le contexte du miracle de l'eau changée en vin est celui de noce à Cana.

### 3.3.2 Traduction

*1 Le troisième jour, il y eut noce à Cana de Galilée et la mère de Jésus était là. 2 Jésus fut aussi invité à la noce avec ses disciples. 3 Le vin ayant manqué, la mère de Jésus lui dit : « Ils n'ont pas de vin. » 4 Jésus lui*

---

[42] *Ibid.*

*répondit : « Femme, quoi entre moi et toi ? Mon heure n'est pas encore là. » 5 Sa mère dit à ceux qui servaient : « Quoi qu'il vous dise, faites-le. » 6 Il y avait là six jarres de pierres, destinées aux rites de purification des juifs, elles contenaient chacune deux ou trois mesures. 7 Jésus leur dit : « Remplissez d'eau ces jarres. » Et ils les remplirent jusqu'au bord. 8 Et il leur dit : « Puisez maintenant et portez-en au maître d'hôtel. » Et ils lui emportèrent. 9 Quand le maître d'hôtel eut goûté l'eau qui avait été changée en vin et il ne savait pas d'où venait ce vin, mais les serviteurs qui avaient puisé l'eau le savaient bien, il appela le marié. 10 Et lui dit : « Tout le monde offre d'abord le bon vin et, lorsque les convives sont gris, le moins bon ; mais toi, tu as gardé le bon vin jusqu'à maintenant ! » 11 Tel fut, à Cana de Galilée, le commencement des signes de Jésus. Il manifesta sa gloire et ses disciples crurent en lui. 12 Après cela, il descendit à Capharnaüm avec sa mère, ses frères et ses disciples, mais ils n'y restèrent que peu de jours.*

### 3.3.3 Structure

A | v. 1-2 : Jésus et les siens invités à la noce de Cana.

B | v. 3-5 : manque de vin et préoccupation de la mère de Jésus.

C | v. 6-8 : le remplissage de six jarres d'eau.

D | v. 9-11 : le miracle de l'eau changée en vin.

E | v. 12 : la descente de Jésus et les siens à Capharnaüm.

Bref : A et B : sont synthétiques.

    B et C : sont aussi synthétiques

    C et D : sont aussi synthétiques

    D et C : sont également synthétiques.

### 3.3.4 Commentaire

Le miracle de l'eau changée en vin est le premier de cette série de miracles, comme c'est écrit : « ταύτην ἐποίησεν ἀρχὴ τῶν σημείων ὁ Ἰησοῦς ἐν Κανὰ τῆς Γαλιλαίας. » (v. 11).

A | vv. 1-12

Les vv. 1-2, nous montrent clairement que Jésus et les siens étaient conviés à cette noce de Cana ; comme c'était la tradition à l'occasion de grandes festivités en Palestine, au temps de Jésus, d'inviter tout le monde, la parenté, les amis, les voisins, et même l'étranger de passage à participer à la joie des époux.[43]

B | vv. 3-5

Les vv. 3-5 montrent que le vin a manqué et c'est ce manque qui a provoqué le souci de la mère de Jésus : « οἶνον οὐκ ἔχουσιν ». La préoccupation de la mère de Jésus à cause de ce manque de vin soulève deux questions : Par sa demande auprès de Jésus, espérait-elle qu'il donnerait le signal du départ, et que se retirant, il inviterait ainsi chacun à faire de même, ce qui mettrait le point final à la fête ; ou attendait-elle un secours matériel, une intervention miraculeuse ?[44]

Selon C. F. MOLLA, suite à la réponse sévère de Jésus, la première possibilité est à écarter.[45] C'est plutôt la deuxième qui est prise en compte, car la mère de Jésus, en paraissant lui faire part de son souci, sous-entend : voici le moment providentiel, c'est l'occasion de manifester publiquement ton autorité et ta puissance.[46] Cette considération implique que la mère de Jésus savait que Jésus pouvait opérer un miracle auquel, elle s'attendait. Pour Henri Van den

---

[43] C. F. MOLLA, *Le quatrième évangile*, Genève, Labor et Fides, 1977, p. 43.
[44] *Ibid.*, p. 44.
[45] *Ibid.*
[46] *Ibid.*

BUSSCHE, cette vue est de la plus haute invraisemblable.[47] En effet, pour H. Van den BUSSCHE, la conversation de Jésus et de sa mère appartient au schéma johannique du récit de miracle.[48] C'est dire que la démarche de la mère de Jésus à son fils, dénote plutôt une situation de désespoir, une situation sans issue ; ainsi toute l'initiative du miracle vient de Jésus et ce miracle se produit contre toute attente.[49]

Il convient de comprendre ici que contrairement à toute attente de la mère de Jésus demandant du vin avec ou sans miracle, le récit johannique d'un miracle oppose toujours à une situation humainement désespérée, à une aporia, une intervention surhumaine de Jésus, inattendue. Donc, le miracle n'arrive qu'au moment où l'homme a reconnu que la situation est insoluble ; il surprend toujours, puisque personne ne l'attend.[50]

L'expression : « τί ἐμοὶ καὶ σοί » (quoi entre moi et toi) du v. 4 est à préciser. La TOB l'a traduite : « *que me veux-tu* »[51] Selon C. F. MOLLA, cette locution est sémitique et elle « *est fréquente dans toute l'écriture (II Sam. 16 : 10 ; 19 : 23 ; Mat. 8 : 29...), qui littéralement équivaut à 'qu'est-ce à toi et à moi ?'* » [52] Quant à son interprétation, il faut retenir celle de l'exégèse protestante ; à savoir que par cette locution, « *Jésus veut tenir sa mère humaine en dehors de sa mission.* »[53]

Que signifie : « οὔπω ἥκει ἡ ὥρα μου » (Mon heure n'est pas encore là), telle est notre traduction. La TOB a traduit : « *Mon heure*

---

[47] H. Van den *BUSSCHE, Jean, commentaire de l'évangile spirituel,* Bruges, Desclée de Brouwer, 1967, p. 140.

[48] *Ibid.,* p. 141.

[49] H. Van den BUSSCHE, *Op. cit.,* p. 141.

[50] *Ibid.*

[51] *TOB* (Nouveau Testament), p. 295.

[52] C. F. MOLLA, *op. cit.,* p. 44.

[53] H. Van den BUSSCHE, *Op. cit.,* p. 142.

*n'est pas encore venue.* »[54] Il faut noter cette remarque de H. Van den BUSSCHE, selon laquelle, dans l'optique de Jean, la dérogation à l'heure est impossible, car l'heure dépend entièrement de la volonté du Père, même si elle commence la journée de Jésus au lieu de la terminer. Les douze heures de la journée de Jésus (11, 9) passent selon le rythme fixé par le Père. Ni sa mère ni Jésus lui-même ne peuvent avancer cette heure, ne fût-ce que d'une minute.[55] En fin de compte, il faut dire que l'heure dont il est question dans ce texte « *s'agit ici d'un fait, d'une date, de l'heure que Jésus, selon Jean ne peut en aucune manière ni retarder, ni devancer.* »[56] Et comme le dit C. F. MOLLA, l'heure de la manifestation totale de Jésus sera l'heure de son élévation à la croix (7 : 30 ; 8 : 20 ; 12 : 23 ; 13 : 1), c'est alors qu'elle sera « affichée » à la surface du monde. Sa gloire est faite d'abaissement et de soumission à celui qui l'a envoyé, elle n'est pas affaire d'ovation et de popularité.[57]

C | vv. 6-8

Les v. 6-8 parlent du remplissage de six jarres d'eau. Il faut remarquer ici que c'est sur l'ordre de Jésus que les serviteurs remplissent les six jarres d'eau jusqu'au bord. Comme dans toutes les sociétés humaines, l'eau sert à plusieurs usages dont l'apaisement de la soif. Dans le quatrième évangile, « *l'eau apparaît toujours comme un bienfait de Dieu.* »[58] Pour P. DIEL et J. SOLOTAREFF, en tant que rituel purificateur, l'utilisation de cette eau n'est plus qu'une convention. Jésus le met devant la réalité de leurs pratiques ; voilà ce que vous faites : votre réceptivité (les jarres) n'est remplie que de la fadeur des conventions moralisantes (l'eau).[59]

---

[54] *TOB* (Nouveau Testament), p. 295.

[55] H. Van den BUSSCHE, *Op. cit.*, p. 146.

[56] *Ibid.*

[57] C. F. MOLLA, *Op. cit.*, p. 44.

[58] E. COTHENET, L. DUSSAUT, P. le FORT, *Op. cit.*, p. 129.

[59] P. DIEL et J. SOLOTAREFF, *Op. cit.*, pp. 91-92.

D | vv. 9-11

Ces versets rapportent alors le miracle de l'eau changée en vin. En effet, comme le souligne H. Van den BUSSCHE :

*Ce signe, personne ne l'a attendu, ni demandé ; c'est pourquoi la mère en est la première, toute surprise. Le récit entier est marqué par la surprise causée tant par la quantité énorme que par la qualité exceptionnelle du vin. Les six urnes dont on précise la capacité, le détail qu'elles étaient pleines jusqu'au bord, l'appréciation flatteuse du maître d'hôtel, l'insistance sur l'incompréhensibilité du cas, tout atteste que ce vin n'est pas uniquement destiné à abreuver les convives.*[60]

Comme il est dit ci-dessus, ce nouveau vin est de qualité supérieure par rapport à l'ancien. Il est qualifié de « τὸν καλὸν οἶνον » (bon vin), en contraste avec celui qualifié de « τὸν ἐλάσσω » (le moins bon). La question ici est celle de savoir quel en est le symbolisme. H. Van den BUSSCHE souligne que dans le Nouveau Testament, le symbolisme du vin est secondaire et plutôt absorbé par l'image du banquet ou de noces. A Cana on trouve les deux : noces et vin, et ils désignent les temps messianiques qui s'accomplissent maintenant en la personne de Jésus.[61] E. COTHENET, L. DUSSAUT, P. Le FORT et al., qui voient l'opposition entre l'eau et le vin, trouvent que cette opposition sert à marquer la succession de deux alliances ; à l'eau de purification des juifs (2, 6) s'oppose le vin de la nouvelle alliance, signe de la joie messianique.[62] P. DIEL et J. SOLOTAREFF les complètent en disant : « *A Cana, l'eau contrastée avec le vin a donc une signification négative ; elle est, par opposition au vin, de goût fade et sans saveur,*

---

[60] H. Van den BUSSCHE, *Op. cit.*, p. 148.

[61] *Ibid.*, p. 149.

[62] E. COTHENET, L. DUSSAUT, P. Le FORT et al. *Op. cit.*, p. 129.

*elle symbolise la platitude de l'esprit. C'est donc l'esprit banal (l'eau) qui anime les convives et va se trouver transformée en enthousiasme spirituel (vin).* »[63] Compris de cette manière, l'eau est alors cet esprit ancien qui caractérisait les juifs dans leurs observances de la torah ; alors que le vin obtenu par le miracle symbolise l'ère nouvelle, celle de la grâce, inaugurée par Jésus et qui transforme l'être entier. S'exprimant sur ce miracle, Frank KERMODE donne cette réflexion :

> *Dans la version de Jean, la transformation de l'eau en vin possède la même force : c'est le premier acte du logos dans le monde, et un exemple de la transformation plus grande à venir. Peut-être s'agit-il de la grâce au-delà de la grâce, du vin messianique de l'être qui remplace le vin inférieur de la Torah, laquelle n'est appropriée qu'au devenir. Ou peut-être la scène décrit-elle la métamorphose de la simple créature par le créateur quand il entre dans son domaine. Elle préfigure, elle en est un archétype-la transformation ultime du devenir en être, la dernière victoire qui restitue le logos à Dieu.*[64]

Partant de cette réflexion, il faut considérer que le symbolisme contenu dans ce premier miracle à Cana est le même. Il oppose l'esprit non transformé de l'être (l'eau) à l'esprit vivifié et transformé par la grâce (le vin).

E | v. 12

Le v. 12 n'a rien de symbolique. Il attire l'attention sur le fait que, après ce premier miracle, Jésus et les siens descendirent à Capharnaüm

---

[63] P. DIEL et J. SOLOTAREFF, *Op. cit.*, p. 90.

[64] F. KERMODE, « Jean », in A. ALTER et F. KERMODE (sous dir.), *Encyclopédie littéraire de la Bible*, Traduit de l'anglais par P. – E. DAUZAT, Paris, Bayard, 2003, p. 550.

où ils n'y demeurèrent, selon la leçon ἔμειναν que nous avons préférée, que peu de jours.

Le code topographique situe Capharnaüm au-dessous de Cana à cause du verbe καταβαίνω (descendre) qui est utilisé par l'auteur. La précision que donne C. F. MOLLA est à retenir. Il dit : « Alors que Cana est situé à quelque deux cent cinquante-six mètres d'altitude, Capharnaüm est à deux cents mètres au-dessous du niveau de la mer. »[65]

### 3.3.5 Synthèse

Le miracle de l'eau changée en vin à Cana est le tout premier miracle accompli par Jésus durant son ministère terrestre. Au-delà de ces deux éléments visibles, l'eau et le vin, le miracle livre en soi une symbolique caractéristique. L'eau naturelle utilisée pour la purification extérieure, représente l'ancienne alliance ; le vin, la nouvelle alliance de grâce, de transformation spirituelle.

## 3.4 La guérison du fils de l'officier royal (Jn 4, 46-54 // Mt 8, 5-13 // Lc 7, 1-10)

Ce miracle est celui de la guérison à distance du fils de l'officier royal à Capharnaüm. Ce miracle qui est le deuxième à Cana a aussi une forte symbolique.

### 3.4.1 Contexte

Le contexte du miracle du fils de l'officier royal de Capharnaüm est le retour de Jésus à Cana de Galilée venant de Jérusalem en Judée.

### 3.4.2 Traduction

*46 Jésus revint donc à Cana de Galilée où il avait fait du vin avec de l'eau[66]. Il y avait un officier royal dont le fils*

---

[65] C. F. MOLLA, *Op. cit.*, p. 46.
[66] Cette traduction vient de la *TOB*.

*était malade à Capharnaüm. 47 Ayant entendu dire que Jésus arrivait de Judée en Galilée, il vint le trouver et le priait de descendre guérir son fils qui se mourait. 48 Jésus lui dit : « si vous ne voyez signes et prodiges, vous ne croirez donc jamais ! » 49 L'officier lui dit : « Seigneur, descend avant que mon fils ne meure ! » 50 Jésus lui dit : « va, ton fils vit. » Cet homme crut à la parole que Jésus lui avait dite et il se mit en route. 51 Tandis qu'il descendait, ses serviteurs vinrent à sa rencontre et dirent : « Ton enfant vit ! » 52 Il leur demanda à quelle heure il s'était trouvé mieux et ils répondirent : « c'est hier, à la septième heure, que la fièvre l'a quitté. » 53 Le père constata que c'était à cette heure même que Jésus lui avait dit : « Ton fils vit. » Dès lors il crut lui et toute sa maisonnée. 54 Tel fut le second signe que Jésus accomplit lorsqu'il revint de Judée en Galilée.*

### 3.4.3 Structure

Ce texte peut se structurer de la manière suivante :

A | v. 46-47 : Retour de Jésus à Cana et demande de l'officier pour la guérison de son fils.

B | v. 48-50 : Réaction de Jésus à la demande de l'officier et la foi de ce dernier.

C | v. 51-53 : Le résultat de la foi de l'officier : la guérison de l'enfant et salut de toute sa maison.

D | v. 54 : Conclusion.

Bref : A et B sont des parallélismes synthétiques

B et C sont également des parallélismes synthétiques.

D sert à marquer la conclusion.

### 4.4.4 Commentaire

A | v. 46-47

Les v. 46-47, commencent par montrer le contexte de ce deuxième miracle de Cana en Galilée. Ces versets montrent le retour de Jésus en lieu où il avait déjà fait un miracle. C'est la nouvelle que cet officier de Capharnaüm a entendue qui le motive à monter à Cana, pour exprimer la préoccupation de son fils qui se mourait. Ce fonctionnaire est supposé de toute vraisemblance être un païen au service d'Hérode Antipas à Capharnaüm.[67] Pour la TOB, « *si l'officier est un païen, il pourrait symboliser l'accès des païens (des étrangers, c'est-à-dire des non-juifs) à la vie, en contraste avec le manque de foi des juifs (cf. 1, 19 note c ; 4, 1-3).* »[68]

Avec cette considération de la TOB, il y a lieu de dire que ce deuxième miracle est typiquement symbolique.

B | v. 48-50

La réaction de Jésus à la demande et la foi sans condition de l'officier sont manifestes dans les v. 48-50. « Ἐαν μη σημεια και τερατα ιδητε ου πιστευτε. » (Si vous ne voyez pas des signes et des prodiges, vous ne croirez pas). Pour H. Van den BUSSCHE, ces mots de Jésus signifieraient : « *A toi aussi, il te faut des signes avant de croire !* »[69] Par cette parole, il faut comprendre que la foi qui se borne à postuler des miracles est insuffisante ; seule la foi sans réticence en Jésus et en sa parole mène à la vie.[70]

Le v. 49 montre l'insistance de l'officier demandant à Jésus d'aller guérir son fils. Il faut remarquer ici qu'il ne demande pas de miracle. Comme le dit H. Van den BUSSCHE : « *Mais l'homme ne pose ni condition ni objection. Il ne sait que deux choses : que son fils est en*

---

[67] H. Van den BUSSCHE, *Op. cit.*, p. 198.

[68] *TOB* (Nouveau Testament), p. 301, note b.

[69] H. Van den BUSSCHE, *Op. cit.*, p. 199.

[70] *TOB* (Nouveau Testament), p. 302, note f.

*train de mourir et que Jésus peut le guérir. Dès que Jésus le congédie sur l'assurance que son fils est guéri, il ne demande pas de caution, il va. Telle est la foi. »[71]*

C | vv. 51-53

Les v. 51-53 donnent le résultat de la foi de l'officier : la guérison de l'enfant de l'officier « ὁ παῖς αὐτοῦ ζῇ » (son fils vit) v. 51 cf. : « πορεύω ὁ υἱός σου ζῇ » (va, ton fils vit) (v. 50 et 53). Mais aussi son salut et le salut de toute sa maison « καὶ ἐπίστευσεν αὐτὸς καὶ ἡ οἰκία αὐτοῦ ὅλη » (il crut, lui et sa maison entière).

Comme il a été signalé ci-dessus, ce miracle de la guérison du fils mourant de l'officier de Capharnaüm a une forte symbolique. C'est ce que P. DIEL et J. SOLOTAREFF voient dans ces lignes qui suivent :

> *Le fils dont il est question (verset 47) est une image symbolique. L'enfant est pour tout homme un espoir, l'espoir de se survivre. L'homme est le symbole de l'esprit. Le fils est donc l'espoir d'esprit. Cet espoir est menacé par la mort, par la banalisation. L'officier se sent donc profondément désorienté par rapport au sens de la vie. Mais il a entendu parler de ce que Jésus propose, et il voulait pouvoir y investir son élan ; cependant, il n'est pas assez convaincu, il lui faudrait un signe extérieur.[72]*

Ce que Jésus propose dans cette citation n'est rien d'autre que la vie spirituelle au-delà de la vie physique donnée au fils de l'officier ; vie spirituelle qui désormais est entrée dans toute sa maison (v. 53). C'est ce que X. LEON - DUFOUR voit de son côté, que la guérison de l'enfant symbolise certes le don de la vie, tel que Jésus peut le faire.[73]

---

[71] H. Van den BUSSCHE, *Op. cit.*, p. 199.

[72] P. DIEL et J. SOLOTAREFF, *Op. cit.* p., 107.

[73] X. LEON – DUFOUR, *Art. cit.*, p. 131.

Dans l'étude de ce texte, on ne peut ne pas voir le lien entre la foi et la vie, aussi bien que l'antithèse de thème mort – vie, de la maladie mortelle à sa guérison.

### 4.4.5 Synthèse

La guérison du fils de l'officier de Capharnaüm en Jn 4, 46-54 invite encore tout lecteur du quatrième évangile de s'élever et de constater une fois de plus, le niveau mystique de l'évangile. Dans l'étude de ce texte, on doit voir le lien entre la foi et la vie mais aussi l'antithèse de thème mort – vie. De la maladie mortelle de l'enfant à la vie accordée, le symbolisme nous invite à voir le passage de la mort à la vie que Jésus accorde à ceux qui croient en lui.

## 3.5  La guérison du paralytique le jour du Sabbat (Jn 5, 1-9)

Après le deuxième miracle de Cana ; celui de la guérison du fils de l'officier (Jn 4, 46-54), la guérison du paralytique le jour du sabbat (Jn 5, 1-9), ouvre les chapitres dans lesquels les miracles opérés par Jésus seront considérés comme œuvre de Dieu et feront de Jésus passible de mort car se considérant l'égal de Dieu.

### 3.5.1 Contexte

Le contexte de la guérison de ce paralytique est celui de fête des juifs à Jérusalem où Jésus monta après le deuxième miracle à Cana.

### 3.5.2 Traduction

*1 Après cela et à l'occasion d'une fête juive, Jésus monta à Jérusalem. 2 Or, il existe à Jérusalem, près de la porte des brebis, une piscine qui s'appelle en hébreu Bethzatha. Elle possède cinq portiques 3 sous lesquels gisait une foule des malades, aveugles, boiteux, impotents. (...4). 5 Il y avait là un homme infirme depuis trente-huit ans. 6*

> *Jésus le vit couché et, apprenant qu'il était dans cet état*
> *depuis longtemps déjà, lui dit : « veux-tu guérir ? » 7*
> *L'infirme lui répond : « Seigneur, je n'ai personne pour*
> *me plonger dans la piscine au moment où l'eau*
> *commence à s'agiter ; et, le temps d'y aller, un autre*
> *descend avant moi. » 8 Jésus lui dit : « Lève-toi, prend*
> *ton grabat et marche. » 9 Et aussitôt l'homme fut guéri ;*
> *il prit son grabat, il marchait. Or ce jour-là était un jour*
> *de sabbat.*

### 3.5.3 Structure

Ce texte peut se structurer de cette manière :

A | vv. 1-3 : La foule des malades de Bethzatha.

B | v. 5 : L'infirme de trente-huit ans.

C | vv. 6-9 : La guérison de l'infirme de trente-huit ans.

Bref : A et B sont des parallélismes synthétiques.

B et C sont aussi des parallélismes synthétiques.

### 3.5.4 Commentaire

A | vv. 1-3

Dans les v. 1-3, il faut remarquer que le code topographique du récit précise qu'à Jérusalem existe près de la porte des brebis une piscine dont le nom préféré par NA[27] est Βηθζαθα (BETHZATHA), soutenu par le codex Sinaïticus (א) et (L), la minuscule 33 et l'ensemble des vieilles versions latines antérieures à la vulgate (it).[74]

La TOB qui a suivi cette tradition manuscrite de NA[27] donne ce témoignage : [75] *« Bethzatha ou Bézatha, nom d'un quartier de Jérusalem situé au Nord du Temple ; des fouilles récentes ont permis de*

---

[74] NA[27], p. 259.

[75] Contre H. Van den BUSSCHE, *Op. cit.*, p. 219, qui a retenu Βηθεσδα (Bethesda) car selon lui, *« il est mieux attesté par la tradition manuscrite et s'accorde très bien à la destination de la localité. »*

*retrouver des ruines de la piscine mais non des cinq portiques. Il y eut à cet endroit un sanctuaire consacré à Sérapis, dieu guérisseur.* »[76]

Etant donné que le terme même de BETHZATHA signifie «*fossé* »,[77] il est « *le symbole du subconscient, fonctionnement malsain du psychisme sous l'empire de l'exaltation imaginative.* »[78]

B | v. 5

Le v. 5, donne la durée de maladie de cet homme. Il était infirme depuis trente-huit ans (τριάκοντα καὶ ὀκτω ἔτη). Cette longueur de temps de souffrance montre à suffisance que le cas était désespéré. Selon C. K. BARRETT, il est vraiment improbable que le nombre de trente-huit soit symbolique.[79] Ce point est aussi celle R. E. BROWN, qui dit que la suggestion que le nombre est symbolique, par exemple les 38 ans d'errance dans Dt 2, 14 n'est pas nécessaire.[80] S'il n'y a rien de symbolique dans ce nombre d'années de souffrance, pour P. DIEL et J. SOLOTAREFF, « *ce paralytique de BETHZATHA est clairement désigné comme malade hystérique dont le subconscient est lourdement chargé.* »[81]

C | vv. 6-9

Les vv. 6-9, montrent le dialogue entre Jésus et l'homme malade de trente-huit ans par procédé de question-réponse ; dialogue qui culmine par la guérison de l'homme infirme. Pour H. Van de BUSSCHE, la question que Jésus pose : « θελεις ὑγιής γενεσθαι ; » (veux-tu guérir ?) (v. 6) est une provocation.[82] « *Jésus ne la pose pas pour encourager l'homme, ni pour l'aider à surmonter son désespoir*

---

[76] *TOB* (Nouveau Testament), p. 302, note i.

[77] P. DIEL et J. SSOLOTAREFF, *Op. cit.*, p. 112.

[78] *Ibid.*

[79] C. K. BARRETT, *Op. cit.*, p. 253.

[80] R. E. BROWN, *The Anchor Bible, The Gospel According to John (Volume 1, I-XII),* London, G. CHAPMAN, 1982, p. 207.

[81] P. DIEL et J. SOLOTAREFF, *Op. cit.*, p. 112.

[82] H. Van den BUSSCHE, *Op. cit.*, p. 221.

*compréhensible : il veut entendre de la bouche même du paralytique la claire affirmation de son état désespéré.* »[83] Il faut comprendre donc ici que la réponse désespérée du paralytique, exprime une lassitude faite de désillusion.[84] C'est à cette réponse donc que Jésus accorde la guérison (v. 8-9).

Y a-t-il quelque chose de symbolique ici ? Raymond E. BROWN répond que certainement quelque symbolisme est possible ; cependant il est difficile de déterminer ce que visait l'évangéliste.[85] Pour C. F. MOLLA, par cette guérison, la parole libératrice atteste que son auteur donne la vie, qu'il est source de la vie.[86] De leur côté P. DIEL et J. SOLOTAREFF, qui voient dans la souffrance du paralytique, ses péchés ; sa guérison n'est autre chose que le pardon, qui lui a été accordé par Jésus qui allège sa culpabilité convulsive et angoissée et le libère de sa convulsion organique.[87]

### 3.5.5 Synthèse

Pendant la longue durée de trente-huit ans, l'infirme malade était dans l'impossibilité de se libérer seul de son mal. Seul Jésus, par une parole le guérit. L'infirmité de cet homme représente la maladie spirituelle ; le péché que personne d'autre ne peut enlever. Seul Jésus pardonne et donne la vie.

## 3.6 La multiplication des pains (Jn 6, 1-15 // Mt 14, 13-21 // Mc 6, 30-44 // Lc 9, 10-17)

Dans les synoptiques, ce récit résulte de la triple tradition ; du fait qu'il est rapporté par les trois évangélistes. Il est dans ce cas *« l'un des*

---

[83] H. Van den BUSSCHE, *Op. cit.*, p. 221.

[84] C. F. MOLLA, *Op. cit.*, p. 74.

[85] R. E. BROWN (Vol. 1), *Op. cit.*, p. 211.

[86] C. F. MOLLA, *Op. cit.*, p. 74.

[87] P. DIEL et J. SOLOTAREFF, *Op. cit.*, p. 110.

*récits les plus connus de l'église primitive. Les évangiles synoptiques le rapportent en l'accompagnant de la traversée du Lac et de la marche sur les eaux : Marc 6 : 31-52 (Mat. 14 : 23-33 ; Lc 9 : 10-7) ; Marc 8 : 1-9 (Mt. 15 :32-39). »*[88]

### 3.6.1 Contexte

Suivant la formule stéréotypée introduite par la formule : « μετὰ ταῦτα » (après cela), le contexte du récit de la multiplication des pains est celui, d'après les disputes précédentes de Jésus avec les juifs à Jérusalem (Jn 5, 15-47).

### 3.6.2 Traduction

*1 Après cela, Jésus passa sur l'autre rive de la mer de Galilée, dite encore de Tibériade*[89]. *2 Une grande foule le suivait parce que les gens avaient vu les signes qu'il opérait sur les malades. 3 C'est pourquoi Jésus gravit la montagne et s'y assit avec ses disciples. 4 C'était peu avant la pâque qui est la fête des juifs. 5 Or, ayant levé les yeux, Jésus vit une grande foule qui venait à lui. Il dit à Philippe : « Où achèterons-nous des pains pour qu'ils aient de quoi manger ? » 6 En parlant ainsi il les mettait à l'épreuve ; il savait, quant à lui, ce qu'il allait faire. 7 Philippe lui répondit : « Deux cents deniers de pain ne suffiraient pas pour que chacun reçoive un petit morceau. » 8 Un de ses disciples, André, le frère de Simon-Pierre, lui dit : 9 « Il y a là un garçon qui possède cinq pains d'orge et deux petits poissons ; mais qu'est-ce que cela pour tant des gens ? » 10 Jésus dit : « Faites-les asseoir. » Il y avait beaucoup d'herbes à cet endroit. Ils s'assirent donc ; ils étaient environ cinq mille hommes. 11*

---

[88] C. F. MOLLA, *Op. cit.*, p. 84.

[89] Nous reproduisons ici aussi la traduction de la TOB.

*Alors Jésus prit les pains, il rendit grâce et les distribua aux convives. Il fit de même avec les poissons ; il leur en donna autant qu'ils en désiraient. 12 Lorsqu'ils furent rassasiés, Jésus dit à ses disciples : « Rassemblez les morceaux qui restent, de sorte que rien ne soit perdu. » Ils les rassemblèrent et ils remplirent douze paniers avec les morceaux de cinq pains d'orge qui étaient restés à ceux qui avaient mangé. 14 A la vue du signe qu'il venait d'opérer, les gens dirent : « celui-ci est vraiment le Prophète, celui qui doit venir dans le monde. » 15 Mais Jésus, sachant qu'on allait venir l'enlever pour le faire roi, se retira à nouveau, seul, dans la montagne.*

### 3.6.3 Structure

A | vv. 1-3 : La grande foule qui suivait Jésus.

B | vv. 4-9 : La recherche de quoi nourrir la grande foule.

C | vv. 10-15 : La grande foule de cinq mille hommes nourrie par cinq pains et deux poissons.

Bref : A et B sont des parallélismes synthétiques

B et C sont aussi des parallélismes synthétiques.

### 3.6.4 Commentaire

A | vv. 1-3

v. 1-3. Il faut noter d'abord ici que l'expression μετὰ ταῦτα sert à relever dans le quatrième évangile un nouveau discours ou un fait à ce qui précède, ainsi Jn 3, 22 ; 5, 1 ; 7, 1 etc.). Cette unité précise aussi le code topographique : « πέραν τῆς θαλάσσης τῆς Γαλιλαίας τῆς Τιβεριάδος » (l'autre rive de la mer de Galilée ou de Tibériade). Comme nous l'avons déjà signalé θαλάσσης τῆς Γαλιλαίας τῆς Τιβεριάδος dit la même chose.

L'autre information qu'il faut retenir ici, ce que la foule suivait Jésus parce qu'elle était attirée par les miracles qu'il faisait. Selon C. F.

MOLLA, l'expression « τῶν μαθητῶν αὐτοῦ » (ses disciples) désigne les apôtres.[90]

B | vv. 4-9

v. 4-9, comme nous l'avons indiqué dans la structure, cette unité montre la préoccupation première, à savoir la recherche de quoi nourrir la grande foule. Comme dans le premier miracle de Cana, il faut voir ici l'aporia ; c'est-à-dire une situation sans issue, l'absence de solution humaine devant la grande foule à nourrir.

Il y a aussi le code chronologique qu'il faut noter ici : « ἦν δὲ ἐγγὺς τὸ πάσχα, ἡ ἑορτὴ τῶν Ἰουδαίων » (la pâque, la fête des juifs était proche). Il y a un élément théologique dans cette indication. En effet, pour C. K. BARRETT, Jean mentionne premièrement la pâque parce que, comme il apparaîtra, certains actes et paroles de ce chapitre ont une signification eucharistique et l'eucharistie, comme dernier souper (cf. 13, 1), doit être compris dans le contexte de la pâque juive.[91] De son côté, H. Van den BUSSCHE voit que par cette indication, la proximité de la pâque rappelle la manne dans le désert comme souvenir de la sortie d'Egypte et de la manne que le Messie allait à nouveau donner.[92]

Partant de cette indication concernant la pâque, l'auteur nous invite à voir autrement Jésus et le miracle qu'il va opérer. Ce miracle est un signe messianique parce qu'il rappelle clairement la manne du désert.[93]

Le v. 6 montre qu'en posant à Philippe la question : « *Où achèterons-nous des pains pour qu'ils aient de quoi manger ?* » au v. 5, Jésus « *le mettait à l'épreuve ; il savait quant à lui ce qu'il allait faire.* » Le verbe utilisé ici pour mettre à l'épreuve est : πειραζειν (τοῦτο δὲ ἔλεγεν πειράζων αὐτον). Selon R. E. BROWN, ailleurs dans les

---

[90] C. F. MOLLA, *Op. cit.*, p. 85.
[91] C. K. BARRETT, *Op. cit.*, p. 274.
[92] H. Van den BUSSCHE, *Op. cit.*, p. 242.
[93] *Ibid.*

évangiles ce verbe a un sens péjoratif de tentation, de test, tromperie.[94] Ceci étant, pour lui, ce verset est naturellement une tentative pour empêcher une quelconque partie de l'ignorance en Jésus.[95] Donc, la question posée par Jésus à Philippe est tout simplement ce que H. Van den BUSSCHE a appelé : « *Humour johannique !* ».[96] Jésus « *savait ce qu'il allait faire* », ceci signifie que le motif de pitié pour la foule telle que rapportée par Mc 6, 34, n'a pas de place ici. Le miracle que va opérer Jésus n'a pas pour but de nourrir la foule, mais de révéler Jésus.[97]

Les chiffres 2 et 5, respectivement nombre de poissons et de pains, ne sont pas choisis au hasard. Selon P. DIEL et J. SOLOTAREFF : « *le deux est le chiffre qui symbolise l'apparition et sa dualité par rapport à l'unité du mystère de l'organisation. Il symbolise par extension les désirs terrestres et leurs promesses, ceux-ci peuvent être positifs et représenter les satisfactions naturelles de la matérialité et de la sexualité, ils peuvent être négatifs et symboliser alors l'exaltation de ces mêmes désirs.* »[98] Dans cinq pains, « *le cinq est, dans sa signification positive, le juste milieu, l'harmonie [...] le pain, ainsi que nous l'avons montré (cf. Introduction), est le symbole de la vérité.* »[99]

C | vv. 10-15

v. 10-15. Ces versets rapportent le miracle fait par Jésus en nourrissant la grande foule de cinq mille personnes, sans compter les femmes et les enfants (Mt 14, 21), par deux poissons et cinq pains.

Comme le font remarquer E. COTHENET, L. DUSSAUT, P. le FORT et al. « *Seul Jésus bénit et distribue les pains (6, 11) ; par contre les disciples sont invités à ramasser les restes dans douze*

---

[94] R. E. BROWN (Volume 1), *Op. cit.*, p. 233.

[95] R.E. BROWN, (Volume 1), *Op. cit.*, 233.

[96] H. Van den BUSSCHE, *Op. cit.*, p. 243.

[97] *Ibid.*

[98] P. DIEL et J. SOLTAREFF, *Op. cit.*, p. 166.

[99] *Ibid.*

*corbeilles.* »[100] Le verbe « εὐχαριστήσας » utilisé ici est significatif d'autant plus qu'il est un terme technique de la célébration de la sainte cène (cf. Jn 6, 23).

A la lecture de récit un fait frappe ; c'est l'ordre de Jésus de ramasser les morceaux restants de sorte que rien ne soit perdu. Dans les synoptiques, cet ordre est absent (Mt 14, 20 ; Mc 6, 43 ; Lc 9, 17). Le verbe συναγειν utilisé au v. 12 (συναγάγετε) et v. 13 (συνήγαγον) est significatif. Infinitif actif de συνάγω ; il signifie : porter ensemble, ramasser, rassembler, comme le grain, les fruits, etc.[101] Le double emploi de ce verbe *« manifeste l'intérêt du narrateur pour le rassemblement, signe de salut par opposition à la dispersion, signe de perte [...] le rôle des disciples, au cours des âges, consiste à faire que ce pain contribue au regroupement des enfants de Dieu (cf. 11, 52) '.*[102]

Le fait que c'est Jésus lui-même qui distribue les pains à 5000 personnes est anecdotique. Il faut y voir le fait que Jésus est le vrai pain du ciel (6, 35-48), Jésus se donne en sacrifice pour être 'mangé' (6, 49-58), il reste présent aux hommes après sa disparition au ciel (6, 60-65).[103] En deuxième lieu, le récit préfigure l'eucharistie.[104]

### 3.6.5 Synthèse

Le miracle de cinq pains qui a nourri une si grande foule de gens au point que douze paniers en furent ramassés en reste, pas question de miettes, mais bien de portions en surnombre,[105] est une image très riche. Il est le symbole du vrai pain ; Jésus, le pain descendant du ciel qui satisfait de façon permanente aux besoins de chacun.[106]

---

[100] E. COTHENET, L. DUSSAUT, P. le FORT et al. *Op. cit.*, p. 132.
[101] *THE ANALYTICAL GREEK LEXICON, Op. cit.*, p. 385.
[102] E. COTHENET, L. DUSSAUT, P. Le FORT et al. *Op. cit.*, p. 132.
[103] X. LEON- DUFOUR, *Art. cit.*, p. 131.
[104] *Ibid.*
[105] H. Van den BUSSCHE, *Op. cit.*, p. 244.
[106] *Ibid.*, p. 245.

A côté de ces actes symboliques étudiés, il faut citer d'autres tels que : la marche sur la mer (Jn 6, 16-21 // Mt 14, 22-27 // Mc 6, 45-52), la guérison de l'aveugle de naissance (Jn 9, 1-41), la résurrection de LAZARE (Jn 11, 1-44), le lavement des pieds (Jn 13, 1-15).

Il y a aussi comme acte miracle, la purification du temple (Jn 2, 13-22 // Mt 21, 12-17 // Mc 11, 15-7 // Lc 19, 45-46). C'est en fait *« le premier acte de Jésus dans une Jérusalem hostile – en un récit factuel, au ton beaucoup moins parabolique que dans l'épisode des noces de Cana, il ne le compte pas au nombre des signes ; mais l'épisode baigne dans une pénombre de sens voilés. »*[107] Quant à sa portée symbolique, X. LEON-DUFOUR voit qu' *« il chasse non seulement les marchands mais aussi le rituel des sacrifices, comme le suggère la brève notation, propre à Jean, 'les brebis et les bœufs'. Jésus met fin au régime de sacrifice de l'ancienne loi. »*[108].

Au chapitre vingt et un, il y a bien entendu le miracle de la pêche miraculeuse dont la portée est ecclésiologique. Ce dernier chapitre est l'épilogue du livre ; placé après la conclusion de l'évangile (20, 30-31), se présente explicitement comme un ajout et doit être lu comme tel.[109]

## 3.7 Bibliographie

Brown, R. E. The Anchor Bible, The Gospel According to John (Volume 1, I-XII), London, G. CHAPMAN, 1982

Bussche, van den H. Jean, commentaire de l'évangile spirituel, Bruges, Desclée de Brouwer, 1967

---

[107] F. KERMODE, *Art. cit.*, p. 551.

[108] X. LEON-DUFOUR, *Art. cit.*, p. 132.

[109] J. ZUMSTEIN, « L'Evangile selon Jean », in D. MARGUERAT (sous dir.), *Introduction au Nouveau Testament,* (3è éd. mise en jour), Genève, Labor et Fides, 2004, p. 347.

Cothenet, E., Dussaut, L., Le Fort, P., et al. Les Écrits de saint Jean et l'épître aux Hébreux, Paris, Desclée, 1984.

Diel, P., et Solotareff, J., Le symbolisme dans l'Évangile de Jean, Paris, Payot, 1983.

Dufour, Xavier-Léon, « Spécificité symbolique du langage de Jean », in Kaestli, J. D., Poffet, J.-M., et Zumstein, J., (éd.), La communauté johannique et son histoire, Genève, Labor et Fides, 1990, pp. 121-134.

Kermode, F., « Jean » in Alter, A., et Kermode, F., (sous dir.), Encyclopédie littéraire de la Bible, Traduit de l'anglais par Dauzat, P.-E., Paris, Bayard, 2003, pp. 540-568.

Letourneau, P., « Les Écrits johanniques », in Mainville, O., (sous dir.), Écrits et milieu du Nouveau Testament, Paris, Médiaspaul, 1999, pp. 229-244.

Molla, C. F. Le quatrième Évangile, Genève, Labor et Fides, 1977

Nouveau Testament : Traduction œcuménique de la Bible (TOB), Les Editions du Cerf

Rahner, K., Vorgrimler, H. Petit dictionnaire de théologie catholique, traduit de l'allemand par P. Démann et M. Vidal, Paris, Seuil, 1970

Zumstein, J. « L'Évangile selon Jean », in : D. Marguerat (sous dir.), Introduction au Nouveau Testament, (3è éd. mise en jour), Genève, Labor et Fides, 2004

# 4

# BIOMIMESIS AND SELF-POIESIS: A RENAISSANCE IN THE BEAUTY OF THE CARING NATURE

*Didier Blasco*

## 4.1 Introduction

Biomimesis is a systemic understanding of cooperation and symbiosis in nature, helping us to adapt respectfully and lovingly our behaviours, in harmony with the living, rooting our actions and choices in the depth of our souls, where the common good is founding an ethics of universal values, in a recognition that all beings are co-creators as earth is a garden of love[110].

Biomimesis is a way of reconciliation with the amazing nature for our modern civilisation, our organisations, and mainly for everyone, as well as a way to draw a renewed inspiration.

---

[110] Mr Didier Blasco who was born in Annemasse (France) and who lives in Sofia (Bulgaria) is Consulting Engineer and Teacher. He has been contributing as expert for various organisations as the Earth Focus Foundation in Geneva (Switzerland); he is alumna of the National Institute of Applied Sciences (INSA) of Lyon (France).

The connection with nature opens beautiful states of mind and feelings, enhancing creativity, intuition. When the words express more than what they describe, because any description is only rendering a specific image of the unlimited, the experience of the caring Nature opens the mind and the heart, beyond our belief's systems. Nature is overwhelming the limiting passions and ideas with a growing empathy and sensibility, thus connecting our heart to the vibrant Life, the beauty of creation. From this intimacy with the ineffable arises an empowering and inspirational wisdom, building sustainability in a peaceful and harmonious manner.

## 4.2 Nature Draws a Path to Sustainable Values

The way driving to biomimesis starts with the existential choice: the love of life, and with its immediate consequence: the hope for an individual well-being. From the personal interest for its own life and with the aim of a durable well-being, an empathetic awareness arises, towards oneself and then towards all beings. The respect of life as awareness of an obvious founding condition for all living grounds personal well-being as respectful integration.

With a holistic understanding of the world, from all the respect due to life and nature arises biomimethics: a systematic of principles for action, founding general values due for a practical and local adaptation, in good intelligence with and for the highest good of all of the living. The focus on nature changes from a dual specialization to a global view where interactions are prominent in understanding the role of each of the multiple members.

Through a mimetic application of the operating procedures of nature, any action draws therefore its inspiration from the most sustainable system ever: the life at work. Fear or destruction are still founding way too many intentions and actions as they lead to a contraction, a vital restriction and a decline of our societies. On the contrary empathy and love can be seen as the foundation of a school of life, with an improved quality of life and higher states of awareness. During this self-development, the respect of the freedom of our choices is fundamental, vouching for the expanding quality of evolution. Through biomimethics, the fruits of free-will are grown out of respect, for the profit of everyone as well as for the good of all the community. Mankind comes again in a dominant place within nature, as a result of its accountable behaviour in driving the world affairs. The fields of application are too many to list all of them.

## 4.3 A Promenade through the Philosophical Roots

The history of sciences underwent a huge turmoil with the philosophical Milesian school. At the turn of the 6th century BC, these pre-Socratic philosophers of Ancient Greece innovated in terms of mental representation, in the build-up of knowledge, hence giving birth to physics, the study of nature: when the mind witnesses the harmonies showed within the world. The mythical tales founding the origins of all phenomena were replaced by innovative concepts. In Delphi, put at the frontispiece of the temple where presides the enthusiastic and sibylline soothsayer, a word of wisdom sounds essential: 'Know thyself'. Man should explore and understand his own being.

Scientific enquiries start developing and planet earth is placed in the centre of the universe through the thought of Anaximander. The shadow of the earth shows a round shape during eclipses, suggestive of its plumpness. The sun and the stars are dancing around the theatre of the vital display surrounding our elders.

Anaximander develops the idea of the 'Arche': the originating substance that encompasses and continuously values all things, generated from an 'apeiron,' a support of unlimited extent and duration for all ephemeral phenomena. The concept will be used later in the

Quantum Field Theory with Max Born's choice of the same word for an accurate representation of the mathematical formulas of his fellow physicist Werner Heisenberg: reality as an emergence coming out of a field of potentialities.

In the 4th century BC, the Delphi sanctuary is still shining brightly, governing the world as Plato will remind us in a cautious tribune to Apollo 'who is guiding the human kind and ruling, through his priesthood, the main part of public affairs'. The supposed atheism of the master Socrates will lead to a capital sentence. The day before Plato joins in as a follower, Socrates has a dream in which a swan would rest on his knees, grow its plumage and eventually take off... Thus it is that Plato will then found his Academy in Athens and lay down the Good as the natural ground. He praises moderation, as the source of wisdom and virtue, learning from the intelligible and its forms to connect with the good beyond the sensible. Then, he also attempts to define logically the best way to govern common life. And his somehow political ethics will draw him into a few troubles. Nevertheless, a more respectful moral code is starting to arise: God that he is, Apollo himself, must go into exile to pay for his murder of the emissary of Gaia: the monster Python.

In Plato's academy, Aristotle becomes a teacher, before founding for the sake of truth, his Lyceum: the Peripatetic naturalist school where he used to teach as he was walking. Making his own out of the Delphi's word inviting to introspection, and giving up with divination and superstition, Aristotle holds on perceptive and cognitive skills to understand the principles of the sensible world. Comprehensibility and congruence are not confined to logic: thanks to his intuition and heightened sensibility, his pragmatism grows richer, in a distinctive way compared to Descartes, who stayed in his rational thinking, consistently with the powerful and scary church that was owning the matters of soul at his time. Aristotle is studying nature with such an acuity that it will even blow Darwin's mind at the height of his glory. Aristotle sees the immanence in the living as a hylomorphism, an essence intimately attached to the body of the being. Looking for the good of man, the main goal in life as such, Aristotle's ethics stays practical, a principle for wise action, useful in everyday's life. In his actual dualism, he makes a distinction between potentiality and actuality. The same idea will arise again in Quantum Mechanics: Erwin Schrödinger's wave function for the probabilities of an event, shrinks into actuality through observation.

Heisenberg complements Plato's idealism and Aristotle's realism:

'In Quantum Physics experiments, we deal with things and facts that are just as real as any phenomenon in daily life. But atoms and elementary particles themselves are somehow not so real; they form a world of potentialities or possibilities, rather than one of things or facts [...] The probability wave [...] which means a tendency for something, a quantitative version of Aristotle's idea of potential. This introduces to a strange kind of physical reality, in the middle between the idea of an event and the actual event, between possibility and actuality'.

Pupil of Aristotle at first, then research fellow and successor as head of the Lyceum, Theophrastus extends the respect of the living, noticing a sensibility and rationality in animals, granting them with an emotional life and a form of psyche.

Closer to our actuality, John Stuart Mill suffers a depression at the age of 20. His education had made him a wonderful 'thinking machine'. In the same movement, it had drained out any form of sensibility and cut him off his inner self. From then on, he will rethink his father's and Bentham's utilitarianism, and reconcile logic to emotional life, so to raise the vitality of the heart!

Finally, for many ancient or contemporary philosophers, appears a more obvious focus towards contemplation of nature or meditative practice; they also draw their inspiration from visions, dreams, special states of awareness and they infuse their philosophy with their personal experiences. Bentham's rational philosophy has died and the comfort of a few cannot be justified and paid through the pain of others: the net balance of well-being is a weak foundation in the build-up of a social morality.

The technocratic control inherited from Descartes is also short, exhilarated at first but ending exhausted and brainwashed through abusive possessiveness of nature, in a knowledge that does not comprehend life, the dichotomy in science excluding all that cannot be constrained in its views. Yet, the principle of love raises from reasonable ground: Stoics and Christians are finally agreeing on this, as a central point of concern in the view of a stable social life, a key nutrient of the soul and thriving soil of a blooming mind. More recently, David Hume also founded on empathy his natural and rational ethics.

At the beginning of the 20$^{th}$ century, the horrors of war undermined the conquering Darwinism and also rushed Albert Schweitzer to express new ethical bases. Following the example of life, his absolute ethics claims its active character. The good of man is now understood as a global concept of the rational and sensible individual, seen as a mixture of different substrates: body, soul and mind, social and interdependent co-creator, raising gradually from passion in a releasing evolution of enhanced awareness. Seating life at the highest rank and bowing to it in reverence, Schweitzer calls for an equality of respect of all the living beings as Good is fundamentally grounded in this devoted love of the living, as the source of a profound spiritual relationship to the world. Through a deepening of this self-respect, Schweitzer is inviting us to meet our inner truth, know ourselves, understand our own being, with the discovery of the evolutive magnificence inhabiting the Living.

# 4.4 A Soft Walk around Sciences

The history of sciences underwent a Renaissance at the beginning of the 20th century, despite Lord Kelvin's concupiscent look at the science of the time that would be quickly completed thanks to little improvements and a few discoveries to come. His radiography of physics was wrong: starting in 1900 with Plank, Albert Einstein will then be a main instigator of this firework, moving up to both front lines of relativity and quantification of photo-electric energetic exchanges. From the 1905 famous year, many theoretical extensions will emerge successfully in Quantum Mechanics. These news will transform the reductionist and mechanical view of the world, inherited from Newton and Descartes amongst others. In 1915, Einstein extends his artwork with the popular and troubling theory of General Relativity that mixes a continuous parametric time in the yoke of a mathematical form, giving birth to the local shape of space-time out of all the surrounding and active energy and matter. The consubstantiality idea applied to matter, space and time is nevertheless truly inspiring. Yet, a momentum is given. A new physics demonstrate a reality made of potentialities, updated in an interaction depending on the observer. Matter is made vibrational energy (De Broglie) and empties of itself. The vacuum is full of energy and virtual particles show noticeable influence (Casimir effect). Certainties are now reserved and only concern the information that one can get about the studied system which stays itself out of reach in its very essence: being simultaneously particle and wave and pre-existing statistically, in an intrinsic uncertainty (Heisenberg's principle). This state of superposition hurts the materialist common sense. Unable to accept this new vision of reality, Albert Einstein proposed in 1935 with Podolsky and Rosen the EPR rebuttal, expressed in 1964 through the famous John S. Bell's inequalities. But in 1982, Alain Aspect confirms experimentally Quantum Mechanics with pairs of entangled photons and causality transcends the space of observation, experiment that will then be confirmed and improved, with 'massive' particles (Anton Zeilinger), on larger scales, and to the point that causality transcends time (delayed choice of Marlan Scully 1998, mobile devices of Antoine Suarez & Nicolas Gisin 2001).

The Quantum Theory is now well established in its non-locality, with the state of superposition, a co-existence of potentialities.

Loosing a part of its objectivity, space-time recovers a platitude, enriched by the relativity of the points of vue. Concurrently, new myths come to birth and expand:

- The big bang, theory which would be seating on less than 5% of all matter-energy in the universe, the 95% being invisible.
- The black holes, absorbing all matter and light but that would evaporate as a result of their brightness.
- A theory of selective evolution that stands still, pending.

Science is hanging loose in its evolution, floating on an ocean of unknown, rocked through the improvement of hypothesis, where any dogma would get rid of the questions that resist any form of integration within its belief system. Yet, the default of Einstein's causality made the naive realism an old-fashioned idea.

Life remains unexplained and never shows twice strictly the same physical occurrence. Objectivity is now a motionless concept, so locked that a higher number of copies will not reanimate it, as much alive as a plaster statue could be, now lost as is the old belly button of the world: the Delphic Omphalos. As would say Einstein: there is no fixed point and the universe has no centre. Reality is not separated from observation and the laws of physics apply to conceptual forms more than to objects.

With a continuous view of the entire universe, David Bohm's quantum potential could found some new determinism, matter seemingly emerging from awareness. The paradoxes of Quantum Physics would be solved in a superposition state, an endless entanglement, shading off the object 'per se,' the properties of the parts and their relationships being defined within the whole system. The concept of identity is now reformed, coming back to Anaximander's word. Intersubjectivity settles the relativity of observation as a main rule and sends back the man of science to social life, with Nature as the main focal point.

## 4.5 Systems Are Everywhere!

The history of sciences knows a step change in the middle of the 20$^{th}$ century, with Ludwig von Bertalanffy's views that focus on the dynamic of interactions in systemics. Detecting interactive systems everywhere, his method is a way to think organised ensembles or complex objects, with different perspectives according to different levels of organisation, mainly taking into account the relationship between distinctive parts. The classical dichotomy, the specialization are dismissed as they are sources of cognitive bias, because of a wounding simplification through their intrinsic reductionism. Isolated systems do not exist. The whole that cannot be shrunk to the sum of its parts. Therefore, the holist properties are back on track in the field of study. A new perspective arises with principles and regulating mechanisms emerging similarly from various scenes. As a new foundation for scientific enquiry, intersubjectivity and a globalizing and aggregating viewpoint save as much useful information as possible. Conceptual isomorphisms, laws or models are transferred in a useful way to skillfully describe some facets of reality so to open new spaces of trans-disciplinary creativity. Systemics extends the hylomorphism philosophy and science initiated with Aristotle, and completed by Leibniz, Goethe or Lamarck. The intelligence of processes grows from the retro-action loops, to self-organisation (shown by Ilya Prigogine in the dissipative open structures), enhancing the classical causality: including teleology or final purpose as an operating postulate. In the systemics' toolbox, we find analogy, metaphor, isomorphism and poetry! A lack of precision of a transposition is not a definitive sentence for its fertility or its relevance. Intuition, imagination, creativity or heuristics, even serendipity, regain the place that they used to occupy since the very beginning of the history of sciences.

## 4.6 General Principle of Biomimetic Action

The fundamentals of biomimethics are now exposed: love, empathy, respect of life, the main place of interactions within an open system, a holist comprehension of the world, a vision of social and personal harmony. Then, understanding how Nature works, life reveals itself through its actions. The renewed glance helps to reproduce principles and to act with the purpose of a respectful integration. Nature expresses life with order, laws and through cooperation. Although their superimposed and simultaneous occurrence does not always make them very obvious, various actions will be easily distinguished as follows.

### 4.6.1 Work and Growth

All of the living is at work and grows, in rhythms and continuously.

A stasis or stagnation is likely a deathly or necrotizing state. The natural balances are dynamic: instable and regulated in their movement. Growth is universal and an inescapable principle of existence that can be expressed at different levels: in a diversification, a creative adaptation according to the different environments or eras. Man is also very skilful in respecting this growth principle beyond the matter: in his knowledge and comprehension of the universe, in his relationships, in his empathy, his well-being, his awareness, with times of expansive and fast progression and others of dormancy and maturing.

### 4.6.2 Nutrition and Nourishment

Nutrition of all the living beings is provided, according to individual preferences and needs. A digesting process ensures the appropriate transformation into nutrients and leads to health and well-being. The emergence of the mammals' lactation is a beautiful and fascinating evolutionary challenge, with the colostrum phase taking place on the first days after birth: a true miracle that doctors keep on exploring, as for the polio oral vaccine.

### 4.6.3 Regeneration

This amazing ability starts in the basic metabolism of the smallest cell which walls allow for the useful elements to enter, and make sure that the metabolite waste is expelled. And hence, quoting Janine Benyus: 'Life creates conditions conducive to Life.'

Recycling is a perfect process in Nature where the waste of one becomes the nutriment of others. In the globalization, the possibility for a trash space disappears; but man is so fast in inventing waste, so as Jean-Paul Sartre pushing back his scrap in a hypothetical social or philosophical nothingness. Yet, The Freudian and Jungian personal and collective unconscious were already well defined! And nothingness comes down to a conceptual dizzy spell, filled with awareness as soon as it is detected, and excluded as *Nature abhors a vacuum*. Thus, with the roundness and finite dimensions of our planet, man is quickly found living on a pile of garbage. So, that might be their hidden purpose: to wake-up the human being and get him back to his accountability in his contribution to the living. Well in advance on the so-called modern man, Nature makes no trash and does a good use of everything: 'Nothing to excess', as says an old word in the Delphi's sanctuary.

### 4.6.4 Healing

To ensure comfort, this natural and surprising upgrading process is to be found at an individual level as well as at a systemic level:

- healing of a wound on the skin: with inflammation, blood coagulation isolating the exposed zone, tissue build-up,
- regulation of eutrophication with cyanobacteria & seaweed,
- adaptation process to aphids of a plant that will harden the surface cells when detecting an aggression,
- On a soil hardened through compaction by the rain that stifles the soil biology, the ventilation will result from thistles, dandelions, or other plants with strong pivoting roots and foliage providing a protective covering to the ground.

### 4.6.5 Protection

This character is constitutive of all the individual bodies, for example under the form of walls, skin, isolators such as hair, down, feathers or grease to keep from the cold and light deflectors for heat protection.... Protection is gained from some collective behaviors of birds, fishes, plants, trees, or animals. It is also seen as resulting from associations between species. In 1988, David Tillman noticed that bio-diversity is much more resilient to the effects of a drought, in a strong positive correlation between diversity and stability in different plots of a grassland field: parametric studies had shown their limits on isolated systems.

Some regulating mechanisms play an important protective role controlling excesses in their moderation effect, through interconnexions that sustain members of a population or ecosystems, when members take it in turns to provide for and support others: such as ivy which sap gives some sugar to bees during winter or also aphids of various species of plants that appear successively during the vegetative time, helping the survival of hover flies.

The coming of a snow coat often precedes a penetrating cold. Likewise the trees that cover their soil with leaves before winter, that will insulate from cold their roots and protect and nourish the aerobic micro-organisms living in the ground, and supplying mineral nutrients, also maintaining a beneficial humidity.

### 4.6.6 Fulfilment of Needs

In combination with the function of protection, the fulfilment of needs is often seen in the harmonious layout of physiologies: cilia and eyebrows to protect the eyes in case of rain fall or sweat, nails or scratches protecting the sensible endings on the feet or the fingers, hair protecting the respiratory system from dust, a hard enamel against abrasion for more resistant teeth, sebaceous glands limiting the drying out of the skin or the burn of the areas exposed to friction. The fulfilment of needs in nature is easier to espy at a systemic level. Many plants are bio-indicators of the characteristic of the soil, of an ecosystem and help in restoring the most conducive conditions for life deployment: they can be seen as a form of healing within the ecosystem.

### 4.6.7 Perpetuation

Healing, nutrition and protection contribute in the survival that will extend beyond the individuals through reproduction of the species. Regeneration and total recycling are also essential in ensuring the perpetuation. Therefore, all the organisation of life contributes in its sustainable continuation in a spirit of cooperation and harmony that combines billions of cells inside a single organism, or billions of organisms inside an ecosystem. To replicate the intelligence at work within Nature and so to help a harmonious integration: that seems to be the purpose of biomimesis.

## 4.7 Self-Poiesis and Other Ways to Articulate Bio-Mimesis

The anchor point settles down on the existential choice. Often unconscious, hidden or repressed, this choice does not result from a relative notion of good or bad, or grow out of fear, which in essence is contrary to life with the resulting narrowing and withdrawal. Life itself is emergence, engagement, coordinated momentum and expansion. Love of life is the founding choice, starting with the love of everyone for its own life.

From this wake-up of awareness, this 'Yes to be', the following step is essential to build up the vision, the project of each life: this is the call for well-being, prevailing as the essential root of existence. To achieve a dynamic harmony with durable and best integration, taking in charge all the levels of a person (the body, the mind and the soul), the respect of life represents the best rational choice. Now focusing towards all of the living, we can describe empathy as growing, and inviting us to love in the awareness of a common heritage.

From this natural agreement will bloom the values: of accountability, sharing, respect, integrity or inclusion, with an essential expression of everyone in a school of life giving the sense, teaching awareness, nourishing the soul out of the good choices, the meeting with other beings and the understanding of nature.

This opening movement, for the common good of self and of the living, initiates the first steps of an ever ascending journey, in a build-up of the being with mind patterns full of vitality, and thanks to self-poiesis, complementary of biomimesis.

Self-poiesis is defined as follows: a practice of human awareness, through actions and choices, where the subject creates and wakes-up in himself the chosen value. Otherwise, the subject becomes the object as a result or product of others, of circumstances, of an environment of life. This practice settles down on the laws of mind: what is placed within awareness will grow:

- We become what we think we are.
- What we fear comes onto us; also, what we hope for!

• Setting an example creates a pattern that we will draw to us attuning to it.

Therefore, the fruits of free-will take all their savour, in this human skill to mould oneself, create circumstances, an environment, relationships and states of mind.

Biomimesis is guiding us to welcome more and more the spirit of life, change our points of view, enjoy the reality, find new ways and transform what is within our power: in a spirit of freedom, with a creative opening full of poetic intuition, in an aesthetic pleasure and a joyful expansion, according to an entertaining diversity where to wander with arousal of our curiosity.

We then attune to life with respect, with the transposition of a universal systemic to the local conditions, and the study of the relationships in the local ecosystem.

At first, it is essential to connect, observe and respect the environment to understand and help nature in its work. In this collusion, it is of first importance to let or to make nature or the natural principles do their work so to help an expected change.

Fighting against life is an exhausting and endless task. Carrying on with the work of nature and focusing its intelligence in the desired direction, with a little patience, will progressively come to a durable transformation with minimum effort, and the achievements will go way beyond expectations. Hereafter, a few guidelines should show the self-realisation of the 'biomimethical' process:

• A goal becomes a mobile horizon.
• A crisis is an opportunity of growth and creativity.
• Symbiosis is stronger than individualism and diversity leads to the multiplication of the possibilities of regulation and to balance.
• A difference is a distinction; inclusion opens new spaces.

- Relationship is key and interfaces are wealthy places for life.
- Gratitude is an unlimited source of well-being.

Let's now have a look at a few biomimethical examples.

## 4.8 The Reconquest on the Desert of Yacouba Sawadogo

The best experts stayed puzzled in their reflection about the progression of the desert in Sahel. International commissions studied the question for a long time, did search and try some possible solutions to fight against this plague that is swallowing gradually this sub-Saharan part of Africa. In vain! Their fight against the desert did not produce significant results.

But, Yacouba Sawadogo loves life. And in his village, life is a synonym of water, the water that comes rarely to wet at times with a few drops the lands hardened like a rock. Instead of fighting against the whole desert, he decided to attract water. Having the dream of water staying long enough in his land, so to grow his mil in the best beautiful manner, Yacouba digs holes, with his single pickaxe. And then he goes further, against the general opinion of the wise men of his village, that call him crazy, that mocks his strange ideas, and swear that the spirits will punish him, as he should not ridicule the old traditions. Yacouba wants to increase the effect of his holes with the incorporation of a few termites in each of them. And he offers them some food as well, and places some split wood, with some organic matter too. The termites do their work and build a dense web of tunnels, ready to infiltrate as much water as possible. Yacouba has also the inspiration to build small walls around his lands, to keep water for a longer time. And when the rain season comes, he seeds in his holes that have become alive and fertile, some mil but also and more importantly some trees, to feed even more termites, and preserve from the burn of the sun, the soil that has become wet again and full of life. Rapidly, his method gives him great results and triple productivity compared to the usual crops. Others in the village start copying his method, and learn more with him. All the village is quickly transformed, and after more time the whole region. After a few decades, Yacouba enjoys the fruit of his ideas, while Nature does its work, in the shadow of a born again forest, listening to singing birds which benefit from the restored life, and which inhabit again this area of Burkina-Faso.

### 4.8.1 Managing Pest and Weeds in Permaculture

Curiously, the 'pests' did not always get that bad consideration that they should be exterminated. And referring to the weeds, their status changed a few decades ago with the apparition of chemicals on the market. In permaculture, they are much better considered. The weeds are useful to know the quality of the soil. They are indicators, as they always have a special function within the ecosystem and help to limit, or redirect the impact of weeds and reduce the action of the pests. With their withdrawal of sap, the aphids cause protective reactions of plants that slow down their growth. An ideal regulation can come through the presence of hover flies that lay eggs close to the aphids, settling the future meat safe for their larvae. For 3000 $m^2$ of raspberry bushes, a few tens of hover flies are enough. A diversity of plants and aphids helps in keeping some active hover flies. In a garden, the idea is to copy this plant diversity, and for example to protect in the same way the raspberry bushes (which may end up producing delicious syrups). With a multiplication of the points of balance and regulation, and in acceptance of a small deduction on the harvest, the pests stay controlled. More, the diversity is also a model and a refuge for the bad years of great misbalance.

The example of slugs is similar. They form a digestive organ for putrid parts of plants or mushrooms. They also activate specific spores. But they can terribly harm some crops. Then, a predator of slugs will be invited in the neighbourhood with some compost, some decaying or split wood. Slugs can also stay remote with crucifer plants turning them too greedy to affect other youngest plants. And a few chicken can regulate slugs too.

Regarding the weeds a coverage with plants can be used (or straw or even canvas sheets) to limit or suppress their seeding. The first function of weeds is often to cover the ground, give some ventilation and protect the soil. This covering of soil has to be made according to the needs of the ground, with hay or straw or wood, or a green fertilizer. All of which will nourish the soil in different ways, and exhausting weeding work will not be necessary. Still, dandelions or purslane are part of delicious salads!

### 4.8.2 Agro-Sylvo-Pastoral Systems: to Restore the Agricultural Soils

The deterioration of soils has accelerated with modern agricultural practices, by ignorance, as a result of heavy mechanization and with the abuse of chemistry. Gradually, the soils have lost most of their biological life: with an acidification and inorganic mineralization resulting from chemical inputs or from irrigation, as well because of an excessive working of the land, burying the aerobic part of the superficial wildlife and exhibiting to air and to the heat of the sun, the anaerobic part of the life of the ground. The life indicators for the soils are heavily falling, and fertility is decreasing: crops are far from reaching the levels that one could expect from the selected seeds. To reverse this downwards movement, new practices are showing their effectiveness:

- Trees and coppices are reinstated in the landscape, in the form of hedgerows, to limit erosion, to increase diversity, to keep wetness and freshness, to host a rich wildlife full of aids for the cultures, to protect from the wind and many deceases, and to grow mycology, useful for ventilation and fertility of the soil.
- The stifling heavy machinery use should be restricted.

- Ploughing should be abolished, allowing life to grow again the aerobic wildlife of the soils that cannot withstand the sun light, and also preserve the essential worms that build the complex of clay minerals and humus particles, helping the culture with enzymatic co-factors, the source of savours and resilience.
- Plants should be used as green fertilizers, like pulses that concentrate organic nitrogen, cover and ventilate deeply the soil and protect it from compaction resulting from the rainfalls.
- Seedling through covering keep away from weeds, preserving the fertilizing biology of the soil.
- Animals are reinstated, fertilizing the ground, helping with their mechanical action.

These 'innovative' practices save important expenses for fuel, chemical inputs or pesticides. In a renewed comprehension of the living and satisfactory for the farmers, they show a significant increase of productivity, helping the soil restoration, the biodiversity and enhancing the beautification of the countryside.

## 4.9 Conclusion

Biomimesis connects with the beauty of the caring Nature, inspiring empathy and nourishing transformative and adaptive mind patterns, an ethical model for sustainability and higher education, for the good of men, of organisations, and of all living beings. The rational build-up of noble values may distract us from the heart of biomimesis: love, empathy, social ethics and relationships giving sense. Beyond the functional analysis of the living, Nature is a guide, a way to let beauty touch our hearts and be moved by sensations, delighted in the sound of singing birds, aroused by the smells, calmed in the vibrant freshness of a forest, and inspired by the mystery of life, journeying within the tissue of existence to perceive in there a teaching, to be resonant of our essence and develop through action in awareness some states of being-ness, some enhanced presence, building up an evolution, a transformation, a way without destination where the path arises from the lucid movement of a character tempered in love, in the freedom of the school of life. Through imitation of nature, the modern man recovers the wholeness of his humanity, grounds himself in values conducive to a durable dynamic future, arises again, and dresses with capital letter the word Human, standing up like the 12-thousand-years-old symbol of our roots in Gobekli Tepe, generic of an interconnected duality, surrounded by the living as in a new hearth, in the warm unity of the earth. This is all the hope of biomimesis: to reconcile men with nature and make in our hearts sound the tune: Life is beautiful!

# 5

# LITOTES, IRONY AND OTHER INNOCENT LIES: TRUSTING TRUTH STRONGER THAN NOT TRUSTING LIES

*Ignace Haaz*

## 5.0 Introduction: Why Could Litotes and Irony Be Considered as Innocent Lies?

There are many ways in which words can transmit an exaggeration of the intended idea or message, as when someone would write a generic and impersonal recommendation letter, which could mean the person hasn't succeeded to be amongst the top students or employees, or short letter of appreciation for service that seems exaggeratedly short, and would be perceived as humiliating, if a few career achievements would be mentioned, without though applauding your performances and commitment to excellence[111]. As for the interpretation of litotes, the negative connotation depends on the meticulous appreciation of the context, including cultural context, and in speech, on the intonation and emphasis, or the (lack of) musicality of the speech[112]. The ironic and

---

[111] Ignace Haaz has been teaching philosophy at the university of Fribourg Switzerland and is currently series editor, programme executive ethics library, publications manager and research expert at Globethics.net.

[112] This chapter is a reworked part of the book: *Philosophy, Poetry and Ethics Education*, Geneva: Globethics.net Philosophy Series No. 1, 2018.

albeit subversive power of exaggerations or understatements, when words are used to bring the interlocutor or the public to unveil a hidden truth, comes close to certain forms of lies, that are often expressed out of sympathy for the auditor, but not for any egoistical interest as of profiting from cheating, or abusing the credibility of a institutional function (as corruption) or reckless abuse of individuals' trust.

There seem to be a world in which innocent half-truth can be expressed in such a way that they lie in a greatest history or narrative, where direct and harsh truth are unlikely to cause serious or widespread offence, because truth is not set as the historical value per se. Let's remind us what S. Kierkegaard showed in his master work on irony in a detailed way: 'according to the Greek view philosophy relates to history in its untruth, as eternal life to the temporal according to the Greek and the antique view in general. [...] eternal life began when one drank to the river Lethe in order to forget the past.[113]'

In the following text we would like to present the philosophical discussion on untrusting lies, which introduces a space for an innocent lie understood as figurative manipulation of the speech: a poetic trope that we would argue could not only be generously used to help us tolerating our sometime deceiving human condition—which is global and universally ours, that of the finitude of human capacity of knowledge and ethical action—but also to maximise our capacity for knowledge formation and adaptation to values.

Concepts formation and communication relates to a collective interplay of different interiorized images, before it comes to the exterior in some well-chosen expressions, in self-mastered way; their origin remain in a mentally latent process of selection of content and ideas, as possible solutions, in a games of compatible propositions. This

---

[113] Kierkegaard, Søren (1989): *The Concept of Irony/Schelling Lecture Notes*, Part I, The Position of Socrates Viewed as Irony, p. 10, New Jersey, Princeton Uni. Press, transl. Howard Hong, 1989.

unconscious material of our life relies on our capacity to identify and quickly switch between different spans, that enable us to focus on complex sets data, all depending very much on figurative manipulations, that should not be confounded with blameworthy and misleading representations.

## 5.1 Trusting Truth Stronger than Not Trusting Lies: Is There Such Thing That of a Total Loss of Credibility: *Falsum in Omnium*?

If to some extend lying is part of human nature, trusting truth should always be considered stronger, all things considered, than refusing to give credit to misleading information:

> 'There are two ways to be fooled. One is to believe what isn't true; the other is to refuse to believe what is true[114].'

But part of a story may be related to questionable episodes of self-evident statements. We find by the Greek fabulist and storyteller Aesop, that liars when they speak the truth are not believed in the famous parable of *The Boy who Cried 'Wolf'*. The story is about:

> a boy tending the sheep 'who would continually go up to the embankment and shout, "Help, there's a wolf!" The farmers would all come running only to find out that what the boy said was not true. Then one day there really was a wolf, but when the boy shouted they didn't believe him and no one came to his aid[115].'

---

[114] Kierkegaard, Sören (1995): *Works of Love*, Kierkegaard's Writings, vol. 16, New Jersey, Princeton Uni. Press, transl. and ed. by Howard Hong and Edna Hong.

[115] *Aesop's Fables*, The Boy who Cried 'Wolf', Fable 151, translation by Laura Gibbs, Oxford UP, Oxford : 2002/2008, p.78, [Chambry 318, Perry 210].

This story made the meaning so clear that 'to cry wolf', is defined as 'to give a false alarm', and no doubt about is allowed about more circumstantial appreciation of the story. Let's imagine as thought experiment, that various consequences could follow in similar situations. *Falsus in uno, falsus in omnibus* i.e. that 'he who lies once is not to be believed twice', follows the first configuration. This obviously self-evident statement is valid but we could define a second configuration where, under some conditions 'to cry wolf' would not mean that for others all my words have lost practical significance and value, because of a single lie. There are reasons to believe this second path more pragmatic and more ethical (charitable), as we can show below.

Anyone who believes in the proverbial warning, and who nevertheless lies, will conclude that the predicted state does not happen, that lying ultimately has no such drastic consequences for two reasons, as S. Dietz shows in her important essay on the value of lies[116]. First, it is not the case that because of a first lie, a second lie should produce a state of being banned of any future communication process, because this could happen only under condition that the second lie is eventually detected, and doesn't remain unrecognized, as many lies are likely to stay. Even a discovered lie usually does not lead to the fact that in fact none of my propositions would be believed; for the audience can generally well differentiate between statements which may be related to the particular interest to which my lie should serve, and other expressions which remain unaffected.

Although it is an essential property of the lie to be audience dependant, we could first imagine that as for shame, lie supposes only an ideal audience: developing a disposition to consider lying a social misbehaviour, and although a concrete audience could always be determinant to assess lie as a token, lie as a type of ethically blameworthy behaviour would depend on other ethical social types of

---

[116] Dietz, Simone (2002): *Der Wert der Lüge*, Paderborn: mentis Verl.

disposition: a network of friendly, love oriented, social behaviours. Lies should not be straightforwardly blamed in such a way that trustworthiness would appear as an absolute state that everybody understands and incorporates in the same way, on the contrary, although nobody is pleased to be fooled and cheated, social life is a subjective construction and it could take a system of trials and errors before one masters a truthful behaviour – opposed to lying, in his domain of family, social, professional, cultural, religious practices. As another fable of Aesop the *Monkeys and the Two Men* shows, strong motives for not telling the truth might as well exist in a given social circle, and it is important to diversify social circles of competencies in order to be immune of social pressure against a set of values that praises truthfulness as central ethical value. As Dietz correctly writes:

> 'the mistrust of a discovered lie is not total in the real world. A discovered lie first leads to the observation that the liar is following certain aims, and second that the liar doesn't expect his project to be discovered therefore he is ready to mask it under a lie. But no hyperbolic doubt, no desperate doubt about the whole world as experience of losing the common ground is likely to happen[117]'.

## 5.2 Brief Philosophical History of the Argument of the Misuse of the Language and the Lie in the Classical Religious Context

### 5.2.1 The Misuse of Language in Relation to the Unity and Purity of the Soul vs. the Modern View

In the classical religious philosophical deontological (duty based

---

[117] Dietz, Simone, *Der Wert der Lüge*, Paderborn: mentis Verl., p. 11. Cf. Amadou Sadjo *L'interdiction du mensonge chez Kant*; Université de Montréal, Mémoire de Master, 2010; http://www.globethics.net/gel/4369959

ethical) integration of Christian morality, lying entails not only that a moral duty is violated under condition of the lack of respect of others freedom, with I. Kant[118], not to be exposed to the possible set-back of interest consequent to a lie; this understanding is complex, as it relates first to the religious/metaphysical belief that there is a unity and purity of the soul, and second to the notion of the integration of the lie to morality as part of social ethics[119]. Lie finally can be analysed as part of a doctrine of law with Kant. Kant morally condemns the lie because in itself, lies constitute the most serious violation of the duty of man to himself: sincerity.

The man who is not sincere, that is to say who deliberately says the opposite of what he thinks not only goes against the finality inherent in the communication, but also, by lying man renounces his personality. By renouncing his personality, man ceases to be a true man, that is to say, in whom thinking and saying overlap, he becomes a semblance of man, he who deliberately says the opposite of what he thinks[120]. This line of argument goes back to St. Augustin (421): *Enchiridion ad Laurentium sive de fide, spe et saritate liber unus* ; (420): *Contra mendacium.*

---

[118] Kant, I., & Wood, A. (1797/1996). On a supposed right to lie from philanthropy. In: Mary Gregor (Ed.), *Practical Philosophy* (The Cambridge Edition of the Works of Immanuel Kant, pp. 605-616). Cambridge: UP. The central text being: Metaphysics of Morals (1797), divided in the Doctrine of Rights and the Doctrine of Virtues. See also: Paton, An Alleged Right to Lie, *Kant-Studien* 45 (1953-54).

[119] See the very detailed presentation of these aspects by Carson: Thomas L. Carson, Thomas L. (2010): *Kant and the Absolute Prohibition against Lying*, Oxford ; New York : Oxford University Press.

[120] Augustinus, Aurelius (421): *Enchiridion ad Laurentium sive de fide, spe et saritate liber unus.* https://www.augustinus.it/latino/enchiridion/enchiridion.htm, Augustinus, Aurelius (420): *Contra mendacium*, all Latin and English texts can be found on https://www.augustinus.it

When we sketch the philosophical historical discussion on truthfulness, one need to introduce Benjamin Constant's controversy compared to Kantian's rigorist view on an unconditional duty of truthfulness. Constant shows that duty to not lie should not be under any condition true, as for example if one would help a refugee to find a shelter, in the context of a totalitarian regime against a duty of solidarity to signal fugitives[121]. One could fail to realize the duty toward one self to live in dignity, but accept it to avoid 'larger evils'. In some cases a principle cannot be applied without in the first place clarifying intermediary principles as the no harm principle that should be considered prior to a right to truth.

In late modernity, there is a second step back from the background of the *(ideal) audience* dependant characterisation of truthfulness or the value of truth in the discourse. We find the argument of the *misuse of the language* as a view that draws the lie out of the moral framework (as morally neutral) on our cognitive capacity of dreaming, of a rhetorical embellishing of words and of an interesting *poetic illusion*, that is a poetic capacity, different from the general and main aim of language. The original idea is that we could imagine some liars as being involved in an activity that certainly uses the language in non-common way, in a ludic and perhaps private way, that could be seen as creative and imaginative, but not focusing on wrongful intentions aimed at fooling others in order to extract some benefit or inflict some prejudice

---

[121] « Le principe moral que dire la vérité est un devoir, s'il était pris de manière absolue et isolée, rendrait toute société impossible [...]. Dire la vérité est un devoir. Qu'est-ce qu'un devoir ? L'idée de devoir est inséparable de celle de droits : un devoir est ce qui, dans un être, correspond aux droits d'un autre. Là où il n'y a pas de droits, il n'y a pas de devoirs. Dire la vérité n'est donc un devoir qu'envers ceux qui ont droit à la vérité. Or nul homme n'a droit à la vérité qui nuit à autrui. » Contant, B. (1797): *Des réactions politiques*, quoted from: Lequan, Mai (2002): « Existe-t-il un droit de mentir ? Actualité de la controverse Kant/Constant », *Études* 2004/2 (Tome 400), p. 140.

or harm. In the next section we will present this view of the misuse of the language in an extra-moral sense more in details, as a linguistic hermeneutic view and question ourselves whether it still makes sense to speak about misuse of language and how far the term lie is appropriate if nobody *else* is being fooled.

We find in Bok (1978/1980) and Dietz (2002) that it might not be so easy to just say that we could put under brackets the ideal audience in a communication process because of 'the domino theory of the lie' that states, on the contrary that lie cannot be morally neutral. The direct consequence of a lie is the destruction of the public trust. But this view doesn't suppose, as Dietz observes it correctly, that there should be a strict interdiction of lie. There could be 'a standard of acceptability of the lie, in at least one single occasion and as case of urgency[122]' (Bok 1978, 1980; Dietz, 2002). Depending on what we understand by public sphere, trust in the public sphere takes different connotations, depending on whether we define the public common ground on a liberal background of benefit related collaboration (as with Locke), on mutual recognition and a community based understanding of human activities (with Hegel), on a common good or virtue based framework (Aristotle, Macintyre), a utility based understanding of public interest (Bentham, Mill), or on an unconscious Will-to-Live (Schopenhauer) etc.

We are particularly interested in the modern philosophical ethical (but not necessarily religious) view of social life elaborated on the notion of mutual recognition, for the obvious reason that it could help us to define the idea reconciliation of the self. Mutual recognition is founding reconciliation, based on an ethical understanding of the personal identity ('of duties toward one self', 'Pflichten gegen sich selbst'). It opens the perspective to draw a relation between the topic of the lie, self-abusing the self and helps to realise that reconciliation is not

---

[122] Bok, Sissela (1978), *Lügen: Vom täglichen Zwang zur Unaufrichtigkeit*, Reinbeck, 1980.

possible without presupposing a clarification of the difference between both the lie and self-abusing.

This optic shows that personal identity and integrity requires for preservation some rational capacities, and relies on the crucial importance of social recognition for the development. Lying, we now understand, could be considered as rational only under certain strict conditions, the limits in which the liar doesn't run the risk of being deceived by his lie, which brings back the key notion of an ideal audience, that is the standard to evaluate the level of acceptability, in relation to the social construction of the framework of mutual recognition and esteem. Kant refers to the weakness of the capacity of understanding and grounds the modern perspective on the lie, in slightly different ways, in the *Doctrine of rights* and the *Doctrine of virtues*, where harmless consequences also qualify for being called lies, giving a rather harsh connotation to the word[123].

Hegel produces a social ethical structure of life, built on the circle of the proto-ethical understanding of life in the family, and explains the basic structure of rights, that are individually interdepending in nature and how rights are related to self-development of our capacities and ethical values in time. Let us come back to why the development of talents is important in the context of the lie.

There are two perspectives in Kant's *Groundwork* toward the ethical obligation not to lie and toward the limit up to which omitting to develop all our rational capacities, including the maxim of not to lie, could be understandable, because although I cannot will a talentless world rationally, there are no rational situation where all human beings should be expected to develop all possible talents at the same time. Let's briefly clarify Kant's view on why lie should be forbidden on the ground of the *categorical imperative* and the moral law, and then see the *aporia* of limitations in 'time, interest, energy' to develop my talents as Johnson

---

[123] Kant, I. (1797), ibid.

and Cureton (2017) pointed out in their important analysis of Kant's moral views on the lie[124].

Although the lie could be understood either as duties toward one self (as we will see extensively below), it can be also seen as duty toward others, and as a *perfect duty* which corresponds to the rule: 'not to act in ways resulting in logical or practical contradictions when universalised'. For example, we have a perfect duty not to steal, since the maxim 'It is permissible to steal' is contradictory as universal law[125]. In the same way, if we understand the lie on the model of failing to keep a promise, then it becomes obvious for Kant that lies can be defined as his rule-based consequentialist ethics requires, - as any maxim or rule, by the condition that it meets the capacity of being universalised in the form of a *universal law*, as the essential condition of what Kant calls the *categorical imperative* (G 4:421[126]). As Johnson *et alii* point out:

> 'The maxim of lying whenever it gets you what you want generates a contradiction once you try to combine it with the universalized version that all rational agents must, by a law of nature, lie when doing so gets them what they want.' (Johnson, ibid.)

---

[124] Johnson, Robert and Cureton, Adam, 'Kant's Moral Philosophy', *The Stanford Encyclopedia of Philosophy* (Fall 2017 Edition), Edward N. Zalta (ed.), forthcoming URL = <https://plato.stanford.edu/archives/fall2017/entries/kant-moral/>.

[125] 'Everyone must admit that a law, if it is to hold morally, i.e. as the ground of an obligation, must carry with it absolute necessity; that the command: thou shalt not lie, does not just hold for human beings only, as if other rational beings did not have to heed it; and so with all remaining actual moral laws; hence that the ground of the obligation here must not be sought in the nature of the human being, or in the circumstances of the world in which he is placed, but a priori solely in concepts of pure reason'. Kant, I. *Groundwork of the Metaphysics of Morals* (2012), Preface, 4:389, Cambridge University Press, p.5.

[126] Kant, I. *Groundwork of the Metaphysics of Morals*, 4:421, ibid.

On the contrary, if we introduce, instead of the paradigm of the promise keeping the framework of the human being as rational agent that is developing his rational capacities, that are not all given a priori and put into practice in an ideal context, but pointing out a situation where some of these capacities lack either time, energy or interest:

> 'we can easily conceive of adopting a maxim of refusing to develop any of our talents in a world in which that maxim is a universal law of nature. It would undoubtedly be a world more primitive than our own, but pursuing such a policy is still conceivable in it. However, it is not, Kant argues, possible to rationally will this maxim in such a world.' [127]

This Kantian interpretation is slightly different from self-development seen as based on some talents that grow under circumstances of a divine grace, and that are correlated to the creation of some new responsibilities. We find in the Gospel of Matthew 14-30 the idea of a process of development of responsibilities and capacities:

> 'You knew that I reap harvest where I did not sow and gather crops where I did now scatter seeds? Well, you should have deposited my money in the bank and I would have received it with interest when I returned'.

This situation entails the new challenge of keeping one's promise, and not to lie or hid one's responsibility, knowing that the situation has changed; development is organically given, one doesn't need to make a choice about what type of development one would prefer; this situation is well described by the father James Alberione (1884-1971), founder of the Society of St Paul:

> 'Where there is talent, there is responsibility as well. As the talents grow day by day, that is, as graces increase, so does our

---

[127] Johnson, ibid.

responsibility. It does become imperative to progress and no stagnate.'

For Kant's explanation, the reason why it is not rational to think a world where rational beings voluntarily fail to develop some of their capacities is that it is not rational not to develop all possible capacities and to aim at a less perfect existence, if we would have the choice to get a fully perfect existence. Either we need judicious picking of the talents that best suit our situation given the limits of our concrete living conditions, or suppose that we are rationally required to develop all our talents, which would join the former view that development is organically given (by God's grace):

> 'Then, there seems to be no need to go further [..] to show that refusing to develop talents is immoral. Given that, insofar as we are rational, we must will to develop capacities, it is by this very fact irrational not to do so.' [128]

We see that Kant's explanation of the immorality of the lie, that is heavily based on our duty to develop our rational capacity needs some additional conceptual clarifications on the unconscious subjective historical drive, that makes the whole process a process of development in tension, and also a process that can be transcended and overcome under some precise conditions. We need to introduce here the poetic dimension of this unconscious process of subjective (individual and collective) drives.

### 5.2.2 Earth Ethics as New Way to Reconcile the Self with a New Kairos in an Non-Christian Way with Nietzsche

One of the original propositions developed by Nietzsche, apart from his sophisticated philosophy of rhetoric and poetry, is to transpose a

---

[128] Johnson, ibid. Reference to J. Alberione: http://loveofstpaul.blogspot.ch/2009/03/saturday-march-21-2009.html

global ethics, that is an ethics of the world related to theological and political affiliations, into a *geo-philosophy* or an *earth ethics* (Schapiro, 2016)[129]. Reconciliation of ourselves should first be understood as philosophy of the future, or positioning ourselves toward 'great events', transformative ways of transcending ourselves, our networks of conventional and statist ideals, into new 'great events', in inhabiting the earth in dynamical ways (one requires mobility in any possible forms) (ibid). Earth is the centre, of an ethics of the future, cultivating an openness, and displacing the way thinking in petty environments serves conservative power balances, hostile to radical transformations of our earthly habitation. The garden is a space that promotes a hedonistic happiness where, as Schapiro shows: 'the dominant themes are the shaping and tending of the natural, with a view to produce a rewarding result as well as the enjoyment of an earthly site[130]'. The garden is related to the innocence of the being, as all human beings have been given a natural place for living in the Garden of Eden, but Nietzsche 'rewrites this narrative and its topos without God or sin' (ibid, p.136). 'Garden happiness' is not an apology of a sensualist ethics, but a place to think the futurity of the human ethos, as becoming without debt ('Unschuld des Werdens'). Nietzsche overcomes the sensual understanding of the garden in *Zarathustra*: "The Three Evils': 'Sensuality: for free hearts innocent and free, the garden-happiness of the earth, all futures' exuberance of thanks to the now', as retroactive effect of the future on the present, as if the future was in preparation and that some sight of the prospective time were given in the present (ibid. p.135).

The historical role of the garden to form modern aesthetics, not only as living poetry and place of natural harmony, but as ethical laboratory

---

[129] Schapiro, Gary (2016): *Nietzsche's Earth: Great Events, Great Politics*, Chicago: University of Chicago Press.

[130] Schapiro, ibid., pp. 150-1.

for an ethics of taste, an ethics of early education, an ethics of good life as healthy embodiment of earthly energies through physical activities, and psycho-therapy through all sorts of repetitive tasks related to gardening, philosophy of climate and humoral medicine, philosophy of the seasons, world transformation as earthly self-transmutation of the garden, economic ethics as place where we learn how to serve the place where we live in simplicity and authenticity, etc.

Part of this reconciliation programme with the earth and the multidisciplinary value related cultivation of our garden relates to an inner garden, an interior development of the self. Sovereignty of the human will over nature should be viewed not only as a pluralistic method for civilizing natural forces, but also as work of the reason on the behalf of reason (Schapiro, p. 162), to shape new metanarratives, to find new *kairos*, new peaceful realisations of the self that builds concepts expected to last for centuries. Nietzsche is critical of the early apocalyptic Christian invention of St. Paul, of the faith being disappointed and turned rigorously to embrace a religion started out of an unworldly foundation, and that Christian faith should ultimately be found in the strong motive of a redemption ethics starting a new world history. But it is far from clear why we could not find a common ground, between both the Christian and Nietzsche's way of realising reconciliation, since after all, this is all about reconciliation. Let's go back to the notion of self-development and see how it could be related to a poetic earth related narrative that would as well secure some important aspects of the heritage of a Christian ethics.

### 5.2.3 Self-Development in a Hermeneutically Given Unconscious Poetical Heritage and our Given Pragmatic Transcendence

The framework of a normative oriented transcendental hermeneutic is based on the romantic understanding of poetry (as for example in a garden poetry, or an earth poetry, etc.), where the poetic dimension of language is not produced by learned elites but by a largely unconscious cultural, socio-psychological background of life on earth. This poetic concept of language was first described by Giambattista Vico (1668-1744). In order to overcome some shortfalls of this framework, and end up opposing Christian reconciliation, as redemption related and Nietzsche's redemption as forming a prehistory of reconciliation, which integrates a deep cultural ethical dimension, one could find in the transcendence and in a pragmatic turn of the language, a common point of relation and mutual accommodation, as Karl-Otto Apel has interestingly suggested.

The first men were poets by necessity, says Vico, who thinks the images of a given language are not essentially spiritual inventions of writers and philosophers but results of concrete needs of the people (Apel, Vico, p. 345)[131]. This non humanistic conception of the language, which gives a deep psycho-sociological axiology to our values, doesn't depend only on formal universal rules, but as well on concrete means to appropriate ethical standards by cultural communities, as Nietzsche also sees by the medium of his earth ethics. But this experimental position should be enlarged by a pragmatic ethical layer, that opens a dimension of transcendence and ethical values on the ground of this popular knowledge that we all share, and this is given in mostly one culture, related to one language at a time but is open to as many languages and cultures as possible, by the simple fact that the spiritual images of a

---

[131] „in der Topik, Metaphorik, Allegorik der humanistischen Bildungspoesie und -Rhetorik die humane und schon auf den aufgeklärten Verstand bezogenen Endphase eines ungeheuren und wilden, aber schöpferischen Phantaisezeitalters [...], einer Zeit, in der all Verhaltensweisen des Menschen: Recht, Gesittung, Kriegsführung, Wirtschaft, Religion durchaus dichterisch waren". Quoted from Woidich, Stefanie (2007): *Vico und die Hermeneutik: Eine rezeptionsgeschichtliche Annäherung*, K&N, note 1062, p. 305. See also: Pender, E. E. 'Plato on Metaphors and Models' in: *Metaphor, Allegory, and the Classical Tradition: Ancient Thought and Modern Revisions*, G. R. Boys-Stones (ed.), OUP, 2003.

language are also excellent candidates for cultural intermediation, as bridges across cultures.

### 5.2.4 Philosophical Correction of Civil Use of Language and the Poetic Language of Concepts 'Begriffsdichtung'

There is a first distinction, found in early Modern philosophy, between conceptual language and rhetorical or poetic language, as we find in Locke's philosophical opposition between the two meanings of words for human being: 'a civil use' and a 'philosophical use': the first being related to the communication of ideas by the means of words, 'in the context of ordinary civil life' in different societies where human being are related one to the other; the second use of words is a true philosophical use of words, as one should do if one would want 'to give precise notions of things'. Human spirit should certainly use this second type of language 'to express in general propositions truth that are beyond doubt and on which the mind could rely and get satisfied with in his quest for truth[132]'.

Knowledge which is a conceptual knowledge, constructed by a philosophical use of words, is opposed to the ordinary language and rhetorical or poetical language that certainly embellish, persuade but that needs philosophical corrections to be reliable[133]. If we draw an analogy between the rhetorical use of language open to conceptual and philosophical correction, such as we find in Locke's antinomy, and the fact that lies are to some extent part of human nature, then the definition of lying could be essentially found as related to the intention to deceive ('the untruthfulness' and 'addressee' conditions). Mahon expresses it

---

[132] Locke, J. *Philosophical Essay Concerning Human Understanding*, Book III, Ch. IX, §3. Oxford: UP, Oxford World's Classics, 1689/2008.

[133] See: my PhD thesis on the various ways poetic and metaphorical languages are understood by modern and romantic philosophers. Haaz, Ignace (2006): *Nietzsche et la métaphore cognitive*, Coll. Epistémologie et philosophie des sciences, L'Harmattan, pp. 119, 84.

below, in his definition and the four systematic characteristics of a lie:

'To lie = def.: to make a believed-false statement to another person with the intention that the other person believes that statement to be true.

[...] there are at least four necessary conditions for lying. First, lying requires that a person make a statement (statement condition). Second, lying requires that the person believe the statement to be false; that is, lying requires that the statement be untruthful (untruthfulness condition). Third, lying requires that the untruthful statement be made to another person (addressee condition). Fourth, lying requires that the person intend that that other person believe the untruthful statement to be true (intention to deceive the addressee condition)[134].'

On the contrary, if we follow with Blumenberg the idea that some metaphorical figures are better ways for making truth statements than the language of propositions, we need to consider poetry self-deceiving as ordinary language, but contrary to ordinary language it is not that it is loaded with ideological fallacies and misleading simplifications. Poetical figures are self-deceiving because of the incommunicability of some emotions, without the system of a standardized and well accepted language. But metaphors can also be seen as an appropriate linguistic vehicle for that what is given under metaphors and rhetorical tropes, which is the nearest to the truth (and the farthest from ideologies). We come close to a second distinction, found in Romantic philosophy, where philosophical knowledge is related to a language of concepts that belongs to the domain of the poetry. Metaphysical understanding of

---

[134] Mahon, James Edwin, 'The Definition of Lying and Deception', The Stanford Encyclopedia of Philosophy (Winter 2016 Edition), Edward N. Zalta (ed.), URL = <https://plato.stanford.edu/archives/win2016/entries/lying-definition/>.

ethical emotions belongs on one side to the domain of our emotional determinations; on the other side it is essentially 'religious edification' and metaphysic as art that opens the creative space of 'the art of a poetry of concepts', and where 'metaphysic has nothing to do either as religious or artistic with the truth in itself' following Schlimgen[135]. If as network of tropes and metaphors philosophical language should be essentially related to our emotional capacity, not to form culpable intentions to deceive others by telling untruth statements, but on the contrary, to tell the most profound truth on value of life, given the premise that the person who does such 'lies' does a statements, that are far more accurate when it comes to form metaphysical values, than non-metaphorical statements. Then, such 'lies', would in fact not qualify anymore for being ethically lies, provided that the person who 'lies' believe the statement to be truth, and there is an optimistic bet that the addressee shares this sophisticated poetic communication.

## 5.3 The Romantic Logic, Epistemology of the Lie and the Value of Games and Spans for Knowledge Formation and Values

Our mental life, we could say our deep neuropsychology, seeks patterns, but many are different from the evidence of causal relations. A central concept of the Romantic theory of knowledge is probably based on this simple observation[136]. The general strategy is to unveil the affective ground of an artistic and scientific creativity, as we introduced it in the previous paragraph, distinct from the cult of truth as *the*

---

[135] See Hans Blumenberg (2010): *Paradigms for a Metaphorology*, Transl. Robert Savage, Cornell University Press. Schlimgen, E. (2000): 'Logik' in: *Nietzsche Handbuch*, Henning Ottmann (Ed.), Stuttgart: Metzler Verl. p. 276.
[136] Main representatives of this Romantic tradition are Neokantian Schopenhauerian philosophers, but we find evidence of similar views as well by: Vico, Humboldt and Gerber. Cf. also *Nietzsche et la métaphore cognitive*, ibid.

supposed key epistemic value.

The assumption is that there is blindness due to lack of attention, or lack of mental focus due to changes, when we analyse the psychological cognitive conditions of knowledge formation, which are proceeding in very conventional and repetitive ways. Romantic knowledge formation on the contrary reconnects with a subjective grounding of our concepts. It is subjective because logical categories: as identity and non-contradiction belong essentially to mental life, before getting a practical transcription in social interactions. Non-contradiction, that is based on a subjectively constituting experience (as opposed to a purely subjective or solipsist notion of knowledge) should also always be based on a correspondence theory of truth, that states that there is a semantic pretention of truth, and there is no denial of the value of the opposition between true and lie, truth and contradiction, as we presented it in what we called the Modern view. How far could truth be seen as redundant? If we follow the proposition of Nietzsche, in his *On Truth and Lies in a Nonmoral Sense*, we would find ourselves totally in the other extreme, where any truth statement is virtually redundant:

> 'Every word immediately becomes a concept, inasmuch as it is not intended to serve as a reminder of the unique and wholly individualized original experience to which it owes its birth, but must at the same time fit innumerable, more or less similar cases—which means, strictly speaking, never equal—in other words, a lot of unequal cases. Every concept originates through our equating what is unequal[137]'.

We understand in comparable views, found in the Romantic logic, that concepts doesn't derive rationally, as logically founding proposition, in some cases. Let's note that the regulative notion of

---

[137] Nietzsche, F. (1873/1976): *On Truth and Lies in a Nonmoral Sense*, Walter Kaufmann's transl., The Portable Nietzsche, Viking Press, 46.

logical identity or of logical non-contradiction doesn't necessarily lose all meaning, on the contrary we would be tempted to say, the main finding of Romantic epistemology is in showing us how observation is key in order to find mnemonic solutions to problems, including how we understand and transmit concepts in ways similar to Simonides of Ceos (c.556-c.468 B.C.E.)[138].

Idris Aberkane uses the concept of a 'span', of the width of human hand: the distance from the end of the thumb to that of the little finger, to represent the utility to base our method of valuation and knowledge formation, on sensual means of ordering them and representing knowledge subjectively. As for mnemonic, truth has its utility but truth needs to be placed in linguistic packaging that helps us to make the best use of it.

There is a great interest to discover an autonomous world of thought and a subjectively bound world of representations, under the conditions: 1) that a non-communicability of subjective representations, or the untruthfulness of images need to be excluded (otherwise if it is not possible anymore to figure out the utility of the representation or the 'lie' if we use it to cheat, and risk to lose the trust of others)[139]; 2) secondly there should be an epistemic value given to the interplay of research formation and results, and more generally to *the model of a game* as the modus operandi of scientific knowledge formation, by opposition to an industrialized process of knowledge and values, based

---

[138] On Simonides see: Cicero, De Oratore, II, lxxxvi. The greatest opponent to this view is G. Frege, by showing a=a is different from a=b, in the same way as 3x4=12 differs from Mark Twain = Samuel Clemens. Some identity statements need further enquiries in order to confirm the identity; therefor there are different semantic relations to explain significance and logic is not purely formal as for Kant, but it relates to knowledge formation and concepts, without extending concepts to subjectively based forms.

[139] See Schlimgen, E. (2000): Logik in: *Nietzsche Handbuch*, Henning Ottmann (Ed.), Metzler Verl. p. 276.

on well-known models. 3) There are strong evidences in neuropsychology and cognitive sciences that education and research should move on the ground of a poetic interplay of concepts, what some call 'neuro-ergonomics', a way to study the brain at work, to open and liberate the human nervous system and the brain, in our understanding of emerging knowledge and values, the unveiling of blind spots and the highlighting of unexpected springs of knowledge formation and ethical values adaptation and resistance.

The poetic and mnemonic power to enhance performance and expand capacities is real. New capacities to produce and cherish knowledge in interaction are to be explored. A knowledge that includes sagacity is vital, because poetic knowledge and values show the priority to focus on the dynamic interplay, in a time when the temptation of trusting artificial intelligence, automated systems is emerging, and when moralizing educational failures is greater than ever, because the quantitative expansion of knowledge is itself becoming problematic. After hundred thousand years of evolution of the brain and our capacity to build on mental representations – our inner poetry capacity, we still have the temptation to ignore it, for the sake of being more scientific.

# 5.4 Bibliography

Aberkane, Idriss (2016) : *Libérez votre cerveau !* Paris : Robert Laffont 2016.

*Aesop's Fables*, The Boy who Cried 'Wolf', Fable 151.

Augustinus, Aurelius (421): *Enchiridion ad Laurentium sive de fide, spe et saritate liber unus.*

— (420): *Contra mendacium*, all Latin and English texts can be found on https://www.augustinus.it

Blumenberg, Hans (2010): *Paradigms for a Metaphorology*, Transl.

Robert Savage, New York: Cornell University Press. 1ˢᵗ éd. in German: Suhrkamp Verl., 1960.

Carson, Thomas L. (2010): *Kant and the Absolute Prohibition against Lying*, Oxford, New York: Oxford University Press.

Dietz, Simone (2002): *Der Wert der Lüge über das Verhältnis von Sprache und Moral*, Paderborn: mentis Verl.

Haaz, Ignace (2006): *Nietzsche et la métaphore cognitive*, Coll. Epistémologie et philosophie des sciences, L'Harmattan.

Kant, Immanuel, & Wood, Alan (1797/1996). On a supposed right to lie from philanthropy. In: M. Gregor (Ed.), *Practical Philosophy*, The Cambridge Edition of the Works of Immanuel Kant, pp. 605-616. Cambridge: UP.

Kierkegaard, Søren (1995): *Works of Love*, Kierkegaard's Writings, vol. 16, New Jersey, Princeton Uni. Press, transl. and ed. by Howard Hong and Edna Hong.

— (1989): *The Concept of Irony/Schelling Lecture Notes*, Part I, The Position of Socrates Viewed as Irony, Kierkegaard's Writings, vol. 2, New Jersey, Princeton Uni. Press, transl. Howard Hong.

Lequan, Mai (2002): « Existe-t-il un droit de mentir ? Actualité de la controverse Kant/Constant », Études 2004/2 (Tome 400).

Locke, John (1689/2008): *Philosophical Essay Concerning Human Understanding*, Oxford: University Press, Oxford World's Classics.

Mahon, James Edwin, 'The Definition of Lying and Deception', The Stanford Encyclopedia of Philosophy (Winter 2016 Edition), Edward N. Zalta (ed.), URL = <https://plato.stanford.edu/archives/win2016/entries/lying-definition/>.

Nietzsche, Friedrich (1873/1976): *On Truth and Lies in a Nonmoral Sense*, Walter Kaufmann's transl. The Portable Nietzsche, Viking

Press.

Paton, H. J. An Alleged Right to Lie, *Kant-Studien* 45 (1953-54). 190-203.

Sadjo, Amadou (2010) : *L'interdiction du mensonge chez Kant*, Université de Montréal, Mémoire de Master, http://www.globethics.net/ gel/4369959

Schlimgen, Erwin (2000): Logik in: *Nietzsche Handbuch. Leben – Werk – Wirkung*, Henning Ottmann (Ed.), Stuttgart, Weimar: Metzler Verl.

Schapiro, Gary (2016): *Nietzsche's Earth: Great Events, Great Politics*, Chicago: University of Chicago Press.

# 6

# LITERATURE, POETRY AND RECONCILIATION: WHY WAIT UNTIL WAR IS OVER?

*Alexander Savvas*

## 6.1 Literature and Poetry Assist in the Healing Process

Literature and poetry can assist in the healing process leading to the recovery of harmonious relations involving humans on both interpersonal and collective levels. Literature or poetry comprises the realm of arts. In this respect, both encompass both analytical, quantifiable aspects, such as the use of grammar or that of prosaic stance, and an abstract, not directly quantifiable aspect, such as the message or enchantment they can transmit through the assembly of words. The accomplishment of a piece of literature, poetry thus require a joint capacity of mastering the technical aspects of language, together with a broader, intellectual, intangible sense of where the reader is invited to wander and the necessary conclusion thereof. Therefore, at the epitome of the reading, both the reader and the writer have shared a moment of spiritual togetherness, even though their conclusions may still differ.

This moment of togetherness is likely to create a fresh, sometimes intimate bond between both parties. An integral yet unavoidable aspect of human life commands that in a situation of conflict, either of interpersonal (argumentative) or of collective nature (open warfare between several groups of people), neither party holds absolutely all the truth, the other absolutely all the wrongs. In fact, neither party is absolutely right, nor absolutely wrong, even though it is evident in some instances to clearly differentiate right from wrong, each party holds at least one key in the necessary common set to open the gates of peace and unlock, terminate either an argumentative or an armed conflict. This is what makes life in society or the nature of world affairs complex and fascinating, with the invention of diplomacy, peace conferences and other forums for mediation on the global level, to prevent war, or couple counselling on the interpersonal level, to avoid divorce.

However, friends in the common sense who have decided to freely frequent each other outside the bond of, say, marriage, seldom require the help of a third party to solve their differences, based on the fact that their bond was freely consented to (such as may indeed be the case in marriage), yet in absentia of any further legal aspects involving society at large. The same process and efforts they have achieved to create the common bond of friendship may be reactivated freely in view to repair a temporary failure in the relationship, or not. What is true on the personal level is of course totally different on the collective level, when large scathes of the population, or even entire populations from different cultures may face each other off in a hostile stance or an armed conflict.

In this respect, the use of written language can be instrumental in view to bring both parties to the conclusion that, albeit the fact that one party may be more inclined to represent the truth, both parties in quite similar way may hold some arguments that can be used in view to achieve a common goal, such as the restoration of peaceful relations, itself leading to reconciliation.

Of course, this evidently suggests an certain degree of literacy on either side, such as the ability to correctly read and write and be prone to consider other people's arguments, such as in literature, or even beyond that, to consider their feelings, such as in poetry. Beyond sympathy, writing to and reading from other people may stimulate empathy, and thus spur the albeit slow, yet necessary self-assessment and self-reinvention process, necessary for mutual understanding leading to reconciliation.

By self-sacrificing some time and efforts writing, explaining and transmitting one's arguments, the writer initiates a personal process of self-questioning and, inevitably, a process of self-restraining. He opens the door to an unarmed reply, thus creating a forum for discussion. Indeed, this sacrifice shows enough humility with the aim of writing down and explaining one's position and it can be self-curing in the sense that it inevitably invites the writer to intimately question his or her own beliefs, before exploring those of the opposite side. By doing so, one frequently realises what went wrong, and what may be enhanced. Interestingly, as it is generally the case when people use their intellect, the outcome is very likely to create a bond, and take the shape of a peaceful, if not friendly, conclusion. Thus, by initiating in his turn a process of self-questioning and self-restraining, the reader finds the possibility to construe the opposing arguments and reply in an unarmed way.

## 6.2 Why not Use Writing to Endeavour Preventing Misery

On numerous occasions, it has become evident that literature and poetry, along with other forms of Art, have been helpful in the necessary recovery and healing process bringing conflicts to a halt. An article from the British edition of 'The Conversation' of October 5, 2014 reads 'When the war is over, literature can help us make sense of it all[140]'.

*Detail of Cavalry Charge[141].*

But why wait until war is over? And even more so, why wait for war to start? Why not use writing to endeavour preventing misery, death and destruction, before trying to heal the wounds of those who survived? And beyond, why accept the scourge of war as a fatality?

As Meena Alexander wrote in an address to the *Yale Political Union* on April 23, 2013:

'In some sense poetry's task is to reconcile us to the world—not to accept it at face value or to assent to things that are wrong, but to reconcile one in a larger sense (...)'

Having said that, it is not for literature, or in this case for poetry to wholly encompass the opposite side's arguments, nor to expect in return

---

[140] Matt McGuire, When the war is over, literature can help us make sense of it all, The Conversation, 5 Oct. 2014, https://theconversation.com/when-the-war-is-over-literature-can-help-us-make-sense-of-it-all-32424

[141] Detail of Cavalry Charge, The Ulysses S. Grant Memorial, the United States Capitol, the National Mall, Washington, D.C by AgnosticPreachersKid - Own work, https://commons.wikimedia.org/w/index.php?curid=10529038

the opposite side to fully encompass ours, but rather to find a common ground of understanding, amidst our differences. The mere fact of writing and reading each other is a form of labour often involving hard work, always humility, leading to self-respect and beyond to respect for other people. By the recourse of this fruitful intellectual process and before initiating or pursuing a conflict, the notions of self-respect, humility and respect for others become evident and in all cases comprise a welcome, valuable flattery to the other side.

Beyond misconceptions stemming from or leading to one's own or other people's woes, and notwithstanding the inextricable differences in points of views at first glance, said flattery suddenly begs to be returned as a favour in an iterative, therefore creative, artistic and most important, peaceful way. Thus, by paying regards to each other's efforts and notwithstanding the sake of one's arguments, literature and poetry may thus be a very fast, uncostly and effective way to prevent conflict or help restore peace.

Having said that, writing literature or poetry represent a creative effort that can heal one's proper woes before assisting in curing others', or create the necessary forum of thoughtful discussions and exchanges germane to the reconciliation process.

# 7

# UNDERDEVELOPMENT AS IDEOLOGY: RACISM, IDEOLOGICAL LIES AND AFRICA'S TRUE POTENTIAL OF DEVELOPMENT

*Ernest Beyaraza*

## 7.1 Nature of Underdevelopment

What is underdevelopment?[142] Generally, underdevelopment is regarded as undermining, retarding, or interfering with the development process of the people. Therefore, to understand the concept of underdevelopment we need to begin with that of development. We need to understand what is 'interfered with' in order to see in proper perspective the process of interference and to appreciate the effects of this interference. In this attempt, I apply the concept of 'transcendence'. I use this concept to refer to the natural human or innate ability by which a person, in whatever circumstances, can change or undergo a process of

---

[142] Prof. Ernest Beyaraza is a Ugandan with B.A. Diploma in Education, M.A., LL.B, and LL.M. from Makerere University, a Diploma in Legal Practice from Law Development Centre (LDC), a Diploma in Administration and Management from Uganda Management Institute (UMI), Uganda, and Ph.D. from the University of Bayreuth, Germany. He taught at Makerere, Kenyatta, Bayreuth, and is currently a professor of Law at Catholic University of Eastern Africa.

development. Without this ability a person would not be able to outgrow or outlive the effects of the strict and effective methods society uses to teach, i.e. hand over its values, or traditions[143] to the new generation, such as drilling, training, conditioning, indoctrination, or even brain washing. At first, any child must be modeled, or patterned to the status quo. A person has no alternative to being influenced by these circumstances. Through the process of socialization a person adopts the belief system of his or her society. Thus, one speaks a certain language and finds other languages strange. One behaves according to the tenets, values, or dictates of his or her society. But, eventually one is able to develop an independent mind. Ultimately, one thinks of the belief system and appreciates it, if it makes sense to him or her. This would be impossible, if what I refer to as 'transcendence' did not exist. Through 'transcendence' one overcomes these influences or the 'environment' and becomes a 'responsible' individual. Being 'responsible', in this sense, means being able to 'respond' or react and become different persons, not just to be 'caring' or 'dutiful' persons. This is in contrast with merely succumbing to the influences, realities, or whatever one may call the world, or natural order in which one finds oneself in life, which, actually, would be inhuman. It is this 'transcendence' that defines human beings and human nature. Brutes do not have this capacity.

I do not employ the term 'transcendence' in the lofty sense, but as an innate capacity or ability. A person has an inborn capacity to transcend what the environment originally makes of him or her. To transcend, according to the Latin root of the term, simply means to go beyond, without clarifying, 'beyond what'. I take advantage of this to insert 'going beyond what a person has been socialized to by the person's

---

[143] The root of the term 'tradition' is the Latin 'traditum'. Tradere means to hand down, i.e. from generation to generation whatever society considers necessary. This includes skills and methods of doing things, values, and general culture.

society, or patterned to by any other circumstances'. Without this 'transcendence' we would all be 'children of our societies'. Instead, we end up being critical of ourselves, families, relatives, societies, and fellow human beings as a whole. Thus, the African people, the Asians, the Europeans, the Americans and other people in the world naturally have certain different outlooks on life due to their different environments, but can 'transcend' them.

By environment I refer to the natural, social, political, educational, economic, and other circumstances that surround human beings as individuals wherever they exist. But due to the 'transcendence' referred to above, individuals from these different backgrounds see one another as persons, or human beings. Many are brought together through academic and other areas where common tenets forge bonds similar to those made by natural societies to unite individuals. In this case, scientists, philosophers, lawyers, artists, and members of other academic fields, or religious beliefs, together with other groups transcend their original backgrounds and get united as professionals, believers, among other unitive factors. In a nut-shell, it is due to 'transcendence' that individual persons are able to break 'societal fetters'. Without this capacity, women would never think beyond their 'social roles' such as being confined to the kitchen. There would be no feminists.

However, a serious consideration of what I mean by 'transcendence' 'transcends' some feminists' view of regarding women as if they were a special species with their own psychology, philosophy, and similar ideas. Yes. Due to certain circumstances, children, the hand carped, whites, blacks, women, men and other categories of human beings may differently think, reason, feel, value things, among others. Some may develop an inferiority and others a superiority complex. The bottom line, however, is that all this build up, however long it takes, and however strong it becomes, can be demolished. It is 'transcendable'. Human beings by nature are transcendent. They can conceptualize their limits and then break through them. 'Transcendence' liberates individuals as human beings, not just women or any other subjugated people. The subjugated are liberated from the psychological dispositions into which they have been forced by their environment. Equally liberated are those who are deceived and flattered that they are 'superior' as human beings, just because they are older, or of a different sex, colour, social status, among other shallow and narrow differences. I try to elaborate my idea of 'transcendence' using a diagram. See the only figure below.

I also use the expertise of students of society to demonstrate the process of human development. Generally, the starting point of students of socio-political and historical movements is the stateless society, referred to as 'state of nature', or 'natural society', from which 'society', which is defined by central organisation or government, evolves[144].

Development in human society is viewed as a many-sided process, which include human and social development. Individual development is assumed to entail increased skill and capacity, greater freedom, creativity, self-discipline, responsibility and material well-being. Some of these aspects are moral categories and are difficult to evaluate – depending as they do on the age in which one lives, one's class origins, and one's personal code of what is right and what is wrong. However, what is indisputable is that the achievement of any of those aspects of personal development is very much tied in with the state of the society as a whole.

Social Development, on the other hand, is based on the observation that everywhere people have shown a capacity for independently increasing their ability to live a more satisfactory life through exploiting

---

[144] See Contractual Law Theorists and Positivists, e.g. Machiavelli (1469 – 1527, *The Prince*):concept of 'stato'; Thomas Hobbes (1588 – 1679, *Leviathan*): concept of 'state of nature as war of all'; J.J. Rousseau (1712 – 1778) : 'born free' but 'everywhere in chains'; John Locke (1632 – 1714 *Two Treatise of Government):* paradise and property; Karl Marx and the subsequent Marxist School

the resources of nature. Every continent independently participated in the early epochs of the extension of man's control over his environment – which means in effect that every continent can point to a period of economic development. Africa, being the original home of man, was a major participant in the processes in which human groups displayed an ever increasing capacity to extract a living from the natural environment. In this connection, a number of historians have written widely on *Historical Development in Africa*[145].

As our major concern in this book is 'poverty amidst plenty', there is a need to narrow down the concept of development to the economic arena. For long, most economists tended to view development as the maximization of economic growth. In this book, I opt for the modification of this definition by Prof. Dudley Seers whose view is that development is a social phenomenon that involves more than increasing per capita output. According to him, development means eliminating poverty, unemployment and inequality[146]. Hopkins and Hoeven[147] reveal that Seer's work at Sussex University influenced subsequent focus on structural issues such as dualism, population growth, inequality, urbanization, agricultural transformation, education, health, unemployment, basic needs, governance, corruption, among others, all of which began to be reviewed on their own merits, and not merely as appendages to an underlying growth thesis. These ideas form part of

---

[145] Walter Rodney (1973) *How Europe Underdeveloped Africa*, Dar es Salaam: Tanzania Publishing House. Fage, J.D. (1978, Knopf 1st American edition) and (2001, Hutchinson) *A History of Africa*. B. Davidson, *Africa in History*. Henri Labouret, *Africa before the White Man*. M. Shinnie, *Ancient African Kingdoms*. M. Panikkar, *The Serpent and the Crescent*. J. Ajayi and I. Espie (editors), *A Thousand Years of West African History*. B. A. Ogot and J. A. Kieran (editors), *Zamani, a Survey of East African History*.
[146] http://cepa.newshool.ed/het/schools/develop.htm.
[147] Hopkins, M. and Van Der Hoeven, R. (1983) *Basic needs in Development Planning*, Aldershot, Gower.

what I discuss under development theories where I add other economists and thinkers that hold the same views as Seers. I try to present development theories in a chronological order as some of these theories were the basis of colonialism among other practices that have underdeveloped Africa. Seers' ideas came up as late as 1969 when a lot of damage had already been done using development theories. The influence of these theories and the beliefs and practices based on them are still a reality in the contemporary world. I find it necessary to examine them in this order since my concern is the 'root causes of underdevelopment in Africa'.

## 7.2 Africa Underdevelopment

According to Walter Rodney, 'The question as to who, and what, is responsible for African underdevelopment can be answered at two levels. Firstly, the answer is that the operation of the imperialist system bears major responsibility for African economic retardation by draining African wealth and by making it impossible to develop more rapidly the resources of the continent. Secondly, one has to deal with those who manipulated the system and those who are either agents or unwitting accomplices of the said system. The capitalists of Western Europe were the ones who actively extended their exploitation from inside Europe to cover the whole of Africa. In recent times, they were joined, and to some extent replaced, by the capitalists from the United States; and for many years now even the workers of those metropolitan countries have benefited from the exploitation and underdevelopment of Africa.'[148]

However, he does not spare African accomplices. 'None of these remarks are intended to remove the ultimate responsibility for development from the shoulders of Africans. Not only are there African

---

[148] Walter Rodney, op. cit. pp. 27 - 28

accomplices inside the imperialist system, but every African has a responsibility to understand the system and work for its overthrow.'[149]

While examples of the accomplices need not be pointed out here, the stories of Kwame Nkrumah[150] and Patrice Lumumba, whose murderers have confessed with gusto, serve as examples of African leaders who were assassinated partly because they did not accept be accomplices, and in order to sabotage their efforts and reverse, derail or retard African development.

Such African leaders' murders, among hosts of other sabotage methods are clear proof of perpetuating underdevelopment in African. While the above examples are taken from the most recent struggles for independence, when certain countries had already been independent, one can stretch this struggle much further in history to include those who perished during the colonial era and even further to include those who resisted the invasion, right from the beginning, such as Shaka Zulu. Difficult to answer questions arise at this juncture. Supposing Shaka Zulu and similar leaders who struggled for the unification of Africa had not been stopped what would have become of Africa?

Development in Africa was part of Walter Rodney's research for his book, *How Europe Underdeveloped Africa*. He opens chapter two of this book: 'How Africa developed Before the Coming of the Europeans up to 15th Century', with the following quotation:

Before even the British came into relation with our people, we were a developed people, having our own institutions, having our own ideas of government[151].

---

[149] ibid. p. 28

[150] *New African*, 'Nkrumah's Legacy', 40 years after the 24th February, 1966 coup in February 2006 Issue. No 448.

[151] Walter Rodney quotes an African, a Gold Coast Nationalist, J.E. Casely-Hayford, 1922.

Rodney argues that although Africa today is underdeveloped in contrast to Western and other countries, this position has been arrived at not by the separate evolution of Africa on the one hand and Europe on the other, but through exploitation. He uses examples to indicate uneven development in Africa itself, where there were empires in one area and hunting groups in other areas, citing the Ethiopian empire vis-à-vis hunting pigmies in Congo forest and Khoisan hunter-gatherers in Kalahari Desert. However, he points out this unevenness even within the same empires, such as Ethiopia where were both literate feudal Amharic noblemen as well as simple Kaffa cultivators and Galla pastoralists. Similarly, the empire of Western Sudan had sophisticated, educated Mandinga townsmen, small communities of Bozo fishermen and Fulan herdsmen. This picture cuts across the whole of Africa. Rodney and many other scholars, besides presenting this unevenness demonstrate the existence of many African 'civilizations', but Rodney prefers using the term 'cultures', arguing that 'civilization' was a term used by European capitalists from the epoch of slavery through colonialism, fascism, and genocidal wars. A culture, according to him is a total way of life, embracing what people ate, wore, the way they walked and the way they talked, the way they treated death and greeted the newborn, with unique features in various localities. It is in this context that when Prof. Mbiti[152] and similar scholars think of African Traditional Religions and try to compare them with Christianity, some other scholars, for example, Okot p'Bitek[153] use African religions and cultures interchangeably and accuse Mbiti of trying to Hellenize them.

However, throughout colonial rule, African cultures were not only disregarded but also undermined. Theories created in the West were

---

[152] John Samuel Mbiti (1969) *African Religions and Philosophy.* London: Heinmann.

[153] Okot p'Bitek (1971) *African Religions in Western Scholarship.* Nairobi:EALB

conveniently used to dominate the people, many of whom became so mentally colonized as to mistake the theories for nothing but the truth. It is, therefore, necessary to examine a number of them as some tend to lead us to the roots of certain detrimental biases, attitudes, beliefs, and practices.

Under discussions on state, I indicate how the African modern state was initiated by colonization, and how the so-called independent state inherited almost all its characteristics from the colonial state. Elsewhere, I show how some thinkers defend colonialism, arguing that the 1960s when Africa became independent were marked by development, particularly economic development which was henceforth mismanaged and destroyed by the new and ignorant African rulers. But, under discussions on 'underdevelopment', I have seen that underdevelopment means interference with development. What needs to demonstrate, therefore, is how interference in Africa by foreign forces is to blame for underdevelopment in Africa.

So, before we leave this brief consideration of 'underdevelopment in Africa', there is a need to reiterate a few areas and cases of interference that clearly account this underdevelopment to-date. As we have seen above, Africa is characterized by 'failing' and 'failed' states. Definitions of these conditions do not only help us to understand what these conditions mean, but also how they can be used to destroy any thriving country. One can clearly see these definitions as embodiments of objectives, goals, and standards in place to guide those engaged in the destruction business. A state 'fails' if it does not have 'physical control of its territory or a monopoly on the legitimate use of force'. Fragile Africa is a very good candidate here. While Africans organised themselves to fight against colonial rule, today 'rebels' can be literally created to occupy parts of a successful country purely to fulfill the condition of lack of 'physical control'. Africa is also quite viable for the 'erosion of legitimate authority to make collective decisions' standard.

Unlike developed countries where political parties are based on clear principles, e.g. the Conservatives vis-à-vis the Democrats, African political parties are, sometimes, based on flimsy grounds or none at all. There is evidence of politicians identified and supported by foreign forces just to throw out of power someone who does not follow their exploitative selfish interests and dictates. Africa is also characterized by sanctions which have successfully helped to the important condition of 'inability to provide reasonable public services'. The same and similar interference have led to 'inability to interact with other states' and being a 'full member of the international community'. All these combined have made the African modern state have the 'central government so weak or ineffective', lack 'practical control over much of its territory', reach the standards of 'non-provision of public services', 'widespread corruption and criminality', 'refugees and involuntary movement of populations', 'sharp economic decline'.

It is not surprising, therefore, that the majority of 'failing', and 'failed' states in the world are in Africa where often peaceful people wake up to find their houses on fire, where wars break out without anyone being aware of who is fighting who and why, where as people run for dear life mining and other methods of looting natural resources start, among other heinous activities right under the 'modern' world's nose. It is not surprising either that chaos in Africa is a luxury affordable by only rich countries. The indicators put in place by *Foreign Policy Magazine* annual index above apply only to 'states determined by membership in the United Nations' which is ratified in international law. Why? Is this because other countries are out of the UN reach or control? Whatever reason given, I find that the social, economic, and political indicators of 'failure' which include demographic pressures, massive movement of refugees, internally displaced peoples, legacy of vengeance-seeking group grievance, chronic and sustained human flight, uneven economic development along group lines, sharp/or severe economic decline, criminalization and/or delegitimisation of the state, progressive deterioration of public services, widespread violation of human rights, security apparatus as 'state within a state', rise of factionalised elites, and intervention of other states or external factors, could easily serve as a useful and reliable list in a good script to be followed by whoever sets out to reduce a state, however vibrant, to its knees. Planners of wars and armed conflicts in Africa are certainly aware of this script and its clear guide-lines. There is no reason why they may not follow them to the letter. As we shall see later, equally plausible documents, e.g. international law, have been similarly criticized for being misused to catch out innocent and unsuspecting leaders, particularly those in Africa, for failing or refusing to heed certain dictates.

In the final analysis, the indicators of state failure are a double-edged sword. On the one hand, they are bench marks. They are a check list. They are reference points. They are standards. Equipped with them one can determine, tell or at least gauge the status of a state under observation. On the other hand, they are guide-lines. They provide a direction of some acts. They do not necessarily indicate. They are assumed. They are there to be followed. While states can use this view to guard against failing, their detractors can use the same to make sure they fail them. For example, those fighting certain states can use the 'indicators' to push the states against the wall by enforcing wrong policies on them, imposing sanctions on them, forcing them into wars and armed conflicts, sabotaging their economic development, among other things that they know very well eventually reduce the states to 'failing', or 'failed states'.

## 7.3 Racial Theorists

There is a need to examine racial theorists, particularly those who were, according to my observation, more prompted to write by new developments in the world influenced mainly by such doctrines as capitalism, colonialism, imperialism, mercantilism, and related activities such as immigration, commerce, wars, slave trade, exploitation, insatiable greed for power and other people's property, among others. These and similar factors distinguished between the foreign rulers and the subjugated indigenous people, the foreign 'haves' and the indigenous 'have-nots', the comfortable foreigners and the suffering indigenous, the well fed foreigners and the hungry hard working indigenous, and so many other unfair, unbalanced, and even embarrassing differences. This situation created a need for justification. Racial theories came in to fill in the gap. In reality, they are 'justification theories', trying to cover up the deliberate unfair dealings. The slavery issue, for instance, has existed all over the world where wars took place and the victors enslaved the conquered. However, there were social avenues through which the slaves could be absorbed in the new societies. This became difficult with the African slaves who were enslaved for commercial purposes, and so there had always to be a marked difference between masters and slaves. This commercial need also led to slave trade, which had never been heard of anywhere in the world before the 8th of August 1444 when a slaves market opened at the West African coast to sell off captured Senegalese victims. This and similar inhuman acts led some theorists to lie that the wars fought in Africa in which the slaves were captured were 'just wars'. The idea of 'just wars' was used because 'just wars' were accepted, and, ipso facto, slavery. The problem, however, was that, as seen above, traditionally slaves were never mistreated as those from Africa were. Due to this challenge, a new lie in form of a theory emerged, namely that Africans were sub-human, and so there was no problem in the human beings using them. This again became a real problem when, for example, some slave masters tricked their wives and abandoned them in certain comfortable places such as hammocks and disappeared with the more attractive black women. In addition to this human weakness, the weak 'justification theories' were watered down by the performance of certain activities that demonstrated the superiority of the slaves over their masters.

Yet another indicator that the racial theorists mentioned above are fake is the fact that the original racial theorists did not write to 'justify' evil activities. Some objectively compared their own races with other races and discovered and exposed aspects in which they thought the latter were superior. A good example is Joseph-Arthur de Gobineau, a French, who argued that all European thought originated in Asia[154]. When it came to racial superiority, the Frenchman gave the first position to Aryans, arguing that the Germanic Aryan is sacred, and that it is the race of the lords of the earth which is furnished with all the energy of the Aryan variety. According to him, the white species has nothing more powerful and active to offer than the Germanic Aryans[155].

This contradictory attitude, however, is characteristic of the whole racist system. For example, as cited elsewhere in this book and other sources, Ibn Rushd, Westernized as Averroes, is established as the Father of Enlightenment. The truth is that the Europe merely developed the foreign ideas and took advantage of them to revolutionize their societies through science and technology. Yet, when the West used these achievements to subjugate the rest of the world, they unashamedly contradicted history by bragging and preaching Euro-centricim, telling

---

[154] Joseph-Arthur de Gobineau (1865) : Les religions et les philosophes dans l'Asie centrale, Paris, Didier et Cie.
[155] Michael D. Biddiss (1970): The Father of Racist Ideology, London: Weidenfeld and Nicolson, pp. 175 176.

lies that everything, including ideas originated from the 'West' whose history of civilization is well documented.

This chauvinism has been expressed by Joseph Chamberlain who conceived the British as the greatest governing race the world has ever seen, and by the Duke of West Minster who praised Imperialism as having become the very latest and the highest embodiment of the British democratic nationalism, adding that Imperialism was a conscious expression of the English race[156]. This justification myth for colonialism and imperialism is further strengthened by Cecil Rhodes who claimed that the English were the leading race in the world and that the more the English populate the world the better for mankind since God chose them to produce a state and society based on justice, freedom and peace. Thus, he claimed God empowered him to colour as much of the map of African British red as possible[157].

The analysis of these views and claims leads to a double-edged contradiction. First, the British colonists and imperialist looted cultural products wherever they went. Their museums still display the loot. Some artifacts have successfully been reclaimed by their rightful owners. This is clear proof of the existence of civilization elsewhere and contradicts Euro-centricism and the claim of originating and spreading civilization. The truth is that the exercise interfered a lot with true civilization, since this is mainly based on internal human development and psychological disposition. It destroyed cultural activities, curtailed development, disoriented people and societies, among other problems. Second, the colonist and imperialists did not only destroy peaceful societies with their systems, ideas and leaders in all forms, but also sowed and still saw seeds of disunity which have created chaos in many

---

[156] See Peter Watson ( 2005) Ideas. A History from Fire to Freud, Phoenix, p. 904.

[157] William J. Stead (ed.: 1902) The Last Will and Testament of C. J. Rhodes, London: Review of Reviews Office, pp. 57 and 97.

societies. This contradicts the claim of producing 'a state and society based on justice, freedom and peace'.

Incriminating evidence of the contradictions includes the following examples: first, pretexts deliberately created to justify colonization. Problems would be started in an unsuspecting society. Colonists would get in to solve them. Then they would stay, arguing the situation would be worse if they left. Second, the brutality and cruelty unleashed on the colonized was unprecedented. Some of the victims have been compensated for these inhuman acts. Third, policies such as divide and rule did not only weaken the strong societies colonists found in place, but have also been inherited and still adversely affect the modern African state. Fourth, the religious and other forms of sectarianism initiated by colonists still bedevil 'former' colonies.

Despite the so many loopholes and contradictions, the racial theories have spread like fire and that their ideas have been used in various ways for mental colonization. There are many ways in which certain mechanisms are still in place to perpetuate the otherwise meaningless racism. 'Agents of imperialism' are not yet in short supply. There is, therefore, a need to expose as much of these theorists as possible.

Those who have based their racial theories on Darwinism have come up with new areas such as 'Social Darwinism' and 'Scientific Darwinism'. Social Darwinism stemmed from Herbert Spencer's thought. He compared the growth of society with that of a factory, and argued that both needed structural differentiation and specialization of functions. According to him, such a structure made society adaptable in the Darwin sense, and pointed out that evolution occurs among societies at every level, resulting in the 'survival of the fittest'. He held that this process application and misapplication of Darwinian thinking to the various cultures around the world.

In this category was Friedrich Ratzel who from a different angle developed a similar argument that all living organisms competed in a

Kampf um Raum, i. e. a struggle for space, in which the winners expelled the losers. He extended this struggle to humans and argued that the successful races had to extend their living space, i. e. Lebensraum, if they wanted to avoid decline.

Modern (scientific) Darwinism, on the other hand, was based on three factors:

a)  the Enlightenment view that human condition was essentially a biological state, as opposed to a theological state;

b)  the wider contact between different races brought about by imperial conquests,

c)  the application and misapplication of Darwinian thinking to the various cultures around the world[158].

One of the biological racist theorists was Jules Virey. In 1841 he addressed the Parisian Academie de Medecine on 'biological causes of civilization', and divided people of the world into two: whites 'who had achieved a more or less perfect stage of civilization', and the blacks (Africans, Asians, and American Indians) who were condemned to a 'constantly imperfect civilization'. He was pessimistic that the 'blacks' would ever achieve 'full civilization'. He went as far as telling a lie that like white people, domestic animals, like cows, have white flesh, while black people, like wild animals, such as deer, have dark flesh. He went on to say that 'just as the wild animal was prey to the human, so the black human was the natural prey of the white human'[159] Pegdon also reports that according to Virey, a doctor of human medicine, slavery, far from being cruel was consistent with nature[160].

---

[158] Peter Watson, op. cit. p. 914

[159] Anthony Pagden (2001) People and Empires London: Weidenfeld and Nicolson, p. 147.

[160] Anthony Pagden, op. cit. p. 148.

Dr. Virey is not alone. His days have not gone, either. Only recently, when I was already carrying out research for this book, I personally met a highly placed medical doctor who gave me a good lecture on the difference between a white person's skin and the skin of a black person. He could not carry out an operation on a black skin, as he did on a white skin, because if he did, there would grow a bigger swelling than then one he was asked to remove. Research had been carried out in the US to find out why black women who pierced their ears, navels and other parts of the body had developed strange swellings after the piercing. The findings show that black skins are so different that such cuts lead to swellings. He could easily cut a swelling from the body of a white person and only a small line, or hardly any shows afterwards. But not so with a black person's skin. As a lay man, I listened with faith and patience, but wondered whether I remembered correctly the nicely healed scars on many bodies I knew. I thought of the so many cuts Africans get daily in their life environment. I thought of women who give birth to so many children. If those repeated cuts leave behind big growths that grow bigger with every birth, then they must be quite a site. Do those dresses cover heaven and earth?

Other racial theorists include Houston Stewart Chamberlain (1855 – 1927) who held that racial struggle was fundamental to a 'scientific' understanding of history and culture. According to him, the history of the West was an incessant conflict between the spiritual and culture-creating Aryans together with the mercenary and materialistic Jews. He thought that the Germanic peoples were the last remnants of the Aryans, who had become enfeebled through interbreeding with other races. This idea was emphasized by that of degeneracy by Max Nardau (1849 – 1923) together with the argument of Joseph le Conte (1823 – 1901) that when two races came into contact one was bound to dominate the other[161].

---

[161] Joseph le Conte (18920) The Race Problem in the South.

Francis Galton (1822 – 1911) made a big contribution to scientific Darwinism by arguing that the essence of eugenics was that 'inferiority' and 'superiority' could be objectively described and measured[162]

George Vacher de Lapouge (1854 – 1936) studied ancient skulls and concluded that races were species in the process of formation. He believed that racial differences were 'innate and ineradicable'. The idea that they could integrate, he claimed, was against the law of biology.[163]

It is important to reiterate the fact that while in certain societies and academic circles these theories were understood to emanate from the competition of thinkers who wanted to be noticed, or those sponsored by exploitative forces to justify and cover up their immoral and shameful activities, in colonized societies, such as Africa, they were and still are being forced down the throats of the victims through various methods as the truth and nothing but the truth.

This has led to sheer biased attitudes of certain people towards other people. Thus, one comes to certain conclusions or assumptions, without any second thought, on the basis of ridiculous things such as colour. Many think they do not need to travel to Africa, for instance, to know how Africans think and what they think about. Arm-chair anthropologists, so-called religious people, historians and even scientists just open their mouths and say anything about Africa. These include L. Ron Hubbard, a science fiction writer and founder of Scientology Church, who extended his 'fictitious' mind to Africa:

'The African tribesman, with his complete contempt for truth and his emphasis on brutality and savagery for others but not for himself, is a no-civilisation'[164].

---

[162] Ivan Hannaford (1996 ) Race: The History of an Idea, Baltimore: John Hopkins University Press, p. 330

[163] Ibid. p. 330

[164] L. Ron Hubbard, *Scientology: The Fundamentals of Thought.*

Where did this gentleman meet such a 'tribesman' with these attributes? Certainly, nowhere! Is it not shameful that according to him being African does not go beyond his figment of the mind? Is it not ridiculous that a scientist merely imagines 'brute' and 'savage' and blindly imputes them on people just because of colour? What does he mean by these terms? What does he mean by 'truth' for which his imaginary African tribesman has complete contempt? How does he determine the completeness of this contempt? How does he come to the conclusion of 'emphasis on brutality and savagery for others but not for himself'? What does he understand by 'civilisation'?

A comparison of reality in the west with this myth in Africa shows the scientist is totally wrong. Well documented activities show real contempt for truth, for example by those who have strived to cover up their theft by creating a 'civilisation' pretext or platform for colonialism and imperialism. One may cite lies upon lies told about 'other cultures'. One may also cite deliberate misinformation, even currently, through sophisticated means such mass media, research, and other fabrications. Who emphasizes brutality and savagery more than people who thrive on killing others through sophisticated wars? We know very well that international law, for instance, was established due to world war atrocities. Refugee law originally came into existence for Western countries. International human law came into existence in the West. Red Cross and other international organisations emerged in brutally and savagery devastated West. These were not 'brute and savage African' wars. It is not Africans who 'savagery and brutally kill others but save themselves' through biological wars, use of chemical weapons, atomic and other bombs, poison, long-range missiles, and other weapons of mass destruction. In South Africa, Whites built huge and high vehicles from which they would torture and terrorize helpless Blacks. There are helicopters which have been designed to throw stones at innocent people protesting injustices against them. Currently, drones are in vogue. So, who really acts with 'emphasis on brutality and savagery for others but not for himself', as Hubbard claims? Does he expect to be taken seriously by any unbiased thinker? He is expected to know that MAD is clear evidence of 'brutality and savagery'. Many are mad about MAD out of fear. Human dignity is out of the equation. Can Hubbard possibly be ignorant of this? Does he tell the truth? Does he distinguish himself from discredited bigots and racists?

Racism is a mere concoction with nothing to do with reality and the truth. This is evident in the fact that while Darwin prescribed a common origin for all races, racists came up with other ideas such as 'inferiority' and 'superiority' of races, 'racial domination', 'eugenics', 'degeneracy', 'Kampf um Raum', 'Lebensraum', 'dependency', among other racist ideas and expressions used to defend socio-political and economic exploitation of some races by others, or to preserve the purity of minority races amidst other races, or to promote outright imperialism and colonialism. The circumstances in which various theorists of this sort lived can support this position. Similarly wrongly used words and expressions include useful ones which have been corrupted or given special meanings in the attempt to achieve narrow and selfish objectives. These include 'intervention', which often is in reality 'interference', 'international community', which often amounts to a collusion of a few influential and selfish countries, 'people power', which is often concocted to hide 'fire power' behind the concoction, 'collaboration', 'trade', 'treaty', 'contract' and so many other good words carrying terrible hidden meanings. In a nutshell, any relationship between nations, corporations, or even individuals, however good and useful, can be misused, if moral uprightness, which will be repeatedly referred to in this book, has been undermined. This situation is compounded by the philosophical problem of 'other minds', and the natural but often naïve human trust.

So, I have presented racial theorist and their theories, not because there is any sense in the theories, but because of three reasons. First, there is a need to prove them wrong, since I am committed to the method of elimination. Second, these theories were used to justify colonialism and imperialism under the guise of 'civilization'. Greedy and ruthless colonists and imperialists ended up being supported by their unsuspecting country men and women abroad who were convinced that the exploiters were doing a good job to infect primitive people with 'civilization' which Okot p'Bitek, a Ugandan thinker, dismissed as 'syphilisation', referring to the introduction of syphilis into highly civilized Africa through this encounter. Many thinkers, up to now, still question the establishing of a huge and sophisticated hospital in Uganda to 'cure' the syphilis hitherto unknown in the country. Third, the theories were assumed to be true. Thus, they guided colonial and imperial activities, and are highly responsible for mental colonization whose disastrous effects are still felt, for example, through the 'superiority' and 'inferiority' complexes they created, planted, nurtured and perennially propped. The attitudes Africans still habour towards themselves and any people of a different colour stem from these theories.

These theories, despite their successes in achieving the objectives for which they were created, i.e. justification of exploitation and mental colonization, remain baseless. It is not quite accurate to dismiss them as biased ideas since they are deliberate concoctions. Their creators knew and know the truth about the humanity of all people, including Africans. If Westerners who first went to Africa were to base themselves on evidence to describe Africa and the African people, the story would be totally different. There is documented civilization in Africa long before Westerners arrived. Yet, this was manipulated to misinform unsuspecting people that nothing ranging from crops, culture, history, education, philosophy – nothing – existed in Africa before colonization and imperialism. Afro-centricism has emerged to counter this Euro-centricism. All the same, the subjugation and exploitation of Africa has continued unabated through other methods, including brute force.

This force is partly due to the internal contradictions within these concocted racial theories which have lead to the natural deaths of the theories. The demise of the theories leaves us as ignorant about underdevelopment as before their concoction. So, we need to look elsewhere for an explanation of African underdevelopment.

A good example of such deaths of racist theories is that of Eugenics. Eugenics originated from social Darwinism but got its definition and elaboration from Francis Galton, Charles Darwin's step-cousin. This theory was first propounded in the *American Journal of Sociology* as recently as 1904. Eugenics can be understood not only as a way of segregating 'natives' whom it dismisses as inferior beings, but also as a means of keeping certain races pure in the face of the rampant immigrations and temptations to mix with other races which could lead to the demise of the minority races. The people were divided into the 'civilized' and 'natives'. The 'natives' were baptized relegated to the naturally less intelligent and capable than the 'civilized' people. Eugenics discouraged marriage between the two groups arguing that the product of the two would be worse than the 'native'.

Eugenics, which was born in USA, died in USA where enumerable successful African Americans of mixed origin emerged. Some Africans sought education from USA and returned to their countries. An example may be cited from Uganda where during colonial rule the highest educated African could not go beyond Primary six. Whoever got to this level qualified to be teacher of others. The teaching was in vernacular. There is an African saying that even bad things can be comparatively better or worse. *Ebibi bihitahitana.* In the colonial context, there is a view that the British were the best colonists. The explanation is that they, unlike other colonizers, they could not take the colonized home due to lack of space. This forced them to initiate institutions within the colonies in order to colonize the people at home, thus leading to higher standards of education together with management and administration within the colonies. All the same, the English language was 'hidden' from the colonized. A view has been expressed that this was intended to protect colonial administrators whose level of education was so low that they could not afford to expose themselves to 'natives'. So, they hid their language and tried to communicate in broken Kiswahili, while unsuspecting Africans thought they were not expected to understand the language of the people who were next to God Himself. Comparative studies show that colonists who easily exposed their language soon faced racial confrontations. For example, in Angola immediately the young went to school, they were told they were no longer Africans. So, they had to avoid African culture and tradition. They had to speak, eat, dance, walk, laugh and do everything *as* 'whites'. They were told to have little to do with relatives and all those who did not have a chance to be pulled out of the cave of darkness. The cat came out of the bag when they went to join their fellow 'whites' in the exclusively 'white' clubs, some accompanied by their girlfriends, only to be embarrassed and ordered out by muscular bouncers as wrong people in right places.

The English approach was perfectly in accordance with the mental colonization plan. The colonists and imperialists wanted the colonized to swallow 'superiority vis-à-vis inferiority theories'. They wanted them to believe that they were slowly developing, but far behind their masters. In the case of language they wanted the colonized to believe that their language and general culture were underdeveloped, unlike those of the masters which had reached the peak. They, actually, had no 'culture'. They were uncultured, uncultivated, uncouth, uncivilized…and that was the reason why the 'cultured' masters had come. So, mastery of the English language meant getting close to the master in terms of development, which would be an uphill task. This belief was later revealed by a widely quoted Uganda who was selected to live in England for some time. When he returned, he 'proved' mental colonization by demonstrating his newly acquired belief that all the people's culture, including language, existed in a straight line at the apex of which was the colonial masters' culture. The goal of everyone was to get to this apex. So, his memorable experience which expressed this thinking was that what he had witnessed was a marvel. The people were so advanced that even the child spoke perfect English. The 'unilateralism' pushed down the throats of the unsuspecting, innocent, mentally colonized people made the victims believe that it would, indeed, be difficult to catch up with their colonial masters who perfectly spoke their language.

A lot was done to discredit Africans and even set them against themselves as incapable or inferior. Everything African was to be discarded. All had to be channeled into the right direction. No one was allowed to resist because no one had a right to be 'uncivilized'. The West had the right and obligation to civilize the rest of the world, among others. 'Civilizing' or Christianizing meant the same thing, namely, Westernizing. One of the ways was by washing their underdeveloped, or 'non culture' off them, as if it were dirt. The contradiction, however, included observations and admissions of a number of well-developed cultural aspects, including African languages and general behavior, in contrast with the immorality the 'civilized' exhibited.

In the case of Uganda, problems arose when Dr. Aggrey of Ghana visited the country and was publicly seen and heard speaking English and laughing with the colonial masters. To make matters worse, he was darker than Ernest Kalibbala who was then the top African teacher in the country. Dr. Aggrey Memorial School was later built in Kampala. Challenged by the liberating visit and associated events, Kalibbala took off to England for further studies only to find himself in Primary Six where he looked like the father or even grandfather of the whole class.

USA saved the situation when he was advised that that was the place where he could best fit. Indeed he did. He got his education, married an African American, and returned to Uganda with a Ph.D. degree to become father of Private Schools. These made a big difference. First, the teaching of English started in Primary three, contrary to the colonial system of starting it in Primary five. Second, private schools in Uganda became far better than Government schools. Under a separate study[165] I have tried to find out what went wrong such that currently private schools have lost their traditional status.

What is most remarkable, however, is that Eugenics has been buried where it was born and died, USA. One of the nails in the coffin of this false and baseless theory is the great victory of invincible President Baraka Obama! When some of us relentlessly celebrated this victory, those without a clue about our views on racist theorists and their theories could easily have marveled at witnessing true and diehard racists.

According to Eugenics, 'natives', wherever they were found, were by nature inferior to the wondering Europeans. These were later grouped as Westerners and described as 'whites', despite the fact that no 'white' person has ever existed in this world. The racist and false description of people as 'white', 'black', 'yellow' et cetera has persisted, as if people were blind. I always pray and hope that I am not branded a racist when I tell the truth that I have never seen a 'white' person. I cannot imagine what colour his shirt or her shoes would be. Who looks like these? So also is the false, yet persistent, reference to the world as 'East' and 'West' regardless of the natural geographical location of the categorized areas. One of the most ridiculous, though, appears to be 'commonwealth' countries which range from the riches to the poorest in the world. The deceitful expression is also a mockery as some of these countries are as poor as me. The 'commonwealth' countries have neither riches nor poverty in common.

---

[165] Education Challenges in Uganda A Comparative Study with Switzerland.

Obama and fellow successful persons of mixed races have buried eugenics forever. It is necessary, however, to point out that there have always been efforts made to hide this truth. If only a small fraction of the successful contributions by Africans both at home and in diaspora were to be officially recognized and revealed, the attitude to Africa and the Africans would change forever. Exploiters of Africa who highly benefit from burning a house and hiding the smoke, despite common knowledge of the covered up truth, are behind this game. For example, fearless African soldiers fought and helped colonial masters to win wars, such as the World War. But the gallant soldiers were not allowed to join the victory parades at their heroic return 'home'. The world needs to join hands to fight racism, which in some places is practiced with impunity, instead of sitting and watching till it knocks right on their doors. The truth is that Blacks of whatever origin, whatever persuasion, whatever qualifications, and of whatever status will continue facing racial discrimination unless and until Africa is free and respected. The African Americans are more than the Israel Americans, but racial discrimination of the two is hardly comparable because of the status of Israel.

His brilliant performance before the presidential race, throughout the campaigns, and during the presidency leave even biased bigots dumbfounded. Due to his African roots, however, the academic cum political giant has doubly suffered. First, the rampant racism has not spared even the president himself. Given the facts and circumstances, the world has a big challenge to stand up against the idiotic and shameful practice. Africans should ask what they can do for their son, and not what he can do for them. There is nothing impressive in racial murders. It is ironical to see tearful and fearful faces of innocent people subjected to racial discrimination in a land that boasts of fathering and championing human rights. The recent words of a victim, whose son was murdered in cold blood, that all he could trust is the Lord tell the tale.

Second, those who built castles in the air and expected immediate assistance, as if he had been elected their own president, have, as expected, been disappointed. They expected better treatment than that received from his predecessors who looked away or offered peanuts. An analysis of a statement that giving Africa money was like throwing it into a rat-hole is true, but has two problems. Number one is given the 'colossal' amount of money that allegedly 'trickles' into Africa, 'rat-hole' is an understatement[166]. 'Gigantic Cave' would suit better the magnitude of the cash flow route 'through' Africa under the guise of 'development aid', for instance. Number two is the idea of 'rats' is wrong. There is not a single rat in the hole. The 'rat-less hole' uninterrupted leads back to the source with massive profits. Such deceit, misinformation and other gimmicks were expected to end with their own being in the driving seat.

When he visited Africa, the president struck the right code in emphasizing strong institutions which are permanent in contrast to strong governments/states which are transient. This might not have sounded well in the ears of dictators or the 'strong' regimes scattered all over Africa. For different reasons, however, even those very far aware from state power have a little problem. As I argue below, many of these regimes heavily depend on Western benefactors. So, who did he

---

[166] 'Colossal' amounts 'trickling' into Africa pose no contradiction problem. The amounts of development aid communicated to the world through mass media often leave listeners wondering whether recipients need any other source of funding to successfully carry out national development duties. The documented declarations are there for any interested party to examine. The amounts are truly colossal. I deliberately describe these as trickles because given the capacity Africa has to generate its own income, foreign funding, however much it is, remains a trickle. The much larger problem, however, is that figures on paper are never reflected in any developmental projects, thus giving the impression that the funds could be given by certain unsuspecting citizens but received back 'via Africa'.

address? The president was on the right course in reminding Africans of their responsibilities, particularly solving their problems. The problem, however, is that many of the problems in Africa are not 'African'. The problems happen in Africa but originate elsewhere. So, the call to one side to solve these problems naturally partly sounded well. African leaders have always clamoured for the opportunity to solve their problems against foreign interference. Political and economic problems cannot be solved by those who create them to enrich themselves. Proxy wars cannot be stopped by those behind arms' trafficking. Beneficiaries cannot stop wars. Deliberately 'wrong' policies are ever enforced on Africa. Local accomplices and international bodies such as IFM, WB, NGOs have been found to more add than solve problems. Some tactics are used to 'aid' foreigners with incredible sums of money 'via Africa'. Africa is tired of being destabilized with impunity and then shamelessly blamed for the ensuing mess.

The unfortunate presence of greedy and ruthless rulers is undeniable. Criticism, wherever it comes from, is welcome. But it is also true that a many of these are stooges imposed on innocent people. They are supported by those who 'milk' Africa through them. It is true that good and dedicated African leaders have been forced to follow wrong policies and forced out of power when they resist, or even assassinated. The history of instability has for time immemorial bedeviled Africa. It is true that one who controls the past controls the future. That is why colonialism and imperialism are jealously guarded and incognito or openly continually enforced. Quite often there is a vacuum of leadership. Chaos is ever present. Rivers and rivers of innocent African blood ever flow. Would be builders of Africa languish in exile. Many are in prisons and humiliated both at home and abroad. Sanctions, too, deprive fragile Africa and easily turn the continent into the playground for exploiters. They have become the life style affecting nationals much more than governments.

In Africa there is no homogeneous population. This translates into inequalities which are real issues in Africa, and explains why growth numbers of a country's GDP are always artificial. People hardly participate in the growth. Africa is characterized by both internal inequalities and being unequal, as a whole, to the rest of the world. All these injustices make Africa special. The continent is identified with gaps. There is a gap between Africa and the rest of the world. Within Africa, there is a gap between leaders and rulers. There is a gap between governments and populations. Often such problems as corruption are mistaken to be part of African culture either because observers expect standards that hardly exist due to lack or weakness of certain institutions, or because they witness cases of taking advantage of helpless people. Above all, what is observable takes place in Africa but the real sources of the crooked plans and the main beneficiaries are often selfish foreign forces.

Under a separate study on 'Ethical Issues in Research', I have shown evidence of some academics employed to misuse their fields in favour of exploiters and to the detriment of the exploited. This explains why certain views by scholars such as Darwin were twisted to misinform the world about innocent people simply to justify exploitation. Similar lies have unashamedly been told against nature by scientists whose calling should be to protect it for the common good. Thus, a blatant lie that equatorial forests are not the lungs of the earth, as was long believed, is common knowledge. The subsequent justified destruction of this forest, effects such as global warming, the notorious floods, among other dangers, all in the name of greed for gains from timber, are also common knowledge.

Colonial anthropologists and their lies are also well known. As I have argued elsewhere, the fact that no anthropologist ever conceded having failed to understand a given society with all its complexities. At this juncture, I only add a theory advanced against 'native' societies simply to justify the anthropologists' untenable approach. Surprisingly, this theory was also used by 'philosophers' who are expected to know and avoid the fallacy of generalization. The theory states that primitive people are confronted by nature and use magic to respond, and that their minds are so 'fixed' that all the natives' answers to life issues are the same[167]. According to this view, therefore, a foreign observer is able to discern these answers and piece them together in the world view within which the 'natives' understand and do things. The serious question that arises is how human beings can possibly have such a 'fixed' and easily predictable mind. Philosophers know that one of the difficult but very important areas of philosophy is knowledge itself. Self-knowledge - 'know thyself' - and the 'problem of other minds' are highly valued and ranked. Many know how ridiculously annoying it is when simplistic minds either out of ignorance or malice concoct schemes and innocently place innocent people therein, or merely frame them.

In the case of armchair anthropologists and similar minds, however, one does not need to labour the point that these foreigners who did not know much about the local people's language, could not discuss anything, among other handicaps had no alternative but to concoct their own 'fixed' world view which they would pretend to use to explain everything about the people under their study. This explains why none of them failed to understand the people he set out to study. Ipso facto, none of them did. If it is so difficult to understand and explain the life of an individual person, what about a much more complex society? The unfortunate thing is that the concoctions have been forced the throat of many unsuspecting people who have ended up believing that they are, indeed, what these liars tell them they are.

---

[167] While such anthropologist may be represented by Frazer, the 'philosophers' may be represented by Horton.

## 7.4 Racism as Ideology

Eurocentricism, modernism, civilization, and other isms that promoted the West at the expense of the rest of the world were highly calculated ideologies. The Oxford Advanced Learners' Dictionary defines an ideology as a set of cultural beliefs, values, and attitudes that underlie and justify either the status quo or the movements to change it. It also refers to as a system of ideas and ideals especially one which forms the basis of economic and political theory and policy. In this regard, we may observe that *the highly calculated theories were intended to create beliefs, values, and attitudes to underlie and justify the movements to change the status quo in the colonies*! This is observation may be corroborated by Webster's Desk Dictionary which defines ideology as the body of doctrines or beliefs that guides a particular individual, class, or culture. It adds that ideology is such a body of doctrines or beliefs with reference to some political and social plan. We can conclude that mental colonization, for example, is an aspect of this plan or plot. There is a dire need to make a thorough study of this plot and its disastrous results which are still growing strong, misinforming, cheating and destroying innocent and unsuspecting people. A good number of the ideas that guide life were created only yesterday with a purpose. Their deconstruction, depending on the purpose and effects, is urgent.

It is regrettable that, as revealed above, racism was concocted and promoted by academic giants and specialists or experts in well-established fields of education. It has been pointed out that this was not by accident. It was by design. There was a selfish need to deceive the world and the most credible were sought out to do the job. There was no ignorance whatsoever about the so-called black race, or the Africans. The theorists knew the truth and nothing but the truth but deliberately twisted it. The evidence of this lies in what the Africans had achieved long before the plots and attempts to erase them off the earth physically, intellectually, politically, economically and culturally were hatched. Whereas a good number of these bizarre theorists are dead, many others still live. Worst of all, they have reproduced themselves and have mentors. It is unrealistic and hypocritical to limit inhuman concepts such as 'terrorism' or 'radicalization' to specific groups and cover up those which are even worse. Sometimes the attacked or hunted down are victims of the injustices. Many of these are just caught in the act of reacting. Many others, however, are merely perceived reactionaries.

The lines in the dust are clear. The sun shimmers on the social constructs whose deconstruction is long overdue. Some social architects thought they were smart when they deliberately and meticulously created heaven and hell on the same planet or even in the same country. They knew very well that hell was required to sustain heaven. The goal of ideology has always been to convince the victims and the beneficiaries alike that hell and heaven inmates occupy their natural positions. However, the ideology has been a glorious failure. The evidence of this failure is clear in resistance after resistance followed by brutal force to keep the people in the ideologically created places and positions.

There are well informed and influential people who have exposed this plot. These include Pope Pius XII and Sheikh Anta Diop. It is imperative to look at 'Pope Pius XII Hope for Black People's Triumph' which reveals the hidden truth about Blacks. Most important, it uncovers innumerable lies about Africa. It is equally imperative to view and listen to the video, Cheikh Anta Diop – The African Origins of Civilisation.

Further information reveals that Africans crossed the Atlantic Ocean and settled in America where they had a lot of influence long before the famous Christopher Columbus 'discovered' the continent. The civilisation in Egypt has been traced to Sub-Saharan Africa. Despite deliberate efforts to destroy the evidence of civilisation on various sites, such as Timbukutu just recently, there is much more that cannot be destroyed. Some looted artefacts are being retrieved from various museums. Above all, there is nothing that can reverse science and technology and then distort or destroy the evidence arrived at through means such as DNA.

Today the true African history is fast being reconstructed. Distortions are being exposed, revised, or totally rejected. Many people have become aware of who are behind the distortions and why. However, it is important to reiterate that as soon as the African liberation struggles led to flag independence, multinationals took over the position of colonising nations. As earlier observed, it is gratifying to note that despite the difficulty, almost impossibility, for any single nation to resist multinationals or the current negative globalisation, efforts have been made to form international resistances against the powerful negative forces. Currently, these organisations are the hope of the world against the cut throat competitive capitalism that has created chaos all over the world.

Pope Francis, too, has warned the world against forces that are in action wholly motivated by the desire to grab other people's property. One strongly feels that this is addressed to Africa. Of the continents whose property has been grabbed, Africa ranks highest.

However, as the world slowly but steadily looks through the strategic ideologies and related unholy alliances, attempts on new ideologies and strategies are being made. One of the most serious is corruption. There are many national and international efforts bent on bedevilling Africa, particularly the leadership, through emphasis on accountability, governance, human rights, among others. They focus on African governments, motivated by the so called corruption. By accountability they limit themselves to monetary issues.

If the concerned organisations were serious, they would have realised that the monetary system, under which corruption emerges, was introduced to Africa through individual property ownership. The African system was communal property ownership. The communal systems were not only physical but also intellectual. Thus, we still talk of certain ethnic groups' land, medicine, political systems, among other systems in which greed for power and property, nepotism, dictatorship, among other aspects of corruption are incompatible and irrelevant.

Whereas the architects of the corruption ideology know the truth mentioned above, they are also aware of possibilities of human manipulability and are experts in the game. They are aware that yesterday people wondered about their aimlessness, as they appeared to be merely wandering around, only for the same people to adore them as the source of everything, the next day. They know how they have introduced corruption through kick-backs, for instance, as they competed for tenders, particularly when big sums of international organisations 'development' funds are involved. They know the game is business, and dirty business at that. Bet still they know how to twist stories and the truth. Thus, corruption which fell like rain, even when big and small were looking, now has its origin in Africa. Many are without shame preaching that Africans are by nature corrupt. Yet, records reveal evidence of concerted searches by powerful governments for 'corruptibility' among 'suitable' rulers to be handed over power to as stooges!

All is drama. It is deliberate. It is deceit. There is no racist who does not know that the hated person is much of a person as anybody else. There is no false theorist who does not know the truth but willingly and knowingly decides to ignore, twist or tell it slant. It is all malice. None of them can ever be excused. The ball is in their camp to continue or change the game.

As regards human manipulability, credulity, and creativity we may refer to the experience of a researcher who gave a curious object to some people with instructions to put it on a table, take three steps backwards and then bow to it three times. Later, when asked by the architect of the game why they went through those steps, the unsuspecting people gave reasons for every action! Today uncountable numbers are deliberately sunk in the Mediterranean Sea. A careful observation reveals these are the cream of their societies. For sure, no one would walk from Kabimbiri to their death in that sea. Yet the song begins and stops with 'illegal migrations'.

If the deceived people are so rich as to pay heavily in the hope of getting better jobs abroad, just as one may give a bribe to be promoted or get a better job at home, why are these rich people described as 'economic' let alone political refugees? If yesterday brain drain sorted out certain significant members of society for employment why are similar brains today sorted out to be murdered? There are many questions, but what appears to be clear is that deliberate efforts continue to be made to destroy economies, political and other systems, and totally destabilize countries.

In the orchestrated confusion multitudes of 'immigrants' are relayed through mass media for propaganda purposes. A few are selected to be drowned as cameras tell the tales that move the world. A few still are selected to share their experiences, including those who have succeeded in 'making it abroad', once the dream of those at the bottom of the sea. The experiences are augmented by selected episodes of wars and all the circumstances that have reduced the people to such abject poverty that they would rather die than stay in such circumstances. When the lesson is home, the stage is set for two things: either 'build governments' that can stabilize the situation, or 'intervene militarily'. 'Build' is significant as it reveals who puts the required governments in place. However, the latter is the 'option' or rather the goal, given who is behind the destabilization and why. The war is ever for the unbalanced world economy. Ever increasing mismanagement of 'powerful' countries' economies always spills over to the economies of the 'weak' and exploited countries for recovery and better life.

Through ideology, the strategy is to put ideas into peoples' minds and hearts. Then the people, including the victims, will do the rest. Once blacks are successfully depicted as a different species, then the people, including the black people, will look for the differences and, strange enough, find them. In no time, they will behave accordingly. Then the stage will be set for discrimination, exploitation, and all that was anticipated by the racial architects. Tools, like fear, will come in handy to implement the theories. These will forcefully reduce the discriminated to their level. This scenario is the mother of all terrorism.

This issue needs a separate and exhaustive study. All systems that have been created to subjugate people are founded on terrorizing the innocent and unsuspecting people. Colonization, apartheid, and all other forms of exploitation are founded on fear. This extends to sexism. Women are subjugated through family violence. Even the strongest are psychologically reduced to believing that they are weaker than the weakest boy they meet. As regards states, the game begins with deceit. Enemies smile. Empty promises are made. False deals are struck.

Faces change when the deceived wake up. Then the friends become Chinese: hammering protruding nails back to their positions. Excuses are devised. When these fail, threats are made. When threats bounce on deaf ears, sabotage is resorted to. When this is too slow, opposition parties, even when they have nothing better to offer, are created and sustained. When the boneless 'politicians' are laughed at by the electorate, coup d'Etas are resorted to. When even the ignoramus coup makers look through the gimmicks, counter coups are staged. The cold war becomes hot. This is the only history Africa has known.

The same history has proved that the psychological cure is second to none when it comes to a psychological disease. The healing process may take time but it is irreversible. The hoodwinked learn to be careful. This truism is expressed in the African dictum that when you are bitten by a snake you fear a hole. When the terrorists and their intentions are exposed the victims of yesterday become the champions of today. Knowledge is power. Understanding undermines strategy. Awareness erodes fear. When fear merits away, courage prevails. The sky becomes the limit. If there is anything to trust it is fear. If there is anything to fear it is fear. Fear subjugates. Fear frees. Fear compares well with a cloud between the eyes and the sun. The big difference is that fear betrays who plants it. This turns fear into a great liberator.

Whoever needs proof need not scratch their heads. Just face the fearless. You do not need to go or look far. Far afield, avoid propaganda. The power of the word still works through mass media misinformation. The victims still abound. Objectively examine colonial resistance wars. Squarely face the liberation wars. Critically assess the life of the brave leaders. Carefully study their so-called 'failures'. Appreciate their martyrdom. Visit activities of the mentally liberated. Look at the resolute of those who now understand the machinations of the exploiters. Listen to those who take liberators as mentors.

Africa can learn from the Acts of the Apostles. Activities that follow knowledge and understanding are immeasurable. Miracles that happen when fear ebbs away are boundless. Ignorance enslaves. Lose it. Knowledge frees. Seek it. Truth liberates. Follow it.

Beware. Ideologues can sell sand in the desert. They persuade Africa to abandon its healthy foods from healthy gardens and consume unhealthy and dangerous fast foods. They bewitch African brains and force them to abandon traditional crops in favour of biologically modified ones whose seeds end up becoming a real problem that places even peasants at the mercy of foreign providers. They deliberately undermine local business, in all forms, to open the door wide for foreign investment. They sell under the guise of giving free. There is nothing free, not only because whatever is given has been paid for, but mainly because accepting 'free' things affects work ethos and leads to ignoring the recipients' own sources and means of livelihood. This leads to total dependence. When you are reduced to this stage, you are forced to pay anything for survival. You cannot respond to set prices, when the providers show their true faces. You cannot argue. Above all, dependence is the most expensive thing as it costs recipients their self-reliance and human dignity.

There are three important things to note. First, meanwhile Africa was bewitched into a deep slumber people were stealthily carried away into dream land! Now, as the continent wakes up and gropes for the way back home, the Socratic allegory of the cave appears to apply. Some return to shadows. There is a need to persist.

Second, there is no need for argument. This has nothing to do with the cliché against arguing with a fool. It is the other way round. All issues are in place, but one sided. In the event of an argument, Africa will be before a judge to argue issues Africa never agreed on. There are many issues Africa is not even aware of – thanks to the hidden agenda policy. Why, then argue? Africa needs to argue internally. There is a dire need to beware of set snares. We hear of corruption, human rights, governance: a cacophony of what exist nowhere in the world except in some people's minds and on paper. These are court issues. Well planned. Well prepared. Court time, parties, the place and other things are kept a secret.

Third, Africa needs to stand resolute. Fear is part of the gain. There is a need to beware of threats. There is a need to look over the shoulder, but not back. Africa needs its own hidden agenda, plots and set goals.

## 7.5 Racism as Class

While racial theories and ideologies are constructed, there is a sense in which racism is lived. This is the most rampant. In traditional societies, encountering people who looked different did not go beyond curiosity. Thus, stories of how unsuspecting Africans cordially received Whites with hidden agenda abound. The Africans saw fellow human beings that only looked different. Before the hidden agenda saga due to capitalism, different races freely mixed[168].

With time the idea of 'class' has graduated from materialism to psychology. The sense of belonging to a benefitting or socially acceptable class is not only naturally attractive, but is especially meaningful to the have nots. It is some sort of consolation. This attitude is not only limited to Western racists but is also evident in some 'Yellow' people who feel inferior to 'Whites' and console themselves as being, at least, superior to 'Blacks'. The contagious disease has devastated Africa where the traditional classlessness has been shuttered. The people, who naturally are men and women, young and old, look alike, speak the same language, enjoy the same culture etc., have been reduced to splitting hairs in the effort of searching for their differences and asserting them in order to benefit materially and monetary, e.g. in the political arena. Thus, modern Africa boasts of strange things such as sexism, tribalism, religious sectarianism, political party alliances, corruption, intrigue, etc. – thanks to colonialism and imperialism, policies such as divide and rule and subsequent related developments.

---

[168] Black people went to other lands long before Slavery and lived a totally different life. The Africans in various islands in the middle of Oceans were not carried there by anyone. Hardly anyone knows when the first Africans in larger lands and Continents such as Australia, the Middle East, the Far East, and other places arrived there. Racism and discrimination are a recent thing. They emerged due to the material and monetary values that ushered in forced labour, competition, selfishness, greed, etc. When people still shared means of production in common, only human values were the principle. Human dignity reigned. With the shift from human values, the material and monetary values create classes of haves and have nots. Life has been reduced to a struggle to keep in the class or join it. Racists, greedy for power and other people's property, take the haves class as their privilege.

## 7.6 Human Development

In order to address the terrible situation of underdevelopment, ideas such as human development and sustainability have emerged. According to the recommendations of the *Brundtland Commission Report (1987)*, sustainable human development means meeting the needs of the present generation without compromising the needs of future generations. Sustainable development becomes possible when economies use resources for the present without destroying the ecosystem or environment, i.e. preserving something for the future.

Human development and sustainable development can be said to be two sides of same coin. One applies to human beings. The other applies to nature. They are in vogue, and the force behind them is United Nations (UN), particularly *United Nations Development Program (UNDP)*. According to UNDP, human development is a process of enlarging the choices for all people in a society. Therefore, human development places people at the centre of the development process and makes the central purpose of development as creating an enabling environment in which all people can enjoy a long, healthy, and creative life. However, there is no agreed definition of development. According to *The UNDP Human Development Report 1990*, development is defined 'as a process of enlarging people's choices and opportunities – being educated, enabling individuals to develop full potential and lead productive and creative lives, having access and command of resources to live decent, health and longer lives.' This generally quoted definition is abstract. It does not explain how resources are organised and accessed in order to live a creative, productive and decent life. *The Human Development Report (1994)* presents sustainable human development as pro-people, pro-jobs, and pro-nature. It gives the highest priority to poverty reduction, productive employment, social integration, and environmental regeneration. It brings human numbers into balance with the coping capacities of nature. It also recognizes that not much can be achieved without a dramatic improvement in the status of women and the opening of all opportunities to women. *The Human Development Report (1996)* emphasizes employment, co-operation, equity, sustainability, security, in the sense of freedom from threats.

The UN focus is creating an environment in which people can live their full potential and lead to productive and creative lives. Environment is physical, socio-political, economic, and cultural. Human development focuses on personal development to create capacities or mental tools in individuals in contrast to communities. This view started in the 1970s when Alternative Approaches were being floated, but did not work out till in early 1980s when the belief in people took root. The principle is that people are the real wealth of nations. A country is rich or poor depending on its people. There are a number of things that must be done to make this possible:

- First, people must be empowered to do things on their own. This needs to be done through education, nutrition, social relations, health, among other mechanisms.
- Second, people's choices must be expanded. This is in terms of services. Ways of gauging development in a given society include finding out whether the people have different alternatives or choices, i.e. expanded services and their affordability, whether they can afford the type of life they want to live, whether they can achieve the type of education they want to have, whether they can get the medical facilities they want to have. Other facilities include sports, trips, holidays, among others. Having no choices is regarded as a sign of underdevelopment. The narrower the choices the more primitive a society remains. Uniform life is a sign of primitivity.
- Third, people need to live a long life. A society's life expectancy is an indicator to its development level.

- Fourth, there is a need for human welfare. For every project, there must be a goal. The purpose or goal of development is human welfare. What constitutes human welfare is not property. Human welfare can improve without economic growth.
- Fifth, there is an individual need to access, or to have means to access services such as education, health, income, among other facilities. Other indicators include security, human rights, etc. Human rights reinforce development.

United Nations' target on human development and sustainable development is correct, though a little long overdue. Despite the achievements, so far, there are setbacks or challenges to human development. These include the challenge of democracy. In many parts of the world, democracy has been reversed or tampered with. There is also the setback brought about by poor health and disease, particularly AIDs. At the beginning of the third millennium, there were 36 million cases of AIDs world-wide, 95% of whom were in developing countries, and 75% in Sub-Saharan Africa. 13 million children were AIDs orphans, 47% of whom were in Sub-Saharan Africa. In addition, the problems of insecurity and crime, in many cities of the world, are ever on the increase. A further hindrance to human development is the rampant armed conflicts. Other challenges include syndicates, networks, trafficking, and many others.

The international bodies were influenced by a number of scholars, including Amartya Sen[169] who have made a big contribution to the *Alternative Approaches to Development* which basically emphasise human development. Joseph Stiglitz[170] supported globalisation but later pointed out its unfairness to the underdeveloped who lack empowerment to compete with the developed world. These thinkers accept the free

---

[169] Amartya Sen, *Inequality Reexamined*, Oxford: Clarendon Press.
[170] Joseph Stiglitz, critic of globalization, free market fundamentalists, WB, and IMF

enterprise necessary for competition, but agree on the need for safeguards and regulations. Competition without regulation ends in corrupt speculation and exploitation of workers and consumers. Real development entails the quality and quantity of materials, goods, the work force, and distribution of income. Regulation is an excellent device. However, those who best circumvent rules and regulations are those who know them inside out. So, without human values, positive law may be a good tool in the hands of some and against others.

# 8

# RESPONSABILIDAD SOCIAL, SOLIDARIDAD, COMUNICACIÓN Y CULTURA EMPRESARIAL: UN MECANISMO DE RECONCILIACIÓN SOCIAL

*Edison Tabra*

## 8.1 Introducción

El presente artículo desarrolla la noción de la solidaridad enfocada a su práctica en los programas de responsabilidad social empresarial y la influencia que ejerce en los procesos de reconciliación entre sus grupos de interés. Dentro de este proceso, la poesía y la escritura poética ejercen un rol primordial porque su estudio permite encontrar la información que sirve para identificar las expectativas de algunos grupos de interés (comunidades indígenas o campesinas) e incluirlos en los objetivos de la empresa. A lo largo del trabajo se plantean una serie de conceptos como la empresa solidaria, la responsabilidad social solidaria de la empresa y la responsabilidad social de los grupos de interés vinculados a la organización empresarial.

Tradicionalmente, la solidaridad se entiende como un instrumento de ejercicio de la caridad que ejercen las personas con poder económico en favor de aquellas que no cuentan con los recursos necesarios para asegurar su subsistencia[171]. La solidaridad es sinónimo de desprendimiento material de los "unos" a favor de los "otros". En la actualidad, tanto las personas como las empresas adoptan la solidaridad como parte de su plan de vida o de funcionamiento, según sea el caso. En dicho plan se prevé practicar una serie de actividades de ayuda a favor de los más pobres o necesitados tales como hacer regalos, subsidiar cursos o actividades de recolección de fondos. En el caso del mundo del derecho se ha empezado a desarrollar la idea de actividades "probono" que buscan realizar actividades a favor de quienes no pueden contratar los servicios jurídicos o con la calidad profesional.

En ese sentido, la solidaridad se comprende como un sinónimo de la caridad. En el mundo empresarial esta versión solidaria se ha implementado en sus programas de responsabilidad social a favor de las comunidades con quienes convive o, aún más, se ha incluido implícitamente como parte de su involucramiento por mejorar el medio ambiente, los derechos humanos y la gobernanza. En estos planes de responsabilidad social rige un componente de solidaridad desde el punto de vista caritativo. Creemos que esta percepción de la solidaridad no corresponde con su real esencia por cuanto la caridad es un componente más de su esencia pero no el único. Por ende, la práctica de una responsabilidad social en base a la solidaridad caritativa por parte de la empresa o de cualquier agente del mercado, estado u otro *stakeholder* no cumple con su función de forma adecuada y eficaz. Por ende, somos de la idea que urge un cambio de visión que redefina a la solidaridad desde su real dimensión y que se traslade luego a la labor social empresarial.

---

[171] Edison Paul Tabra Ochoa is a leading Lawyer, extrajudicial moderator and a lecturer in Corporate and Business Law at the School of Law of the Pontifical Catholic University of Peru (PUCP). He holds a Ph.D. and a M.A. in Culture and Government of Organizations by University of Navarra (Spain), and a L.L.M. in Business Law by Pontifical Catholic University of Peru (PUCP).

Esta propuesta de cambio de paradigma solidario resulta urgente de hacer por cuanto la solidaridad influye en la responsabilidad social y contribuye a la práctica de otros principios como lo es la reconciliación. En el ámbito de la práctica de la responsabilidad social, la solidaridad ha contribuido al desarrollo de procesos de reconciliación entre la empresa con sus grupos de interés. En especial, la industria minera ha hecho uso de la responsabilidad social para implementar procesos de reconciliación con la población afectada por problemas afectados por su actividad: contaminación, despojo de tierras, incumplimiento de acuerdos, maltrato o indiferencia, bajos sueldos, entre otros. En muchos casos por la creencia que la empresa tenía la percepción de que su compromiso con la sociedad era el pago de los tributos al estado. En muchas ocasiones ello contó con el apoyo del marco jurídico del país de residencia o el apoyo de los gobiernos de turno.

Como consecuencia en América Latina se generó un fuerte malestar y descontento con la presencia y actividad empresarial el cual fue canalizado en la política por grupos de extrema izquierda. Dichos grupos se aprovecharon del resentimiento social de la población para obtener réditos políticos e implementar una serie de reformas "anti inversión" empresarial que lejos de favorecer los intereses de la población, contribuyeron con incrementar sus problema o necesidades sociales.

Hoy en día gracias a la responsabilidad social, el empresariado tiene una nueva oportunidad de incluir los intereses sociales dentro de sus objetivos económicos. Pero ello requiere de demostraciones reales por parte del empresariado en el sentido de que sus prácticas de responsabilidad social beneficiaran a la mayoría de la sociedad. Ello requiere de un proceso previo de reconciliación entre la empresa con la sociedad que demuestre su "sinceridad corporativa" por desarrollar su actividad económica en el país de residencia sin perjudicar los intereses del país y de la sociedad. La reconciliación con el apoyo de la responsabilidad social no involucra un "olvido" de los errores que cometió la organización empresarial en el pasado sino en un involucramiento real por unir sus intereses con los de la sociedad. Ello debe reflejarse en su forma de gobierno donde debe incluir criterios de transparencia y seguridad, un adecuado programa de cumplimiento de las leyes nacionales y compromisos internacionales, la implementación de mecanismos de promoción y ejercicio de los valores corporativos por parte de sus directivos y empleados, el uso de sistemas de atención eficiente de los reclamos y las denuncias de sus clientes, la exigencia de compromisos sociales a los proveedores, la colaboración con los programas de atención social de los gobiernos, entre otros.

De esa manera, creemos que la responsabilidad social que las empresas en el marco de un nuevo de solidaridad contribuirá con una adecuada reconciliación entre empresas y la sociedad. En estas líneas de trabajo esbozaremos la tesis de proponer un nuevo concepto de solidaridad que aplicado a la idea de "responsabilidad social" colabore con los procesos de reconciliación empresa-sociedad y favorezca la satisfacción mutua de sus intereses. En otras palabras la incorporación de todos los elementos que conforman la solidaridad propiciará una adecuada práctica de la responsabilidad social empresarial que, a su vez, logrará un proceso reconciliador entre las organizaciones empresariales, la sociedad y otros grupos de interés. De esta manera, será posible el restablecimiento de la comunicación entre dos agentes sociales que se necesitan mutuamente y que es importante que establezcan una adecuada comunicación y sobretodo convivencia.

De acuerdo a esta perspectiva, se espera que el lector pueda encontrar las ideas que involucran el trabajo de la solidaridad y vincularlas al uso del proceso de reconciliación que toda empresa requiere de implementar en sus actividades comerciales, que le permitan interactuar con sus grupos de interés y permanecer en el mercado en el mayor tiempo posible para beneficio suyo y de toda la sociedad.

## 8.2 Fundamentos teóricos de la práctica solidaria en la vida empresarial

### *8.2.1 Antecedentes evolutivos de la solidaridad*

La actual noción de la solidaridad podemos encontrarla en Aristóteles quien desarrolló la virtud de la amistad entre las personas de una comunidad. La amistad, entendía el filósofo griego, era sumamente importante porque constituía la búsqueda de la sociabilización del ser humano. La sociabilización permite el bienestar de quienes la practican por medio de la virtud de la amistad. Su ejercicio requiere de la igualdad, la libertad y gratuidad: el ser humano necesita encontrarse en una situación social de similitud con quien entabla amistad. En los tiempos de Aristóteles esta noción igualitaria se refería a las clases sociales de las personas. Sin embargo, actualmente podríamos afirmar que la amistad se refiere a aquella que es ejercitada por personas en situación de "igualdad" humana. Es decir, el único requisito para la práctica de la amistad es que sea propia de los seres humanos y movidos por su libertad de socializar. A ello podríamos agregar a la gratuidad que se presenta por la preocupación desinteresada entre las personas que comparten amistad y poseen lazos en común.

Ya con los romanos se desarrolló la noción solidaria que engloba la noción contractualista de la solidaridad. El término latín *in solidum* lo usaron para referirse a las obligaciones presentes en todo acuerdo contractual entre los deudores y acreedores. En este sentido, la obligación solidaria se refiere a aquel compromiso que los deudores tienen con sus proveedores de cumplir sus obligaciones de acuerdo al criterio de la unidad. Es decir, cualquiera de los deudores cumplir la totalidad del compromiso adquirido ante el acreedor. En esta noción de obligación descansa el otro elemento que constituye a la solidaridad moderna: la unidad propia de las obligaciones jurídicas que compromete a dos o más personas a cumplir la obligación total ante su acreedor. Por su parte, Ciceron y Marco Aurelio añaden la idea de apoyo mutuo y beneficio propio que las personas deben de practicar el uno hacia el otro.

Por su parte, Santo Tomas de Aquino añade que los hombres deben practicar las virtudes para el alcanzar su bienestar individual. Ello no sucede cuando el bienestar es colectivo ya que en este caso, el ser humano deberá renunciar a sus ambiciones personales en favor del bien común. En este punto, la "renuncia" es sinónimo de "sacrificio" en favor de los demás o de la comunidad y es un elemento que, más adelante se integra en la noción de la solidaridad y que se consolida en las ideas de sucesivos pensadores.

Así destacamos a John Locke quien resalta la renuncia de las libertades personales que ejercen los seres humanos a cambio de someterse a las reglas jurídicas de la autoridad política. En otros términos es la renuncia de "egoísmos" individuales a cambio de alcanzar objetivos comunes. Por su parte Thomas Hobbes justifica que dicha renuncia se debe a la necesidad de dejar de lado el "estado de naturaleza" a uno donde no exista conflictividad o, por lo menos, no sea la regla general.

Stuart Mill agrega que la renuncia o sacrificio de la persona se debe a la necesidad "utilitarista" por alcanzar su felicidad. Por su parte, Durkheim aporta una visión sociológica de la solidaridad al integrarla como parte de la división del trabajo y la búsqueda de la cohesión social. A diferencia de los demás pensadores, Durkheim usa el término de "cohesión" en vez de "unidad" para referirse al rol que ejerce cada persona en favor de la sociedad.

Esta función social de la solidaridad es ampliada por los solidaristas franceses quienes le asignan un rol político-social al entenderla como un mecanismo regulador de la convivencia de los seres humanos. Las personas poseen lazos en común (nacionalidad) que las obliga a dejar sus libertades individuales en favor de la sociedad. Esto significa la "uniformización" de las libertades individuales por medio de las leyes para convertirlas en una suerte de libertad "colectiva" resguardada por el derecho. De esta forma, a través del derecho, los estados pueden garantizar una libertad colectiva y uniforme para todas las personas.

Por su lado, la doctrina social de la iglesia aporta una visión solidaria más humana e individual. Juan Pablo II la relaciona como la virtud que permite alcanzar el bien común del ser humano. Y esta búsqueda del bien común implica la necesidad de lograr cambios en la persona y en el ambiente que le rodea. Estos cambios no solo son en la esfera privada sino trascienden en la colectividad donde se desarrolla la idea del bien común de la sociedad. Además la solidaridad integra los conceptos de reciprocidad, gratuidad y sociabilidad con el fin de lograr la unidad necesaria entre las personas a fin que las lleve a cumplir sus fines (bien común).

Como vemos la solidaridad comprende el desarrollo de diversos criterios que no necesariamente han sido usados para calificar determinadas conductas o hechos como solidarios. En este sentido, en primer lugar, podemos afirmar que la práctica de la solidaridad requiere del requisito de la gratuidad que implica el involucramiento de la persona en los problemas de otra persona o de la sociedad misma sin esperar una contraprestación directa. También, la sociabilidad entendida como el medio ambiente donde la persona se desarrolla y depende, en cierto modo, del aporte de la persona para cuidar su estabilidad. Además, la libertad es importante porque permiten asegurar que la solidaridad se ejerce por propia iniciativa y deseo de la persona de ejercerla sin presión alguna. Igual sucede con la idea de la igualdad que involucra que las personas asumen un régimen de convivencia uniforme con las leyes.

De esta forma aseguran o pueden cumplir o alcanzar sus objetivos y de los demás integrantes de la sociedad. Este compromiso individual del ser humano requiere ser garantizado a fin de asegurar un adecuado cumplimiento por parte de toda la sociedad. En ese sentido, la ley se constituye en el mecanismo aglutinador de la solidaridad social de las personas y en un instrumento garantista de sus libertades. Creemos que la práctica conjunta de estos elementos desempeñará un rol importante en la actividad empresarial y en la práctica de su responsabilidad social.

### 8.2.2 La solidaridad y la empresa: la empresa "solidaria"

La empresa tradicionalmente ha sido definida como el escenario de unión de los elementos capital y mano de obra que hacen posible el desarrollo de una actividad de explotación de un recurso o brindar un bien o servicio que el mercado requiere con el fin de obtener utilidades. También, una perspectiva jurídica la ha conceptuado como el conjunto de contratos que configuran el desarrollo de una actividad económica o, desde visión ética, como el conjunto de personas que hacen posible el desarrollo de actividad empresarial.

Evidentemente estas perspectivas, unas más que otras, han imperado en los círculos académicos y, quizá, no permiten la discusión de otros puntos de vista. Por ende, la discusión del término "empresa solidaria" genera dudas y suspicacias debido a la confusión con la caridad. Se prevé que el uso de este adjetivo está relacionada a las actividades de apoyo o ayuda social que realiza a favor de la comunidad donde tiene su residencia. Sin embargo, no es usual relacionarla con el desarrollo de su actividad económica debido a la presunción de su pertenencia a las labores sociales.

En efecto, es comprensible y, en cierto modo razonable, pretender que un valor relacionado a la caridad se vincule con un proceso productivo económico. Sin bien hoy en día se discute la necesidad de incluir el elemento ético en la práctica empresa, lo cierto es que no es posible el desprendimiento del factor económico. Sin embargo, en este ensayo podemos encontrar diversos principios éticos que configuran la solidaridad, que la empresa los ejerce como parte de su cultura organizacional y que practicados en conjunto nos llevan a la idea de su ejercicio en la actividad empresarial. Es decir es posible encontrar los elementos de la solidaridad como parte de la cultura de valores que una empresa cumple con el fin de hacer posible su actividad económica.

La cultura organizacional se relaciona principalmente con el conjunto de principios y valores que una empresa ha implementado para facilitar el trabajo de su actividad empresarial. La cultura organizacional o empresarial resulta importante rescatar porque es producto de la autorregulación que ejerce el titular de la empresa movido por la importancia de implementar los valores que se requieren para el funcionamiento óptimo de su organización. Lo rescatable de este fenómeno es que no existe una exigencia legal del gobierno de implementarla como requisitos para hacer posible el funcionamiento de la empresa. Entonces podemos afirmar que, como todo acto de autorregulación, nace de la libertad de quien decide crear y organizar una empresa. Pero esta libertad se ejerce bajo el amparo de las leyes de un país que garantizan la igualdad que, se presume, "igual" en toda persona que desee hacer actividad empresarial en un país.

Por ende podemos afirmar que la empresa nace siendo "solidaria" porque va en sintonía con la libertad de la persona de implementar los valores que su empresa requiere para su funcionamiento de acuerdo a un ordenamiento jurídico que garantiza la misma igualdad a otras personas que deseen hacer lo mismo. Aquí podemos afirmar que por medio de los principios vinculados a la solidaridad se garantiza un equilibrio entre los intereses del titular de la empresa y los de la sociedad.

Además de la libertad y la igualdad, la unidad es otro de los elementos solidarios que se necesitan para el funcionamiento óptimo de una empresa. La unidad implica unir los esfuerzos de los integrantes de una organización empresarial para cumplir con sus objetivos. Por medio de su práctica, sus miembros (directivos y empleados) pueden hacer aportes sus esfuerzos intelectuales y físicos para lograr el bienestar de la organización (bien común). Dicho bienestar no es únicamente de la empresa, o de su titular, sino de todos quienes se involucran en su trabajo. Este involucramiento puede ser entre quienes pertenecen a la empresa o, también, están relacionados a su actividad (grupos de interés).

Desde esta última perspectiva, la unidad como parte de la solidaridad permite el cumplimiento mutuo y reciproco de las expectativas de los miembros de la organización empresarial. Y este punto es importante porque hoy en día en Sudamérica hay la creencia los beneficios de la actividad empresarial no solo pertenecen a quienes la ejercen sino de aquellos quienes permiten hacerla posible. Por ende a través de la práctica de la responsabilidad social se debe involucrar a todos los grupos de interés, directos a indirectos, a facilitar la labor empresarial en armonía con sus intereses.

Desde esta perspectiva, la gratuidad es un elemento importante de la solidaridad que creemos ha sido el valor más trabajado y, por ende, relacionado con la solidaridad entendida como caridad. La gratuidad plantea un desprendimiento, un "dar" sin "esperar nada" a cambio. Así, la gratuidad, bajo la forma de caridad, implica en un valor de regalar algo sin exigencia de una contraprestación. Esta idea no considera dos aspectos que conforman la solidaridad y, por tanto, no podría afirmarse que son parte de ella. El primero es que en la solidaridad impera la unidad para el cumplimiento de compromisos y metas que luego redundarán de forma directa en la actividad empresarial (reciprocidad). Mientras que la gratuidad no prioriza el factor trabajo en común para recibir algo a cambio o por lo menos no de forma directa.

El segundo factor es el fin en sí mismo. Para el caso empresarial, mientras que la práctica de la caridad tiene un fin altruista y, hasta en parte una actividad residual propia de la empresa; la solidaridad a través de sus elementos si ocupa una parte importante en el quehacer de su actividad comercial y está inmersa en el logro de la rentabilidad. Por ende, creemos que la solidaridad y la caridad no pueden confundirse como dos valores similares porque, sobretodo, restringen la aplicación de sus componentes de manera efectiva para el desarrollo de sus actividades. También, impera la sociabilidad como un factor de ejercicio de la solidaridad en la empresa. Como la organización, la empresa es un centro de interacción social que reúne las expectativas personales de las personas y requiere de la sociabilidad para el cumplimiento de estos fines.

Otro aspecto que debe de rescatarse es la importancia de las leyes en la sociedad y en la empresa en concreto debido a la visión contractualista que aporta la solidaridad. En esta visión, cada uno de los grupos de interés posee deberes y derechos que deben de cumplir para el éxito de la actividad empresarial. En este sentido, desde la perspectiva solidaria, la legislación en materia mercantil debería promover normas que incentiven el cumplimiento de los grupos de la empresa (directivos, empleados, proveedores, clientes, entre otros más) y sancionar cualquier atisbo de no hacerlo.

Esta ideas nos llevan a entender que argumentar la existencias de empresas solidarias implica conceptuar a aquellas organizaciones que de forma libre implementan la práctica de una serie de valores como la unidad, la gratuidad, la libertad, la igualdad, el cumplimiento de compromisos y la sociabilidad en la actividad empresarial en la búsqueda de su bien común. Creemos que la cultura organizacional es el medio ideal de transmisión de los valores solidarios que requiere la actividad en conjunto de la empresa y para beneficio de todos sus integrantes. Aún más, la práctica de estos valores debe ir acompañada de una sólida legislación que incentive su práctica y sancione su incumplimiento. Como vemos la idea de solidaridad trasciende más allá de la caridad.

## 8.3 La responsabilidad social empresarial "solidaria"

La cultura organizacional corresponde a la práctica de la responsabilidad social que toda empresa implementa para demostrar su involucramiento con los principales problemas que aquejan a la sociedad (medio ambiente, derechos humanos y gobernanza). En ese sentido la organización implementa el ejercicio de determinados valores y los traslada a sus integrantes. En ese sentido, los valores éticos colaboran con la responsabilidad empresarial hacia la sociedad. Más aún si consideramos que la responsabilidad es una virtud o valor que las instituciones, como las empresariales, desarrollan en la sociedad por el poder económico que ostentan.

El ejercicio del poder económico de las empresas reclama que se ejerza de forma no arbitraria. Es decir, a diferencia de otros agentes de mercado, el sector empresarial posee un poder sustentado en la tenencia del capital que puede generar proclividad a usar en beneficio propio pero que perjudique los intereses de aquellos que conviven con ella de forma directa o indirecta. Por ello, la responsabilidad social se ha convertido en un mecanismo de limitación al poder económico empresarial en base al respeto de los intereses de quienes conviven con ella. Sin embargo, creemos que este enfoque restrictivo no es el adecuado porque genera los riesgos de desincentivo a la inversión empresarial en aquellas zonas que, precisamente, requieren capital para su desarrollo económico y social.

La responsabilidad social no debe constituirse en el conjunto de mecanismos de restricción de los derechos económicos de quien invierte sino, al contrario, debe constituirse en un factor de motivación de creación de valor económico y social tanto para quien invierte como para los grupos de interés que pueden verse beneficiados por dicha inversión. En esa dirección, la responsabilidad social empresarial debe constituirse en el factor de creación e imposición propia de mecanismos de autorregulación que le permitan comportarse acorde a sus valores corporativos pero acorde a las expectativas de los grupos de interés con quienes convive en un país o área determinada. Asimismo, la práctica responsable con la sociedad debe plasmarse en una conducta preventiva de generación de daños o remediarlos.

En este sentido, la responsabilidad social solidaria comprende la inclusión de sus valores corporativos para que sean utilizados para garantizar un adecuado comportamiento organizacional ante la sociedad y colaborar con el desarrollo de su actividad de forma adecuada. Solo de esta forma se podría afirmar que la práctica social y responsable cumple con el estándar de "solidaria" y con las implicancias que ello genera como son la mejora de la valoración social o la reputación corporativa.

En primer lugar, la práctica del valor como parte de la responsabilidad social implica que los integrantes de una empresa han dejado de lado sus objetivos individuales a cambio de cumplir los objetivos de la organización. Este acto de "unidad" no significa que la persona renuncie a sus principios o valores sino que concuerda con ellos y le permite practicarlos dentro y fuera de la organización. Este criterio de unidad en la empresa va acompañado por su ejercicio por todos sus integrantes. Ahora bien, este criterio puede favorecer el ejercicio de los programas de responsabilidad social por cuanto le permite atender los intereses de sus grupos de interés. Al contrario de la teoría de la agencia que privilegia la generación de valor económico al inversionista, la unidad debe integrar y asociar los intereses de todos los *stakeholders* sin hacer discriminación alguna.

La unidad o "espíritu de cuerpo" solo es posible de alcanzar si se asocian los intereses en común o lazos en común entre quienes administran, laboran y dependen de una organización. Por ende, la responsabilidad social solidaria es propender a la unidad de los intereses de todos sus *stakeholders* sin importar la labor que realizan dentro o fuera de la empresa. Así, por medio de la unidad, la organización encontrará la senda del bien común acorde a la justicia tomista donde cada miembro suyo recibe el beneficio o rentabilidad de acuerdo a su aporte. El bien común se convierte en la meta que debe seguir la empresa para lograr el bienestar de sus integrantes. Debe constituirse en el medio que justifica el fin ya no solo de la empresa sino el fin de sus grupos de interés que conforman. Por tanto, somos de la opinión que un cambio de la misión de la responsabilidad social empresarial es necesario de hacer: propugnar el cambio de promover la responsabilidad social de la empresa hacia una responsabilidad social de los grupos de interés de la empresa.

Nuestra propuesta es coherente con la noción de la solidaridad y con la visión *stakeholder* que se trabaja en la actualidad. Asimismo, la búsqueda del bien común implica el ejercicio de la unidad que, a su vez, solo será posible si los grupos de interés asocian sus esfuerzos en favor de alcanzar el bienestar de todos y, para ello, adoptan la decisión de renunciar a sus intereses particulares a favor de uno colectivo que sea aquel que beneficie a todos.

El éxito de la empresa debe ser señal que constituye un beneficio para todos sus integrantes. En este sentido, cada uno de los grupos de interés de la empresa (internos o externos) debe aportar su cuota de responsabilidad para con la empresa y cumplir con su función. Y el cumplimiento de la responsabilidad dependerá de la puesta en práctica de normas que garantizarán que cada grupo de interés acredite haber alcanzado sus objetivos. En primer lugar las normas autorregulatorias que muestran cómo el titular de la empresa organiza, implementa y certifica la práctica de los valores en su organización. En segundo lugar, las normas metaregulatorias promoverán los incentivos legales para la práctica adecuada de los valores con el fin de prevenir sanciones legales. Por último, las normas regulatorias que consistirán aquellas que los gobiernos promulgan para hacerlas obligatorias a las empresas.

En este escenario, las normas garantizan los compromisos que los grupos de interés adquirieron con la empresa. Así, los estándares de responsabilidad social empresarial lejos de certificar el cumplimiento de los avances hechos por la organización en materia de protección de medio ambiente, derechos humanos y gobernanza; también deberían reflejar el aporte de los grupos de interés para el cumplimiento de sus actividades. En ese sentido, la responsabilidad social deja de ser exclusiva de las empresas y pasa a depender de los grupos de interés que se encuentran vinculados a ella.

Así, se destaca la responsabilidad social de los empleados, o de los sindicatos, la responsabilidad social de los directivos o administradores de la empresa, la responsabilidad social de los proveedores o contratistas, incluso de aquellos a quienes subcontratan, la responsabilidad social del inversionistas, la responsabilidad social de los gobiernos o estados, la responsabilidad social de los clientes, la responsabilidad social de las empresas competidoras y la responsabilidad social de la comunidad en general.

La responsabilidad social de los empleados implica que como grupo de interés interno posee el compromiso de colaborar con el trabajo de la empresa por medio del aporte de sus conocimientos. Desde la perspectiva de la responsabilidad social solidaria los empleados aportan sus conocimientos y técnicas en favor de cumplir los objetivos de la empresa pero pensando en los intereses del resto de los grupos de interés. De acuerdo a los criterios de unidad y gratuidad, los empleados identifican y uniformizan sus intereses a los de la empresa pero colaboran a que ésta, a su vez, los armonice con los de la sociedad. Así los empleados o sus sindicatos que cuentan con un perfil social solidario adoptan decisiones pensando en los intereses de sus agremiados pero considerando los del resto de los grupos de interés. No nos referimos cuidar los intereses de los inversores sino de los proveedores, clientes y el estado, entre otros quienes podrían ver perjudicados sus intereses por la actividad de los sindicatos (huelgas).

Por su parte, la solidaridad en los directivos se materializa en el ejercicio de la gestión de acuerdo a los intereses de los *stakeholders*. Además la adopción de decisiones se asocia a implicar e incluir los demás intereses de los grupos de interés con los del inversionista o propietario de la empresa. Desde nuestra perspectiva, el reto de los administradores es el ejercicio correcto de sus poderes de gestión en favor de todos los grupos de interés, incluidos los competidores. Esta función requiere de directivos que cuenten con sólidos valores solidarios que le permitan resistir la presión de favorecer los intereses de uno de sus grupos de interés. Sobre todo ellos deben contar con la suficiente capacidad asociar e integrar los intereses de los *stakeholders* en favor del bien común.

Por su parte, la responsabilidad social de los proveedores o contratistas comprende el cumplimiento de sus compromisos que van más allá de los acuerdos contractuales con la empresa. De acuerdo a la idea de la responsabilidad social solidaria, el compromiso de un contratista con la empresa y con los grupos de interés de ella va por acreditar que cumple con las expectativas de la sociedad de cuidar el medio ambiente, proteger los derechos humanos y ejercitar una adecuada gobernanza. Esta obligación social solidaria del proveedor se justifica en la necesidad de proteger la marca o la reputación de la empresa que ha contratado sus servicios profesionales o técnicos. La marca encierra la labor económica y social que una empresa realiza en favor de sus grupos de interés y debe, por tanto, cuidarse de cualquier intento de dañar su prestigio porque en el fondo perjudica a todos quienes dependen de ella.

La responsabilidad social solidaria del inversionista implica que toda aquella persona que desea invertir su capital debe involucrarse en la problemática de la empresa donde aportará su capital. Para ello, los inversores deben conocer el significado de los valores ligados a la solidaridad como son la unidad, la gratuidad y el bien común, los cuales

les debe brindar las capacidades de invertir en aquellos negocios que no perjudicarán los intereses de los demás grupos de interés ni tampoco aquellos que los perjudique a ellos mismos.

La responsabilidad social de los gobiernos o estados plantea una serie interrogante en su discusión: ¿acaso el trabajo de los gobiernos no es social?. En efecto, los gobiernos gestionan los recursos públicos para la satisfacción de las necesidades básicas de su población. Creemos en este punto que la responsabilidad social de los estados debe descansar en balancear adecuadamente los intereses de los grupos de interés que se encuentran en el territorio. Es decir, los estados pueden privilegiar a los grupos desfavorecidos pero ello no significa que se deba excluir a aquellos que poseen mayores recursos. Definitivamente, los gobiernos se equivocan cuando gobiernan con los grupos de poder y descuidan a los demás. Por ello, somos de la opinión que la responsabilidad social desde la perspectiva solidaria debe asociar y unir los esfuerzos necesarios para priorizar satisfacer las expectativas de todos sus grupos de interés sin distinción alguna.

Por su parte, la responsabilidad social de los clientes descansa en la creencia que ellos reciben una atención adecuada por parte de la empresa. En ese sentido, los valores de la solidaridad proponen el ejercicio de una conducta activa por parte suya en su calidad de consumidor. Así, la noción del consumidor "responsable" denota una conducta activa y preocupada por los problemas que aquejan a la sociedad y que se vinculan con los productos de su preferencia. El consumidor solidario puede ejercer la capacidad de renuncia de sus gustos y preferencias de su producto en caso que perjudique los intereses de la sociedad pero asimismo los intereses de la empresa. En este último caso, un consumidor responsable solidario no usaría productos falsificados de su marca o producto favorito a pesar que le reporta un ahorro económico.

Por último, la responsabilidad social solidaria de las empresas competidoras en general también pasa por el ejercicio de valores basados en el respeto hacia ellas y en el compromiso de no competir de forma irresponsable y de cumplir la legislación comercial al respecto. La unidad de ellas, expresada a través de suscripción de compromisos, de no competir de manera desleal señala el desprendimiento de obtener una ventaja individual a cambio de armonizar los suyos y el de los demás competidores. Por último, la responsabilidad social solidaria de la comunidad podría sintetizarse en cumplimiento de los compromisos con la empresa y en el ejercicio de las conductas éticas hacia esa dirección.

## 8.4 La responsabilidad social "solidaria" como instrumento de reconciliación de los *stakeholders* en el sector minero

En la parte introductoria de este capítulo explicamos el rol que desempeña la solidaridad como medio facilitador de la reconciliación entre los miembros de una sociedad. En el medio empresarial, la responsabilidad se ha convertido en un mecanismo de reconciliación entre la empresa y sus grupos de interés motivada por la errónea comunicación que la primera entabló con los segundos, la comunidad, que generó un fuerte sentimiento de hostilidad a la presencia empresarial en su territorio.

En el caso del sector minero peruano han sido frecuentes los casos de conflictos sociales entre las empresas, muchas de ellas de capitales extranjeros, y las comunidades campesinas. El motivo del surgimiento de estos conflictos fue el inadecuado manejo ambiental, el incumplimiento o violación de los derechos humanos, en especial los laborales, y una inadecuada gobernanza que se caracterizó por prevenir. Así según la Defensoría del Pueblo en el 2017, el 66,4 de los conflictos sociales en el Perú fue de tipo socioambiental. De este grupo, 63,1% de los conflictos tiene relación con la industria minera mientras el 14,9 corresponde a las actividades de explotación de hidrocarburos[172].

A abril de 2018, las estadísticas que presenta la Oficina de la Defensoría muestran que el panorama de los conflictos sociales ambientales no ha variado mucho de acuerdo a la estadística que presentan[173]:

PERÚ: CONFLICTOS SOCIALES, SEGÚN TIPO, POR PRINCIPAL AUTORIDAD COMPETENTE, ABRIL 2018
(Número de casos)

| Tipo | TOTAL | % | Gobierno nacional | Gobierno regional | Gobierno local | Poder Judicial | Org. Const. Autónomo | Poder Legislativo |
|---|---|---|---|---|---|---|---|---|
| TOTAL | 196 | 100.0% | 126 | 36 | 19 | 5 | 8 | 2 |
| Socioambiental | 127 | 64.8% | 104 | 19 | 3 | 0 | 0 | 1 |
| Asuntos de gobierno local | 20 | 10.2% | 0 | 1 | 16 | 1 | 2 | 0 |
| Asuntos de gobierno nacional | 17 | 8.7% | 17 | 0 | 0 | 0 | 0 | 0 |
| Comunal | 10 | 5.1% | 1 | 7 | 0 | 0 | 2 | 0 |
| Otros asuntos | 8 | 4.1% | 0 | 1 | 0 | 3 | 4 | 0 |
| Asuntos de gobierno regional | 7 | 3.6% | 0 | 7 | 0 | 0 | 0 | 0 |
| Laboral | 4 | 2.0% | 2 | 1 | 0 | 1 | 0 | 0 |
| Demarcación territorial | 3 | 1.5% | 2 | 0 | 0 | 0 | 0 | 1 |
| Cultivo ilegal de coca | 0 | 0.0% | 0 | 0 | 0 | 0 | 0 | 0 |
| Electoral | 0 | 0.0% | 0 | 0 | 0 | 0 | 0 | 0 |

Fuente: Defensoría del Pueblo - SIMCO

En ese sentido, las industrias como la minera e hidrocarburos en el Perú viven bajo permanente riesgo de que se produzca un conflicto con la comunidad donde realizan sus labores. En ese sentido muchas de las causas de los conflicto se asocian al incumplimiento de compromisos por parte de empresas mineras, el impago de compensaciones económicas a las comunidades, el incumplimiento de labores de remediación ambiental, la ampliación de establecimientos de complejos de producción, entre otros.

Creemos que estos casos difícilmente curan las heridas "sociales" producto de la decepción de la sociedad por el incumplimiento de los compromisos por parte la empresa minera o de hidrocarburos. Estos

---

[172] Disponible en: https://www.defensoria.gob.pe/temas.php?des=3#r

[173] Defensoría del Pueblo. Reporte de Conflictos Sociales n° 170, abril de 2018, pp. 8.

conflictos sociales generan el riesgo de no solucionarse en un corto plazo y, si sucede así, tiene grandes posibilidades de reiniciarse de nuevo y durar hasta lograr la salida de la empresa del lugar de explotación. Desde el punto de vista social, la industria minera y la de hidrocarburos no comprenden las expectativas reales de la población o no desea satisfacerlas o, quizás no está en capacidad de cumplirlas.

Por su parte, la comunidad asume la percepción que el empresariado es un agente que ha expropiado sus tierras o es un vecino que no cumple el protagonismo social que su poder económico le permite. O más aún las empresas son vistas como un medio alternativo de generación de recursos materiales  tanto para la población y los gobiernos locales. Los actuales programas de responsabilidad social se utilizan como mecanismos de certificación del cumplimiento de buenas conductas o hechos en favor de los grupos de interés. Sin embargo, estos programas de responsabilidad no cumplen con remediar la percepción negativa que la población tiene de la empresa y que no se soluciona hasta, en algunos casos, cuando abandone su asentamiento minero o de hidrocarburos.

En este punto, creemos que los programas de responsabilidad se equivocan si implementan procesos de conversación sino existen un auténtico proceso de reconciliación sincero entre la empresa-comunidad. La reconciliación se asocia al acto en que las personas optan por amistarse otras vez y compartir dicha amistad en el desarrollo de sus actividades. En ese sentido la solidaridad como parte de la responsabilidad social empresarial debe de propugnar la reconciliación de la empresa pero, principalmente, de los grupos de sus interés. Por ende, las prácticas de responsabilidad social deben de incluir mecanismos que logren el restablecimiento de la amistad entre todos los miembros, directos e indirectos, de la empresa.

En este punto, el enfoque responsable, social y solidario reconciliará a los integrantes de la empresa por medio de la práctica de valores en común como la unidad, la gratuidad y la búsqueda del bien común. De esta manera, su práctica otorgará un beneficio en común para todos los *stakeholders* de la empresa y a su vez les permitirá el ejercicio de una responsabilidad social acorde a su condición.

## 8.5 La poesía y la escritura poética como instrumento de reconciliación social en el sector minero

Las humanidades juegan un rol importante en la práctica de la responsabilidad social empresarial porque permiten que la empresa conozca los intereses de una parte de sus grupos de interés que por razones sociales o educativas tienen dificultad para expresarlos de forma directa, sincera y pública. En este caso nos referimos a las comunidades campesinas o indígenas que, muchas veces, por temor no pueden expresar sus puntos de vista o reclamos a la empresa. En muchos casos esperan que sea la organización empresarial quien tome la iniciativa para solucionar sus expectativas y al no sucede ello se genera un sentimiento de defraudación social que genera, con el tiempo, conflictos sociales.

Por ende, la empresa como institución más preparada y sofisticada debe asegurarse de contar con los medios necesarios para prevenir los conflictos, manejarlos adecuadamente y reconciliarse con sus *stakeholders*. Ello la obliga a buscar mecanismos que le permitan conocer las expectativas e intereses reales de ese segmento de grupos de interés y buscar la manera ideal de solucionarlos. De esta manera se evitará que dichos grupos sean manipulados por movimientos políticos que lejos de resolver sus expectativas contribuirán al incremento del nivel de conflicto social.

En este punto, los programas de responsabilidad social empresarial deberían podrían involucrar el estudio de la poesía y escritura poética como medios para entender la identidad, la idiosincrasia y las costumbres de sus grupos de interés y comprender su percepción sobre los aspectos que tienen relación con la actividad de la empresa pero que no pueden transmitírselos en condiciones normales por sus limitaciones sociales y/o culturales. De esta manera, los otros *stakeholders*, inversores o directivos, estarán en capacidad de identificarse con ellos y establecer adecuados canales de comunicación. Solo de esta manera con valores ligados a la solidaridad la empresa desarrollará un adecuado programa de responsabilidad social que lograra una eficaz y permanente reconciliación con sus integrantes.

## 8.6 Síntesis

Este artículo ha desarrollado el aporte de la solidaridad al trabajo de la responsabilidad social empresarial como medio de lograr un eficaz proceso de reconciliación entre los grupos de interés que poseen relación con las organizaciones empresariales. Asimismo, la noción de solidaridad no debe entenderse como sinónimo de la caridad sino de la práctica de los valores de la unidad y el bien común. Estos valores hacen posible la práctica solidaria en la empresa del ejercicio de su cultura organizacional y a quienes la conforman directa o indirectamente.

La cultura organizacional conforma el conjunto de valores que son parte de la responsabilidad social de una empresa y que le permiten a sus grupos de interés integrar, conciliar y reconciliar sus intereses. Es en este ámbito donde la escritura y poesía son el mecanismo eficaz que usualmente utilizan un grupo de los *stakeholders* de la empresa para transmitir sus opiniones o intereses al resto. En el Perú existen muchos conflictos socio-ambientales, principalmente, en la industria minera y de hidrocarburos donde los procesos de reconciliación encuentran necesario acudir al estudio de la poesía y a la escritura poética. Como medios de expresión cultural, ambos permitirán conocer las expectativas de una parte de los grupos de interés para facilitar la convivencia entre todos y favorecer el bien común acorde a la actividad empresarial.

# 8.7 Bibliografía

Alvira, Rafael (1992), *¿Qué es el Humanismo Empresarial?* en el *Humanismo en la Empresa*, Ediciones RIALP, Madrid.

Alvira, Rafael (2008), "Social Justice and the Common Good Within and Between Different Spheres of Society", en Archer, Margaret y Donati, Pierpaolo (eds), *Pursuing the Common Good: How solidarity and Subsidiarity can work together. The proceedings of the 14th Plenary Session 2-6 May 2008*, The Pontifical Academy of Social Sciences, pp. 605-617.

Alvira, Rafael (2009), "El Bien Común y Justicia Social en las diferentes Esferas de la Sociedad", *Revista Empresa y Humanismo*, vol. XII n° 2/09, pp. 61-80.

Amengual, Gabriel (1993), "La Solidaridad como alternativa. Notas al concepto de solidaridad", *RIFP*/1, pp. 135-151.

Andrés López, Gonzalo y Molina de la Torre, Ignacio (2000), *Introducción a la Solidaridad Internacional*, Universidad de Valladolid, Valladolid.

Aristóteles, *Ética a Nicómaco,* Araujo, María y Marías, (ed. y tr.), (1981), Centro de Estudios Constitucionales, Madrid.

Argandoña, Antonio (1990), "Razones y formas de la solidaridad", en Fernández, Fernando (coord.), *Estudios sobre la Encíclica "Sollicitudu rei socialis"*, pp. 333-355.

Argandoña, Antonio (1998), "La Teoría del *Stakeholder* y el Bien Común", *División de investigación* n° 355, IESE Business School, pp. 1-13.

Argandoña, Antonio (2005), "Empresa, Economía de Mercado y Responsabilidad Social", *Documento de Investigación* n° *600*, IESE Business School, pp. 1-18.

Arnsperger, Christian (1997), "Altruisme Solidarité: L'économie a-t-elle besoin d'une Métaphysique?", en *Éthique Sociale. Éthique Sociale Chrétienne, Ethique et Solidarité. Actes du Colloque d'Aix-en-Provence, 3-4 Juillet*, Libraire de l'université d'Aix-en-Provence, pp. 181-198.

Audier, Serge (2007), *Leon Bourgeois. Fonder la Solidarité*, Editions Michalon, París.

Baldwin, Peter (1992), *La Política de Solidaridad Social: Bases Sociales del Estado de Bienestar*, Ministerio de Trabajo y Seguridad Social, Madrid.

Bilgrien Vianney, Marie (1999), *Solidarity. A principle, an attitude, a duty? or the virtue for an interdependent world?*, American University Studies, Series VII Theology and Religion, vol. 204, Peter Lang Publishing, Inc., New York.

Blais, Marie-Claude (2007), *La Solidarité : Histoire d'une Idée,* Gallimard, París.

Bourgeois, Léon [1912 (1998)], *Solidarité*, Presses Universitaires du septentrion, Villeneuve d'Ascq.

Chevalier, Jacques (1992), "La Resurgence du Theme de la Solidarité ", en *La Solidarité: un Sentiment Républicain,* PUF, pp. 113-135.

Colom, Enrique (2001), *Curso de Doctrina Social de la Iglesia.* Ediciones Palabra, Madrid.

Comte, Auguste, *Discurso sobre el Espíritu Positivo*, Marias, Julian (versión y prólogo) (1988), Alianza Editorial, Madrid.

Cortina, Adela (1990), *Ética sin Moral*, Tecnos, Madrid.

Cortina, Adela (1994), *Ética de la Empresa*, Trotta, Madrid.

Cortina, Adela y otros (1996), *Un Mundo de Valores*, Generalitat Valenciana, Valencia.

De Lucas, Javier (1993), *El Concepto de Solidaridad*, Fontamara, México.

Donoso Cortes, *Donoso Cortés (antología)*, Tovar, Antonio (selección) (1940), *Ediciones fe*, Madrid.

Durkheim, Emile (1982), *La división del trabajo social*, Akal editor, Madrid.

Duvignaud, Jean (1986), *La Solidaridad. Vínculos de Sangre y Vínculos de Afinidad*, Fayard, París.

Galindo, Ángel (2002), "La Rentabilidad de la Empresa, compatible con el Trabajo Humano y con un Reparto Solidario del Beneficio", en *La Responsabilidad Social del Empresario. Aportaciones a la Doctrina Social de la Iglesia*, Acción Social Empresarial, Madrid, pp. 215-250.

Galindo García, Ángel (2010), "Lógica del mercado, del Estado y del don en el horizonte de la sociedad civil", en Galindo, Ángel y Flecha, José-Román (coords.), *Caridad en la verdad*, Universidad Pontificia de Salamanca y Fundación Pablo VI, pp. 137-172.

García Roca, Joaquín (1998), *Exclusión Social y Contracultura de la Solidaridad*, Ediciones HOAC, Madrid.

Gide, Charles (1932), *Curso de economía políticas*, Librería de la Vda de Ch. Bouret, 8va edición, París.

Gomez Ligüerre, Carlos (2007), *Solidaridad y Derecho de Daños. Los Límites de la Responsabilidad Colectiva*, Thomson Civitas, Madrid.

Gómez Pérez, Rafael (1993), *Cuestiones Básicas de Doctrina Social de la Iglesia*, Unión Editorial, Toledo.

González, Manuel Jesús y otros (2007), *Ciento Cincuenta Años, Ciento Cincuenta Bancos: 1857-2007*, vols I y II, BBVA, Madrid.

Hobbes, Thomas, *Leviatan*, Moya, C. y Escohotado, A. (ed.) (1983), Editorial Nacional, 2ª edición, Madrid.

Locke, John, *Dos Ensayos sobre el Gobierno Civil*, Abellán, Joaquín (1991), Espasa Calpe, Madrid.

Melé, Domenèc (1992), *Empresa y Economía al Servicio de Hombre: Mensajes de Juan Pablo II a los Empresarios y Directivos Económicos*, EUNSA, Pamplona.

Melé, Domènec (2002), "Humanismo cristiano en dirección de empresas: Objeciones y respuestas", en Borobia, J. J.; Murillo, J. L. y Terrasa, E. (eds.), *Idea Cristiana del Hombre*, EUNSA, Pamplona, pp. 385-392.

Moreau de Bellaing, Louis (1992), "Le solidarisme et ses commentaires actuels" en *La Solidarité: un Sentiment Républicain*, PUF, pp. 85-107.

Morrison, Key (2006), *Marx, Durkheim, Weber. Formations of Modern Social Thought*, SAGE Publications, Second edition, California.

Puy, Francisco (1995), "Las Formulas del Principio de Solidaridad", en Ballesteros, Jesus y otros (Coord.), *Justicia, Solidaridad, paz. Estudios en Homenaje al Profesor José María Rojo Sanz*, Facultad de Derecho de la Universidad de Valencia, pp. 727-745.

Ratzinger, Joseph (2004), *La Fraternidad de los Cristianos*, Ediciones Sígueme, Salamanca.

Renouvier, Charles, *Science de la morale*, Fedi, Laurent (revisión), (2002), Fayard, París.

Sequeiros, Leandro (1997), *Educar para la Solidaridad*, Octaedro ediciones, Barcelona.

Soulet, Marc-Henry (2004), "De Quelques Enejux Contemporains de la Solidarité", en Soulet, Marc-Henry (éd.), *La Solidarité: Exigence Morale ou Obligation Publique?*, Academic Press Fribourg, Fribourg, pp. 9-20.

Spinoza, Baruch (2010), Tratado Político, Villaverde, María José (intr.) y Tierno Galvan, Enrique (est. prel. y trad.), Tecnos, Madrid.

Tabra, Edison (2017), Ética y solidaridad, Globethics, Geneva.

Tabra, Edison (2017), Responsabilidad social y gobierno corporativo en la empresa solidaria, USIL, Lima.

Tischner, Józef (1983), *Ética de la Solidaridad*, Ediciones Encuentro, Madrid.

Vidal Fernández, Fernando y Mota López, Rosalía (2002). "El Voluntariado Social Primario en el Paradigma Dinámico de la Solidaridad", *Revista Miscelánea Comillas*, n° 116, vol. 60, pp. 703-768.

Vidal, Marciano (1992), "Ética de la Solidaridad", *Moralia Revista de Ciencias Morales*, vol. XIV 3-4 Julio-Diciembre, pp. 347-362.

Vidal, Marciano (1996), *Para Comprender la Solidaridad: Virtud y Principio Ético*, Editorial Verbo Divino, Estella.

Vieira, Domingos Lourenço (2006), *La Solidarité au cœur de L'éthique Sociale: La Notion de Solidarité dans L'enseignement social de l'Église catholique*, Éditions Mare & Martin, París.

Zamagni, Stefano (2009), "Fraternidad, Don y Reciprocidad", *Revista Cultura Económica*, Año XXVII. n° 75/76, Agosto-Diciembre 2009, pp. 11-29.

Zubero, Imanol (1996), "Construyendo una sociedad solidaria: Una propuesta para el análisis y la acción", *Cuadernos de Trabajo Social,* n° 9, Universidad Complutense de Madrid, pp. 303-327.

Zubero, Imanol (2003), "Solidaridad", en Ariño, Antonio (Ed.), *Diccionario de la Solidaridad,* Cuadernos de Solidaridad n° 2, Tirant lo Blanch, Valencia, pp. 463-475.

# 9

# VALUE CONSTRUCTION THROUGH POETRY IN RWANDA: POETIC VOICES IMAGINING THE SPACE BEYOND NORMALITY

*Andrea Grieder*

## 9.1 Introduction

'In my childhood, I didn't have someone to share', says Janvier Nsabimana, the young participant to the *Kigali Vibrates with Poetry*, a tri-monthly poetry competition that takes place annually in the capital of Rwanda[174].

'I shared with myself, in my poems.
I shared with my paper and my pen.
I used to write and then, I read my poems.
The more I read, the more I felt well.
I started feeling good.'[175]

---

[174] Dr Andrea Grieder in anthropologist and has established herself as an international expert with experience in the field of art, poetry and reconciliation in the context of post genocide Rwanda; her PhD research: *Collines des mille souvenirs*, 2016, 410pp., (Geneva: Globethics.net, www.globethics.net/theses-series) has planted the seeds of this present publication.

[175] Personal conversation with the poet, April 2018, Kigali.

What began as an inner poetic conversation, eventually found its way to the stage of the 9th edition of the public event in October 2018. His poem: *My home, why don't you care for me* was awarded for the best poem in Kinyarwanda[176].

If poetic creativity has its root in the lack of a possible sharing, a social or inter-relational sharing, we may understand that *talent* expresses an act of transcending the void, aiming consciously or unconsciously to enter into a space of understanding and of recognition, the collectivity.

We also consider that the conversation with oneself generates an inner truth to be shared, knowledge about the self and the society, that grows out of an intuitive wisdom, born in the intimate space of the self, in dialogue with the poetic soul.

## 9.2 To Sustain Poetically in that History

It is widely accepted that poetic writing contributes to create an inner emotional stability, and a sphere of self-sustainability. We can mention Haikus, the traditional of form of poetry in Japan, which is based on a philosophy of harmony, it's depth lies in a poetic contemplation of nature, it's poetic genius in its expression of a moment of illumination. Furthermore, poetry therapy is using the creative process of poetry as a healing process (De Coulon 2009, Leedy 1995).

On a larger scale, within historical contexts of tragedies and violence, poetry is a powerful way of giving meaning to experiences of loss, death and trauma. In his poems, capturing the breaking (rupture) within America brought by September 11 2001, Lawrence dramatize 'the challenge of maintaining one's self in a world in the hold of dehumanizing forces' (Fred Muratori, 2006). Over the last twenty-four years, Rwanda's powerful poetic tradition is contributing to bring its

---

[176] 9th Edition, 31st October 2018.

people out of the ashes of the genocide against the Tutsi in 1994. From South Africa to Colombia, from Iran to Japan, many are the places where the poetic feather is used as an arm against oppression, war and violence on a large social scale as well as a voice that keeps people 'alive.'

Out of an impulse urge to hold on in life or as a meditation on history, the poem expresses the self's capacity to thrive as a story. As Henry James would advise: 'the only thing is to live in the world of creation – to get into it and stay in – to frequent it and haunt it.' We can put it this way: With poetry, we find the strength to stay poetically in that history we live in.

Poetry is in this sense a call for each of us to discover his or her own tools of engagement with the world, forged in the crucible of personal experience, sociocultural context and language.

## 9.3 The Poetic Moral Self

We are often caught up in a finite, un-chosen and often distorted world. With all its different forms, poetry is a manifestation of our capacity, even though in limited way, to transform the world creatively into a meaningful world for itself. Paul Ricoeur speaks about the poetic moral self, as the 'radical capacity, at the very ontological core of human being, for creatively transforming the meaning of its own already fragmented and given historical identity' (John Wall, 2005: 26). The poetic self is both, passive and active, oscillating between freedom and finity. The limits imposed by social structure and narrowing the scope of its agency are world-conditioned and self-inflicted at the same time: 'by choosing blind self-enslavement to narrow elements within them and failures of meaning of its own' (John Wall, 2005:26). We cannot other, then facing the task of 'narrating our own already tragically narrated identity, a task that we could not reject even if we tired, not even in suicide' (John Wall, 2005:26) Our poetic expressions makes as truly human, in the sense of using the potential of creating our own poetic stories. With Paul Ricoeur, we can say: 'Human beings are called by their own primordially created depths to exceed historical evil and tragedy through the ongoing creative transformation together of their word' (John Wall, 2005). Creativity (in its positive drive, along with all its destructive power) expresses our humanity as well as creates that humanity. Among the dimensions are the self's capacity to interpret symbols, traditions and narratives. Laurence Joseph (2005), a prominent lawyer-poet, stresses that every époque has to create its own metaphors, to give meaning of humans historical and embodied world.

In this sense, being poet expresses a moral attitude, as it is the manifestation of our creative capacity. Being creative is an ethical value in itself. Creating meaning out of experience, where the rule is that rules need to be rooted in specific experiences, the ethical wisdom grows out of real life moments.

This ethics of poetic creativity challenges the ancient dispute between ethnicists and poets over reason and emotions, to consider that knowledge and values can be rooted in emotions and intuitive intelligence. It defies the Greek and Biblical Separation of ethics and poetic image-making as well as contemporary conceptions of moral life as grounded in fixed principles and preconstituted traditions (John Wall, 2005) to root value creation in concrete moments of experiences.

## 9.4 Poetic De-Construction

Within the vision of poetics contribution to ethics, Paul Ricoeur develops the concept of moral creativity, poetically complex process of positively and negatively meaning de-construction of the self and its relationship with the world. Moral creativity is in the end an original and necessary religious capability for responding anew to the tensions within and between selves in the world by forming over time, in love and hope, an ever more radically inclusive humanity.

The positive component expresses that the new social order demands endlessly to be formed. There is no way to live in the world without taking part, from birth onward, in systems of shared languages, culture, power and economics, and these systems are shaped between us no matter how 'other' form each other we are. The negative component expresses that social world must constantly be deconstructed form the point of view of those groups it subjects to marginalization (source).

The voices from the margins need to find poetic empowerment in the affirmation of a positive original capacity for social creativity in themselves. John Wall calls for a poetics of hope, the impossible possibility for the shared creation of a reconciled human world together.

## 9.5 Exploring the Space of the Possible

'Poetry Changed the World' writes Elaine Scarry (2014) on ethics of poetry. Scarry argues that empathy, pro-contra argumentation which is expressed in debate poetry, as well as in beauty are among the characteristics in which poetry reduce injuries throughout history. Poetry is an invitation to empathy in the sense that it expresses the capacity of literature to exercise and reinforce our recognition that there *are* other points of view in the world, to make this a powerful habit. In her award winning book *Ethics of Storytelling* (2018), Meretoja speaks about the ethical potential of storytelling in the development of our perspective-awareness and capacity of perspective-taking.

Furthermore, Meretoja speaks of the power of narratives to cultivate our sense of the possible. The *Ethics of Storytelling* analyses how narratives enlarge and diminish the spaces of possibilities in which we act, think and re-imagine the world together with others. Her reflections find an echo in Ricoeur's thinking on the *Poetics of Possibilities*.

'As poetic beings, we can hope for the impossible possibility of the 'new creation' of our distorted social systems in the direction of human reconciliation of an ever more radical and excessive form' (John Wall, 2005:23).

I argue with the voices in Rwanda, that the space of possible can be understood in two dimensions: (1) through their capacity to question and challenge *normality* and (2) through their power of using poetic imagination to connect people in the process of sharing experiences.

## 9.6 Poetic Voices in Rwanda

Social marginalization is frequently described as a call for a world transformation. Poetic voices in Rwanda are voices from the margins; they reflect the contours of their marginalization as well as the call for a transformation. The voices we listen to at this point are voices from the world of refugees, of modern nomads and of disability. All of them, question and challenge *normality*, as well as they also long for normality. This longing is human beings cry for recognition and belonging, at the same time, it is artistic paradox. With our sensual capacities of seeing and hearing, disability challenges us in making us aware that normality is a sensual experience. The voices from disabled poets question the possibility of seeing beyond the disability.

## 9.7 Conclusion

'The hope for social transformation is fundamentally also a question of the shape and meaning of society's shared social imagination' writes John Wall (2005: 23) in reference to Paul Ricoeur. With the poems in Rwanda, we explored the imaginative space opened by the poets. In a first time, the wall of prejudice needs to be broken down, so that the acceptance of the own situation is not only an inner poetic process but find its voice in the public space. Questioning our sense of normality, is a value, an ethical potential of poetry. Beyond normality is a call for more active poetic writing beyond the reactive writing. We argue that social transformation needs the voices from the margins to challenge not only our sense of normality, as a sensual and social experience, but also contributes to an acceptance and valorization of differences. The poetic flow of the poet need to join the flow in the social world, where we accept that a new order is based on values of poetry and creativity.

## 8.8 References

Coulon, de Jacques. 2009. *Exercices pratiques de poésie-thérapie pour retrouver son calme, récupérer de l'énergie, libérer sa créativité.* Payot.

Lawrence, Joseph. 2005. *Into It: Poems*, Farrar, Straus and Giroux, New York.

Leedy, Jack J. 1995. *Prinzipien der Poesietherapie. In Poesie und Therapie. Über die Heilkraft der Sprache. Poesietherapie, Bibliotherapie,* Literarische Werkstätten. Junfermann-Verlag. Paderbron.

Meretoja, Hanna. 2018. *Narrative Hermeneutics, History, and the Possible*, Oxford: UP.

—. 2018. *Storytelling and Ethics: Literature, Visual Arts, and the Power of Narrative*, New York: Routledge.

Muratori, Fred. 2006. Book Reviews. Fred Muratori reviews Lawrence Joseph's Into It, and Codes, Precepts, Biases, and Taboos: Poems 1973-1993, In *American Book Review*, Vol. 27, Number 6, September/October 2006.

Scarry, Elaine. 2014. Poetry Changed the World. Injury and the Ethics of Reading. In: *The Humanities and Public Life*, ed. Peter Brooks. New York: Fordham University Press.

Wall, John. 2005. *Moral Creativity. Paul Ricoeur and the Poetics of Possibility*. Oxford University Press.

# CONCLUSION

In his 'Letter to Menoeceus' Epicurus writes: 'Let no one be slow to seek wisdom when he is young nor weary in the search of it when he has grown old. For no age is too early or too late for the health of the soul[177].' When it comes to evaluating the value of poetry for life, the quarrel between philosophy and poetry, which is both old and venerable, shows that it doesn't make much sense to choose one over the other, but for sure our ability to be filled with wonder, which is central in the poetic form, should be taken seriously[178].

Is poetic discourse a divine language, as it was common to call the short and musical form of poems in verse? This question should not be used for narrow controversies, based on the irrational and 'magical' virtue of poetry, to bound human communities together, by the only means of the expression, as shown in Plato's *Ion*[179]. No need to consider poetry irrationally as the expression of an unknown and mysterious god,

---

[177] Epicurus, Letter to Menoeceus, translated by Robert Drew Hicks.

[178] For a good overview: Barfield, R. (2011): *The Ancient Quarrel between Philosophy and Poetry*, Cambridge: University Press, 278pp.

[179] Plato, Ion [536a] 'You, the rhapsode and actor, are the middle ring; the poet himself is the first; but it is the god who through the whole series draws the souls of men whithersoever he pleases, making the power of one depend on the other. And, just as from the magnet, there is a mighty chain of choric performers and masters and under-masters suspended by side-connections from the rings that hang down from the Muse.' Plato. *Plato in Twelve Volumes*, Vol. 9 translated by Harold N. Fowler. Cambridge, MA, Harvard University Press; London, William Heinemann Ltd. 1925.

to recognize that inspiration (in Greek: enthousiasmós), although not as informative as a demonstration (epideixis), has a certain advantage, as consequence of the dispossession of a more scientific type of knowledge: the ignorance of the poet gives him an assurance to communicate better, not having to present anything else than the emotions as experience of the tragedy. The poet is dispossessed of the true means of recollecting the ideas, he is an 'ideomaniac' to borrow the expression of F. Nietzsche[180], since the poet speaks 'as if he would have been present' during certain events (as the epic events described by Homer). The public perfectly knows that he is being exposed to a harmless deception, of a narrative that is not that of the pilot of the soul who is mastering human knowledge, as based on a pretension for truth and sound reasons. But why then should we choose a type of enthusiasm of a lower kind, compared to religious and prophetic enthusiasms, which are based on true love, as Plato invites us to consider in priority in the *Phaedrus*[181]?

Poetry as a literary genre should be considered as good, since it is part of the form of didactic excellence by helping us to love knowledge for its beauty and not only for its demonstrative perfection, as a non-doctrinal critical approach. Criticizing 'circumstances that exist in the world' or as 'a poetic critique of factually existing circumstances' supposes a place outside de boundaries of the systematic thinking[182].

---

[180] Nietzsche, F. (1882), *The Gay Science*, book V, 357.

[181] Plato, *Phaedrus*, 247c 'the region above the heaven was never worthily sung by any earthly poet, nor will it ever be. It is, however, as I shall tell; for I must dare to speak the truth, especially as truth is my theme. For the colourless, formless, and intangible truly existing essence, with which all true knowledge is concerned, holds this region.'

[182] Richard Eldridge, *Notre Dame Philosophical Reviews*, Michael Hampe, *What Philosophy Is For*, (Michael Winkler tr.), University of Chicago Press, 2018, xi, p.257.

What are these problematic factual circumstances that deserve poetic attention?

We have proposed in our book eight perspectives, ordered in what we called as second part: Essays on poetry.

In the part II, Section 2 on Christian aesthetic, the main argument is to consider Christian art not as exclusively bound to the European framework, but as poetic thinking. Art can help to unmask the essence of something; such art transcends any given culture. The grounding principle of Christian love being across cultures, as Christoph Stückelberger describes it, this idea consequently implies a dose of acculturation, or distance toward discourses and cultures which may limit the motivating power of the principle; but art does it without relying on demonstrative and systematic means as poetry. Art speaks first and by excellence to our sensibility.

In part II, section 5 interpreting concepts as related to poetry, Ignace Haaz quotes Aberakane (2016) and shows that poetry participates in constituting 'excellence' as a 'delightful' mode of experience, transforming the language of knowledge into a game, which by definition 'encourages and prolongs assiduous practices'[183]. Images and inspirations are used as spans, to better recollect the essential part of a discourse, allowing the release of our memory from the unwanted residual information. If Martin Luther King had not started his speech with 'I have a dream', a poetic and prophetic proposal and inspiring invitation, but he would have said: 'I have a five-point plan', a 20pp. strategy, his speech would not have entered History. Similarly, Saint-Exupéry invites us to catch the very essential when he says: 'building a boat isn't about weaving canvas, forging nails, or reading the sky. It's about giving a shared taste for the sea, by the light of which you will see

---

[183] Aberkane, Idriss (2016) : *Libérez votre cerveau ! - Traité de neurosagesse pour changer l'école et la société*. Robert Laffont, pp. 160-162

nothing contradictory but rather a community of love[184]. By addressing poetic figures in the discourse, communication is done in a shorter and far more efficient way, fulfilling much better the expected semiotic function of denotation (to point at the correct object, not the discourse around it). Better than a technical manual, because based on pragmatic context and experience, poems can help us to understand the main issues related to building a boat which, of course is only a metaphor for expressing the key conditions of good leadership.

Fables, maxims, aphorisms often contain moral intentions, but without always delivering its message as explicitly as the storyteller, and without the function of social censorship of rhetoric, used by lawyers and teachers, let's think especially about irony as means to uncover truth. The eight sections of parts I and II, section 1 could be read as exemplifications of this minimalistic moralism: 'as if, between the lines, the intuition [...] that the fable [or the poem, is] moving away and ravishing in man the child he was and who is dormant; as if he was trying to awaken in him the part of childhood that sleeps and dreams. Poetry (in the form of the fable) 'claims from its adult reader that it plays to make the child to hear it'[185], while the moral tales aim to raise the childlike simplicity to the height of the adult responsibility.

The playful nature of many poems is therefore an invitation to the discovery, a labyrinthine itinerary but not an arrogant pedagogical injunction, which is likely to fail. At the gentle invitation of the sensibility and the imaginary it is much harder to resist. The ludic nature of many poems or poem-based short maxims is based on the pleasure of discovery, the development of interpretation skills, a hermeneutic of the speech, on the side of the receiver of these stories. A tolerance for

---

[184] Saint-Exupéry, Citadelle, *Oeuvres*, Gallimard, translation by S.M. Colowick, 1953, p. 687.

[185] Patrick Dandrey, Un hédoniste inquiet, *Jean de la Fontaine*, Société éditrice le Monde, Hors-Série, Mai-Juin 2018, p.18.

solutions that are rarely without a dose of ambivalence opens a critical distance on the level of learner and also it opens a form of critical re-evaluation of values.

The poet aims at the same time a higher target than the ordinary language, since he wants to achieve the transformation of the vehicle of his ideas and of his models of behaviour. Progressing time not fully in transparent ways but masked, since the public knows the innocent nature of his poetic posture, the fable becomes a laboratory of narratives, where the critical spirit can be developed more accurately than in dogmatic and systematic communications, and poetry has a sustainable meaning, being a perpetual mobile of the self-understanding. Most fables are addressed to young people, which raises specific challenges as Divya Singh in part II, section 1 articulates this specific condition of being addressed to children; but outside fairy tales, nursery rhymes and cartoons, fables keep a virtue of religious edification and their function of catharsis of the passions is very useful for the young adults as well. In part I, section 6 and part II, section 9 Andrea Grieder presents her experience with *Kigali vibrates with Poetry*, a poetry competition in Rwanda particularly efficient to work on restorative justice processes, and the integration of vulnerable young people often living in refugee camps. Poetry is able to bring reconciliation in tragic personal life itineraries.

Le Clézio describes the activity of the poet as moved by the desire to change the world, which he realizes essentially by changing the language and changing himself, but also by finding himself, in a new configuration of sense, in accordance with a metaphysical characteristic, shared by all human beings, to giving oneself a meaning and continue to persevere in one's existence. He is like 'The shaman, [who] at the moment of ecstasy, hears the spirits coming to him, in a galloping noise, in an unknown rum or that anguishes and delights him.' It is again the central idea of two types of enthusiasms as Wong has well described, one related to the wise attitude of not abandoning the characteristic of reason based knowledge and discourse, the other presenting the possibility to adopt the kind of tragic imitation that doesn't exclude a Dionysian excess (hybris)[186].

The fabulist is continually in a state of creative childhood that is his spiritual strength, his ability to represent, as in a mirror, the human and social pathologies of the world in which he lives. By his judicious use of words, he also manages to free himself and produce truths that sound like religious revelations. From similar symbolic postures, Kashindi establishes a detailed canvas in part II, section 3, which is applied to isolate Christian religious symbols in the form of biblical analysis in the New Testament.

The romantic perspective of philosophical concepts as based in poetry is a perspective presented by Ignace Haaz (II, 5), who places it in the framework of the history of the metaphysics of the subject, after the development of the natural sciences, as a rediscovery of the importance of the imagination and self-narrative, but which at the same time questions a strong view of individual autonomy of the secularized subject, that is to say of the man placed in a history different from that of the grace of a god who reserves for us capacities of developments that only He knows. A notion of duty to keep our promise should be placed in relation to our capacity to keep a promise and that of our self-development, which are not always aligned. One may have the ideal value to keep a promise but lack the energy for self-development needed to fully fulfil and realise a promise. A way to invest minimal effort on the emotional side is be inventive and playful when it comes to borrow ammunitions from poetry, rhetoric and the philosophy of language. By

---

[186] Wong, K. K. (2001): *Zwei Arten von „Enthusiasmus„ bei Platon in Ion und Phaidros, Nietzsches „Die Geburt der Tragödie aus dem Geiste der Musik' und die „Mimesis' bei Platon und Aristoteles*, Thesis, Eberhardt-Karls-Universität Tübingen, p. 64.

adopting a minimalist attitude toward morals and truth, Ignace Haaz doesn't mean compromising on essential values, but rather keeping the head straight and using innocent lies, similar to the use of irony, do diminish affective investment with counter-values. Instead of seeing innocent lies as a blind exploitation of the trust given by the scheme of collaboration and human exchange, on the contrary irony and litotes are ways to promote values by means of pretending to ignore them, and to work in service of a truth that goes beyond special interests.

History as an anthropological collective narrative leads to the idea that history is written in the mode of regional ethnographic self-understanding of the peoples. The disadvantage of a historiography (as the German term: *Geschichte*) that lacks the ambition to project itself into models of historic utopia (in German: *Historie*), is the temptation of the naturalistic fallacy, of attributing natural characteristics to Man-crafted artefacts. Excessive cultural conservatism or the temptation of religious fundamentalism finds its way in similar mindsets. The instrumental use of history as an ideological channel of information is not avoidable at a time when the information society and the internet make the plurality of forms of communication unavoidable, even if microclimates of information exist with their wall of censure, excluding certain tubes of transmissions of these channels, as the GAFAs in China.[187]

Ideology should always be considered as crystallizing an unwelcome outgrowth of the process of invention of the collective narrative of one or more peoples, one or more poles of civilization on the global scale. We know that the poet-artist depends as the child on a protector (the Fouquet of La Fontaine). What will happen if the misleading use of images, which transform reality, which in turn is used as pretext and entry of a system of constraint, exploitation, education to impotence and criminal organisation on a wide human scale? Part of similar fallacy is

---

[187] GAFA stands for Google, Apple, Facebook and Amazon.

the reduction of all different times to the present. The difference between present view of any given object and sustaining properties across different times was already the interrogation in the centre of Orwell's collection of texts entitled *On Truth*, where differences between peoples or individuals are compared to and transcribed in temporal persisting properties of the same person: 'what have you in common with the child of five whose photography your mother keeps on the mantelpiece? Nothing, except that you happen to be the same person'[188]; the consequence of a relative immediacy of all information, inherent to our society of communication, creates an illusion of thinking, but it disengages from deep critical thinking. Our ideas about our home and our culture, that seem to be different from those of a person we meet by accident in a distant travel, have much more in common, given our common history as homo sapiens, but they also seems radically different if we focus on the complexity of the experience of being a Man.

Prior to the Nuremberg trial there did not exist a formulated code of ethics for medical research on human beings, and the *Essay on the inequality of the human races*, a dissertation of Arthur de Gobineau, argues, in the external form of scientific language, the plausibility of the foundation of the theories of the hierarchy of ethnic groups and peoples. A theory known to be untrue, because of the fallacious use of the Darwinist selection to draw a value judgement, that of inequality as norm, which cannot be ground on empirical observation, but on normative egoism which is a moral psychological optic on the hierarchy of values. Part II, section 7 authored by Ernest Beyarza discusses the instrumental use of colonization in Western and Central Africa that aided the promotion of ideologies, such as the one from Gobineau, to engage a historical process of underdevelopment, which is an invented fiction, because the majority of individuals constituting a people are not born without comparable capacities to learn, without will to live and

---

[188] Orwell, G. (1998/2017): *On Truth*, London: Harwill Secker, p.37.

overcome oneself, without being able of integrating values that make it possible to project oneself into the future in an efficient way to plan and develop individually and collectively. Consequently, unless rhetorical equality and inequality are defined as poles capable of graduation (as when we say 'we are all equal but some are more equal than others'), the ideology of inequality is false but learned helplessness is a proven and dangerous doctrine[189]. Utopias built on the biased rhetoric of colonialism, the theories of conspiracies that feed extremist heresies of the twentieth century, show that playing on our unconscious fears is something that can be planned on a large scale, and that these language pathways, rich in images are the alleys of ignorance and fear, in the situation of privations and struggle for (economic) survival.

The scandal of the instrumental use of Facebook, where anecdotes of millions of users were gathered to foresee political preferences and to manage a campaign of presidential elections in the USA, shows how easy it is to increase even further the control of targeted channels of information, including the work of experts of information technology (data mining), for private group egoistical interest. Autobiographical narrative as seemingly insignificant individual stories escaped the sphere of intimacy of our reading rooms and individual smartphones. A solution against the amalgam of 'popular' opinions for the benefit of a dominant social minority is to always try to overcome the psychological barrier of comparison. It is possible by promoting the experimentation to live in the shoes of someone from a different ethnic group, as Griffin has convincingly shown (*Black Like Me*, 1961).

In the business sector, as Tabra shows in part II, 8 corporate social responsibility (CSR) and corporate communication and culture shows not only the different ways how companies manage their business processes to produce an overall positive impact on society, but also that

---

[189] As the 'we can' attitude, the 'we cannot' attitude can spread quickly and pervert trust and the will to self-develop.

becoming part of a process of communication and corporate culture focusing on how the image an enterprise is shared to the public is as important as the reconciliation process in which the parties need to engage with. If CSR covers sustainability, social impact and ethics, then the narrative behind the corporate culture is as important as the normative ethical dialogue this culture is realizing by solidarity mechanisms inside and across other stakeholder institutions.

The critical spirit of yesterday should be renewed by the critical spirit of today, without losing on the way the well-established principles, without which the values that go through the test of time are lost. In the dense forest of images and self-narratives of our global space of communication, many simplistic images demote the vivid metaphors of poets and moralists, who present the discourse in action, as a dead letter. This regression is already observable in vulnerable social groups and in children's stories, as part II, section 1 shows, where Divya relates an image that provokes a moral shock, such as the familiar figure of the wolf eating the grandmother, without foreseeing and assuring that catharsis works in a harmless way, that is to say without providing contexts where history would have real reasons to scare.

In a world where 25% of American adults admit to not having read a book in 12 months, reading and interpreting a text probably means that among the remaining 75% reading a book has been at best a cognitive process that has mobilized passion, as 'delighting excellence', but reading is unlikely to be associated with the love of knowledge, with mastery as an active integration of concepts, or simply with pure wonder (except if we take car tuning manuals for self-developmental tools).

Yet we all have the same decoding systems, when we consider the History of Evolution in the light of hundreds of thousands of years of perfecting our brain and nervous system: the challenge of our day is to reconcile mass information with the ability to contextualize and transmit knowledge or narratives, without soliciting the signal of pain, which is never the best way to learn, this is possible by imitating the harmony and hidden treasures of nature what Blasco part II, section 4 calls 'biomimethics'.

Dr I. Haaz,

*Globethics.net*

# LIST OF CONTRIBUTORS

**Christian Anieke** is professor of English. He is the founder and current Vice Chancellor, Godfrey Okoye University, the University of the Catholic Diocese of Enugu, Nigeria.

**Ange Theonastine Ashimwe** born 1999 is the Winner of *Kigali vibrates with Poetry*, Edition 7, 2017 by Transpoesis, in Kigali (Rwanda).

**Ernest Beyaraza** is a Ugandan scholar with B.A. Diploma in Education, M.A., LL.B, and LL.M. from Makerere University, a Diploma in Legal Practice from Law Development Centre (LDC), a Diploma in Administration and Management from Uganda Management Institute (UMI), Uganda, and Ph.D. from the University of Bayreuth, Germany. He taught at Makerere, Kenyatta, Bayreuth, and is currently a professor of Law at Catholic University of Eastern Africa, Nairobi (Kenya).

**Didier Blasco** who was born in Annemasse (France) and who lives in Sofia (Bulgaria) is Consulting Engineer and Teacher. He has been contributing as expert for various organisations as the Earth Focus Foundation in Geneva (Switzerland); he is alumna of the National Institute of Applied Sciences (INSA) of Lyon (France).

**Anisie Byukusenge** has graduated in translation and interpreting at the University of Rwanda in 2017.

**Andrea Grieder** in anthropologist and has established herself as an international expert with experience in the field of art, poetry and reconciliation in the context of post genocide Rwanda, where she works as director of Transpoesis; her PhD research: Collines des mille souvenirs (Globethics.net: 2016), has motivated the project of gathering of the present texts.

**Ignace Haaz** has been teaching ethics and philosophy at the University of Fribourg (Switzerland) after his doctoral studies in the philosophy of rhetoric at the University of Geneva. In charge since 2013 of the ethics online library (over 7 million documents: www.globethics.net/library) and of Globethics publications (www.globethics.net/publications).

**Obiora Ike** is Executive Director of Globethics.net in Geneva. He has held several academic posts, most recently as Professor of Ethics and Intercultural Studies at the Godfrey Okoye University Enugu/Nigeria. He is the President of the Club of Rome (Nigeria Chapter) and chairs the government of Enugu State Economic Advisory Committee.

**Mulolwa Kashindi** teaches New Testament exegesis at the Faculty of Theology of the Evangelical University in Africa (UEA). He is currently Executive Director of the Higher Pedagogical Institute of Uvira (ISP-Uvira) in RD. Congo.

**Lion King** born in 1999 was awarded with the Nyirarumaga Trophy, in July 2017 with an overall and overwhelming convincing poetic performance in Kigali (Rwanda).

**James Luchte** is a philosopher, author, writer and poet. Visiting Professor of Philosophy at Shanghai University of Finance and Economics from July 2014-August 2017, he is also on the Board of Advisers of the Nietzsche Circle, a global philosophical community, based in New York.

**Deivit Montealegre** is currently Programme Executive Globethics.net South America and PhD. Candidate at the Instituto Superior Evangélico de Estudios Teológicos (ISEDET) in Buenos Aires (Argentina). His training and previous formation include the Tao Fong Shan Centre, Hong Kong, in governance and management for the economy of the life, and Deivit is a specialist in ecumenical studies from the University of Geneva (Switzerland).

**Janvier Nsabimana** born in 1994, in the Democratic Republic of Congo (DRC) is a young poet who lives in the Nyibiheke Refugee Camp in Easter Province of Rwanda and is currently following studies in Business of Hotel and Tourism Management.

**Ange Sankieme** holds a double doctorate: in Law from the University of Berne, in African, Congolese, European and Swiss law, and in Theology from the University of Basel on migration in the European Union and Switzerland.

**Alexander Savvas** was born in Geneva in 1967. He studied International Relations and French in the United States and Switzerland. He has been working in the financial sector since 1997.

**Divya Singh** is Chief Academic Officer at STADIO Holdings, Divya Singh holds an LL D, a Master in Tertiary Education Management. Among her keynote experiences, she is advocate of the High Court of South Africa and former vice Principal at the University of South Africa.

**Dicky Sofjan** is core doctoral faculty, Indonesian Consortium for Religious Studies (ICRS), Graduate School of Universitas Gadjah Mada (UGM) in Yogyakarta, Indonesia.

**Christoph Stückelberger** is President and Founder of Globethics.net, Executive Director of Geneva Agape Foundation GAF, and Professor of Ethics in Moscow/Russia, Enugu/Nigeria, Beijing/China, Member of Ethics Committees, Advisor to Institutions and Ethics Institutes.

**Edison Paul Tabra Ochoa** is a leading Lawyer, extrajudicial moderator and a lecturer in Corporate and Business Law at the School of Law of the Pontifical Catholic University of Peru (PUCP). He holds a Ph.D. and a M.A. in Culture and Government of Organizations by University of Navarra (Spain), and a L.L.M. in Business Law by Pontifical Catholic University of Peru (PUCP). He is author of three books dedicated to solidarity corporate governance: Solidarity and Corporate Governance (JM Bosch, 2015); Responsabilidad social y gobierno corporativo en la empresa solidaria Social (USIL, 2017), and Ética y solidaridad: Perspectivas históricas y normativas (Globethics, 2017).

## Globethics.net

Globethics.net is a worldwide ethics network based in Geneva, with an international Board of Foundation of eminent persons, 173,000 participants from 200 countries and regional and national programmes. Globethics.net provides services especially for people in Africa, Asia and Latin-America in order to contribute to more equal access to knowledge resources in the field of applied ethics and to make the voices from the Global South more visible and audible in the global discourse. It provides an electronic platform for dialogue, reflection and action. Its central instrument is the internet site *www.globethics.net*.

Globethics.net has four objectives:

**Library: Free Access to Online Documents**
In order to ensure access to knowledge resources in applied ethics, Globethics.net offers its *Globethics.net Library*, the leading global digital library on ethics with over 4.4 million full text documents for free download.

**Network: Global Online Community**
The registered participants form a global community of people interested in or specialists in ethics. It offers participants on its website the opportunity to contribute to forum, to upload articles and to join or form electronic working groups for purposes of networking or collaborative international research.

**Research: Online Workgroups**
Globethics.net registered participants can join or build online research groups on all topics of their interest whereas Globethics.net Head Office in Geneva concentrates on six research topics: *Business/Economic Ethics, Interreligious Ethics, Responsible Leadership, Environmental Ethics, Health Ethics and Ethics of Science and Technology*. The results produced through the working groups and research finds their way *into online collections* and *publications* in four series (see publications list) which can also be downloaded for free.

**Services: Conferences, Certification, Consultancy**
Globethics.net offers services such as the Global Ethics Forum, an international conference on business ethics, customized certification and educational projects, and consultancy on request in a multicultural and multilingual context.

# www.globethics.net ∎

# Globethics.net Publications

The list below is only a selection of our publications. To view the full collection, please visit our website.

All volumes can be downloaded for free in PDF form from the Globethics.net library and at www.globethics.net/publications. Bulk print copies can be ordered from publictions@globethics.net at special rates from the Global South.

The Editor of the different Series of Globethics.net Publications Prof. Dr. Obiora Ike, Executive Director of Globethics.net in Geneva and Professor of Ethics at the Godfrey Okoye University Enugu/Nigeria.

Contact for manuscripts and suggestions: publications@globethics.net

# Global Series

Christoph Stückelberger / Jesse N.K. Mugambi (eds.), *Responsible Leadership. Global and Contextual Perspectives*, 2007, 376pp. ISBN: 978–2–8254–1516–0

Heidi Hadsell / Christoph Stückelberger (eds.), *Overcoming Fundamentalism. Ethical Responses from Five Continents*, 2009, 212pp. ISBN: 978–2–940428–00–7

Christoph Stückelberger / Reinhold Bernhardt (eds.): *Calvin Global. How Faith Influences Societies*, 2009, 258pp. ISBN: 978–2–940428–05–2.

Ariane Hentsch Cisneros / Shanta Premawardhana (eds.), *Sharing Values. A Hermeneutics for Global Ethics*, 2010, 418pp. ISBN: 978–2–940428–25–0.

Deon Rossouw / Christoph Stückelberger (eds.), *Global Survey of Business Ethics in Training, Teaching and Research*, 2012, 404pp. ISBN: 978–2–940428–39–7

Carol Cosgrove Sacks/ Paul H. Dembinski (eds.), *Trust and Ethics in Finance. Innovative Ideas from the Robin Cosgrove Prize*, 2012, 380pp. ISBN: 978–2–940428–41–0

Jean-Claude Bastos de Morais / Christoph Stückelberger (eds.), *Innovation Ethics. African and Global Perspectives*, 2014, 233pp. ISBN: 978–2–88931–003–6

Nicolae Irina / Christoph Stückelberger (eds.), *Mining, Ethics and Sustainability*, 2014, 198pp. ISBN: 978–2–88931–020–3

Philip Lee and Dafne Sabanes Plou (eds), *More or Less Equal: How Digital Platforms Can Help Advance Communication Rights*, 2014, 158pp. ISBN 978–2–88931–009–8

Sanjoy Mukherjee and Christoph Stückelberger (eds.) *Sustainability Ethics. Ecology, Economy, Ethics. International Conference SusCon III, Shillong/India*, 2015, 353pp. ISBN: 978–2–88931–068–5

Amélie Vallotton Preisig / Hermann Rösch / Christoph Stückelberger (eds.) *Ethical Dilemmas in the Information Society. Codes of Ethics for Librarians and Archivists*, 2014, 224pp. ISBN: 978–288931–024–1.

*Prospects and Challenges for the Ecumenical Movement in the 21st Century. Insights from the Global Ecumenical Theological Institute*, David Field / Jutta Koslowski, 256pp. 2016, ISBN: 978–2–88931–097–5

Christoph Stückelberger, Walter Fust, Obiora Ike (eds.), *Global Ethics for Leadership. Values and Virtues for Life*, 2016, 444pp. ISBN: 978–2–88931–123–1

Dietrich Werner / Elisabeth Jeglitzka (eds.), *Eco-Theology, Climate Justice and Food Security: Theological Education and Christian Leadership Development*, 316pp. 2016, ISBN 978–2–88931–145–3

Obiora Ike, Andrea Grieder and Ignace Haaz (Eds.), *Poetry and Ethics: Inventing Possibilities in Which We Are Moved to Action and How We Live Together*, 271pp. 2018, ISBN 978–2–88931–242–9

# Theses Series

Kitoka Moke Mutondo, *Église, protection des droits de l'homme et refondation de l'État en République Démocratique du Congo*, 2012, 412pp. ISBN: 978–2–940428–31–1

Ange Sankieme Lusanga, *Éthique de la migration. La valeur de la justice comme base pour une migration dans l'Union Européenne et la Suisse*, 2012, 358pp. ISBN: 978–2–940428–49–6

Nyembo Imbanga, *Parler en langues ou parler d'autres langues. Approche exégétique des Actes des Apôtres*, 2012, 356pp. ISBN: 978–2–940428–51–9

Kahwa Njojo, *Éthique de la non-violence*, 2013, 596pp. ISBN: 978–2–940428–61–8

Ibiladé Nicodème Alagbada, *Le Prophète Michée face à la corruption des classes dirigeantes*, 2013,298pp. ISBN: 978–2–940428–89–2

Carlos Alberto Sintado, *Social Ecology, Ecojustice and the New Testament: Liberating Readings*, 2015, 379pp. ISBN: 978-2-940428-99-1

Symphorien Ntibagirirwa, *Philosophical Premises for African Economic Development: Sen's Capability Approach*, 2014, 384pp. ISBN: 978-2-88931-001-2

Jude Likori Omukaga, *Right to Food Ethics: Theological Approaches of Asbjørn Eide*, 2015, 609pp. ISBN: 978-2-88931-047-0

Jörg F. W. Bürgi, *Improving Sustainable Performance of SME's, The Dynamic Interplay of Morality and Management Systems*, 2014, 528pp. ISBN: 978-2-88931-015-9

Jun Yan, *Local Culture and Early Parenting in China: A Case Study on Chinese Christian Mothers' Childrearing Experiences*, 2015, 190pp. ISBN 978-2-88931-065-4

Frédéric-Paul Piguet, *Justice climatique et interdiction de nuire*, 2014, 559 pp. ISBN 978-2-88931-005-0

Mulolwa Kashindi, *Appellations johanniques de Jésus dans l'Apocalypse: une lecture Bafuliiru des titres christologiques*, 2015, 577pp. ISBN 978-2-88931-040-1

Naupess K. Kibiswa, *Ethnonationalism and Conflict Resolution: The Armed Group Bany2 in DR Congo*. 2015, 528pp. ISBN: 978-2-88931-032-6

Kilongo Fatuma Ngongo, *Les héroïnes sans couronne. Leadership des femmes dans les Églises de Pentecôte en Afrique Centrale*, 2015, 489pp. ISBN 978-2-88931-038-8

Alexis Lékpéa Dea, *Évangélisation et pratique holistique de conversion en Afrique. L'Union des Églises Évangéliques Services et Œuvres de Côte d'Ivoire 1927-1982*, 2015, 588 pp. ISBN 978-2-88931-058-6

Bosela E. Eale, *Justice and Poverty as Challenges for Churches: with a Case Study of the Democratic Republic of Congo*, 2015, 335pp, ISBN: 978-2-88931-078-4

Andrea Grieder, *Collines des mille souvenirs. Vivre après et avec le génocide perpétré contre les Tutsi du Rwanda*, 2016, 403pp. ISBN 978-2-88931-101-9

Monica Emmanuel, *Federalism in Nigeria: Between Divisions in Conflict and Stability in Diversity*, 2016, 522pp. ISBN: 978-2-88931-106-4

John Kasuku, *Intelligence Reform in the Post-Dictatorial Democratic Republic of Congo*, 2016, 355pp. ISBN 978-2-88931-121-7

Fifamè Fidèle Houssou Gandonour, *Les fondements éthiques du féminisme.*
*Réflexions à partir du contexte africain,* 2016, 430pp. ISBN 978–2–88931–138–
5

Nicoleta Acatrinei, *Work Motivation and Pro-Social Behavior in the Delivery of*
*Public Services Theoretical and Empirical Insights,* 2016, 387pp. ISBN 978–2–
88931–150–7

# Texts Series

*Principles on Sharing Values across Cultures and Religions,* 2012, 20pp.
Available in English, French, Spanish, German and Chinese. Other languages in
preparation. ISBN: 978–2–940428–09–0

*Ethics in Politics. Why it Matters More than Ever and How it Can Make a*
*Difference. A Declaration,* 8pp, 2012. Available in English and French. ISBN:
978–2–940428–35–9

*Religions for Climate Justice: International Interfaith Statements 2008–2014,*
2014, 45pp. Available in English. ISBN 978–2–88931–006–7

*Ethics in the Information Society: the Nine 'P's. A Discussion Paper*
*for the WSIS+10 Process 2013–2015,* 2013, 32pp. ISBN: 978–2–940428–063–2

*Principles on Equality and Inequality for a Sustainable Economy. Endorsed*
*by the Global Ethics Forum 2014 with Results from Ben Africa Conference*
*2014,* 2015, 41pp. ISBN: 978–2–88931–025–8

# Focus Series

Christoph Stückelberger, *Das Menschenrecht auf Nahrung und Wasser.*
*Eine ethische Priorität,* 2009, 80pp. ISBN: 978–2–940428–06–9

Christoph Stückelberger, *Corruption-Free Churches are Possible. Experiences,*
*Values, Solutions,* 2010, 278pp. ISBN: 978–2–940428–07–6

—, *Des Églises sans corruption sont possibles: Expériences, valeurs, solutions,*
2013, 228pp. ISBN: 978–2–940428–73–1

Vincent Mbavu Muhindo, *La République Démocratique du Congo en panne.*
*Bilan 50 ans après l'indépendance,* 2011, 380pp. ISBN: 978–2–940428–29–8

Benoît Girardin, *Ethics in Politics: Why it matters more than ever and how it*
*can make a difference,* 2012, 172pp. ISBN: 978–2–940428–21–2

—, *L'éthique: un défi pour la politique. Pourquoi l'éthique importe plus que jamais en politique et comment elle peut faire la différence*, 2014, 220pp. ISBN 978–2–940428–91–5

Willem A Landman, *End-of-Life Decisions, Ethics and the Law*, 2012, 136pp. ISBN: 978–2–940428–53–3

Corneille Ntamwenge, *Éthique des affaires au Congo. Tisser une culture d'intégrité par le Code de Conduite des Affaires en RD Congo*, 2013, 132pp. ISBN: 978–2–940428–57–1

Elisabeth Nduku / John Tenamwenye (eds.), *Corruption in Africa: A Threat to Justice and Sustainable Peace*, 2014, 510pp. ISBN: 978–2–88931–017–3

Dicky Sofjan (with Mega Hidayati), *Religion and Television in Indonesia: Ethics Surrounding Dakwahtainment*, 2013, 112pp. ISBN: 978–2–940428–81–6

Yahya Wijaya / Nina Mariani Noor (eds.), *Etika Ekonomi dan Bisnis: Perspektif Agama-Agama di Indonesia*, 2014, 293pp. ISBN: 978–2–940428–67–0

Bernard Adeney-Risakotta (ed.), *Dealing with Diversity. Religion, Globalization, Violence, Gender and Disaster in Indonesia*. 2014, 372pp. ISBN: 978–2–940428–69–4

Sofie Geerts, Namhla Xinwa and Deon Rossouw, EthicsSA (eds.), *Africans' Perceptions of Chinese Business in Africa A Survey*. 2014, 62pp. ISBN: 978–2–940428–93–9

Nina Mariani Noor/ Ferry Muhammadsyah Siregar (eds.), *Etika Sosial dalam Interaksi Lintas Agama* 2014, 208pp. ISBN 978–2–940428–83–0

B. Muchukiwa Rukakiza, A. Bishweka Cimenesa et C. Kapapa Masonga (éds.), *L'État africain et les mécanismes culturels traditionnels de transformation des conflits*. 2015, 95pp. ISBN: 978–2–88931– 042–5

Dickey Sofian (ed.), Religion, *Public Policy and Social Transformation in Southeast Asia*, 2016, 288pp. ISBN: 978–2–88931–115–6

Symphorien Ntibagirirwa, *Local Cultural Values and Projects of Economic Development: An Interpretation in the Light of the Capability Approach*, 2016, 88pp. ISBN: 978–2–88931–111–8

Karl Wilhelm Rennstich, *Gerechtigkeit für Alle. Religiöser Sozialismus in Mission und Entwicklung*, 2016, 500pp. ISBN 978–2–88931–140–8.

John M. Itty, *Search for Non-Violent and People-Centric Development*, 2017, 317pp. ISBN 978–2–88931–185–9

Florian Josef Hoffmann, *Reichtum der Welt—für Alle Durch Wohlstand zur Freiheit*, 2017, 122pp. ISBN 978–2–88931–187–3

Cristina Calvo / Humberto Shikiya / Deivit Montealegre (eds.), *Ética y economía la relación dañada*, 2017, 377pp. ISBN 978–2–88931–200–9

Maryann Ijeoma Egbujor, *The Relevance of Journalism Education in Kenya for Professional Identity and Ethical Standards*, 2018, 141pp. ISBN 978–2–88931233–7

# African Law Series

D. Brian Dennison/ Pamela Tibihikirra-Kalyegira (eds.), *Legal Ethics and Professionalism. A Handbook for Uganda*, 2014, 400pp. ISBN 978–2–88931–011–1

Pascale Mukonde Musulay, *Droit des affaires en Afrique subsaharienne et économie planétaire*, 2015, 164pp. ISBN: 978–2–88931–044–9

Pascal Mukonde Musulay, *Démocratie électorale en Afrique subsaharienne: Entre droit, pouvoir et argent*, 2016, 209pp. ISBN 978–2–88931–156–9

# China Christian Series

Yahya Wijaya; Christoph Stückelberger; Cui Wantian, *Christian Faith and Values: An Introduction for Entrepreneurs in China*, 2014, 76pp. ISBN: 978–2–940428–87–8

Yahya Wijaya; Christoph Stückelberger; Cui Wantian, *Christian Faith and Values: An Introduction for Entrepreneurs in China*, 2014, 73pp. ISBN: 978–2–88931–013–5 (en Chinois)

Christoph Stückelberger, *We are all Guests on Earth. A Global Christian Vision for Climate Justice*, 2015, 52pp. ISBN: 978–2–88931–034–0 (en Chinois, version anglaise dans la Bibliothèque Globethics.net)

Christoph Stückelberger, Cui Wantian, Teodorina Lessidrenska, Wang Dan, Liu Yang, Zhang Yu, *Entrepreneurs with Christian Values: Training Handbook for 12 Modules*, 2016, 270pp. ISBN 978–2–88931–142–2

# China Ethics Series

Liu Baocheng / Dorothy Gao (eds.), 中国的企业社会责任 *Corporate Social Responsibility in China*, 459pp. 2015, en Chinois, ISBN 978–2–88931–050–0

Bao Ziran, 影响中国环境政策执行效果的因素分析 *China's Environmental Policy, Factor Analysis of its Implementation*, 2015, 431pp. En chinois, ISBN 978–2–88931–051–7

Yuan Wang and Yating Luo, *China Business Perception Index: Survey on Chinese Companies' Perception of Doing Business in Kenya*, 99pp. 2015, en anglais, ISBN 978–2–88931–062–3.

王淑芹 (Wang Shuqin) (编辑) (Ed.), *Research on Chinese Business Ethics [Volume 1]*, 2016, 413pp. ISBN: 978–2–88931–104–0

王淑芹 (Wang Shuqin) (编辑) (Ed.), *Research on Chinese Business Ethics [Volume 2]*, 2016, 400pp. ISBN: 978–2–88931–108–8

Liu Baocheng, *Chinese Civil Society*, 2016, 177pp. ISBN 978–2–88931–168–2

Liu Baocheng / Zhang Mengsha, *Philanthropy in China: Report of Concepts, History, Drivers, Institutions*, 2017, 246pp. ISBN: 978–2–88931–178–1

# Education Ethics Series

Divya Singh / Christoph Stückelberger (Eds.), *Ethics in Higher Education Values-driven Leaders for the Future*, 2017, 367pp. ISBN: 978–2–88931–165–1

Obiora Ike / Chidiebere Onyia (Eds.) *Ethics in Higher Education, Foundation for Sustainable Development*, 2018, 645pp. IBSN: 978-2-88931-217-7

Obiora Ike / Chidiebere Onyia (Eds.) *Ethics in Higher Education, Religions and Traditions in Nigeria* 2018, 198pp. IBSN: 978-2-88931-219-1

# Readers Series

Christoph Stückelberger, *Global Ethics Applied: vol. 4 Bioethics, Religion, Leadership*, 2016, 426. ISBN 978–2–88931–130–9

Кристоф Штукельбергер, *Сборник статей, Прикладная глобальная этика Экономика. Инновации. Развитие. Мир*, 2017, 224pp. ISBN: 978–5–93618–250–1

# CEC Series

Win Burton, *The European Vision and the Churches: The Legacy of Marc Lenders*, Globethics.net, 2015, 251pp. ISBN: 978–2–88931–054–8

Laurens Hogebrink, *Europe's Heart and Soul. Jacques Delors' Appeal to the Churches*, 2015, 91pp. ISBN: 978–2–88931–091–3

Elizabeta Kitanovic and Fr Aimilianos Bogiannou (Eds.), *Advancing Freedom of Religion or Belief for All*, 2016, 191pp. ISBN: 978–2–88931–136–1

Peter Pavlovic (ed.) *Beyond Prosperity? European Economic Governance as a Dialogue between Theology, Economics and Politics*, 2017, 147pp. ISBN 978–2–88931–181–1

## CEC Flash Series

Guy Liagre (ed.), *The New CEC: The Churches' Engagement with a Changing Europe*, 2015, 41pp. ISBN 978–2–88931–072–2

Guy Liagre, *Pensées européennes. De « l'homo nationalis » à une nouvelle citoyenneté*, 2015, 45pp. ISBN: 978–2–88931–073–9

## Copublications & Other

Patrice Meyer-Bisch, Stefania Gandolfi, Greta Balliu (eds.), *Souveraineté et coopérations: Guide pour fonder toute gouvernance démocratique sur l'interdépendance des droits de l'homme*, 2016, 99pp. ISBN 978–2–88931–119–4 (Available in Italian)

## Reports

*Global Ethics Forum 2016 Report, Higher Education—Ethics in Action: The Value of Values across Sectors*, 2016, 184pp. ISBN: 978–2–88931–159–0

*African Church Assets Programme ACAP: Report on Workshop March 2016*, 2016, 75pp. ISBN 978–2–88931–161–3

*Globethics Consortium on Ethics in Higher Education Inaugural Meeting 2017 Report*, 2018, 170pp. ISBN 978–2–88931–238–2

*This is only selection of our latest publications, to view our full collection please visit:*

# www.globethics.net/publications